STUDIES IN COMMUNICATION

VOLUME I

Studies in Mass Communication & Technology:
Selected Proceedings From the Fourth
International Conference On Culture
and Communication

COMMUNICATION AND INFORMATION SCIENCE

A Series of Monographs, Treatises, and Texts

Edited by
MELVIN J. VOIGT

University of California, San Diego

STUDIES IN COMMUNICATION

VOLUME I

Studies in Mass Communication & Technology:
Selected Proceedings From the Fourth
International Conference On Culture and
Communication, Temple University, 1981

Edited by

SARI THOMAS
Temple University

ABLEX Publishing Corporation
Norwood, New Jersey 07648

Library of Congress Cataloging in Publication Data

International Conference on Culture and Communication
   (4th : 1981 : Temple University)
   Studies in Communication.

   (Communication and information science)
   "Selected proceedings from the Fourth International Conference on Culture
and Communication, Temple University, 1981."
   Bibliography: v. 1, p.
   Includes index.
   Contents: v. 1. Studies in mass communication & technology.
   1. Communication—Congresses. 2. Culture—Congresses.
I. Thomas. Sari. 1949-   . II. Title. III. Series.
P91.I57 1981   302.2   83-25746
ISBN 0-89391-133-X (v. 1)

Printed in the United States of America.

ABLEX Publishing Corporation
355 Chestnut Street
Norwood, New Jersey 07648

Contents

Introduction

SARI THOMAS

The Conference on Culture and Communication is a multi-disciplinary meeting which endeavors to explore the commonality of many fields from a communication perspective. The Conference schedules daily paper presentations and symposia on Communication Theory; Research Methodology and Philosophy of Social Science; Interpersonal Interaction; Government, Industry, and Culture; Communication and Ideology; Mass Media and Acculturation; Art as Cultural Artifact; and Education and Communicational Competence; and offers special evening lectures.

*   *   *

. . . communication might be considered, in the broadest sense, as the active aspect of cultural structure. (Birdwhistell, 1970, p. 251)

The Conference at which papers in these volumes were delivered is designed to present scholarly efforts that, when taken together, reflect study of the basic interactive paradigm as suggested above by Birdwhistell. This model, in brief, proposes that the social universe may be examined from two interrelated perspectives; first, exteriorly, as *culture,* and second, interiorly, as *communication.* In this sense, culture may be seen as the *structure* of human organization at any given point in time or space, and as comprising (1) material conditions, (2) standardized actions (e.g., medical practices, agricultural techniques), and (3) worldviews and values. Clearly, none of these aspects of culture is a static phenomenon, and, even when they appear to be stable and unchanged over time, a considerable amount of energy must be expended (although not necessarily consciously) to maintain that order. The *system* that is and produces that energy (for maintenance *or* change) may be understood as *communication.*

This theoretical model does not stray far afield from more classic understandings of both "culture" and "communication". In certain schools of anthropology, for example, culture is generally thought of as ". . . the component of accumulated resources, immaterial as well as material, which the people inherit, employ, transmute, add to, and transmit." (Firth, 1951, p. 27) In the field of communication, the phenomenon of communication is ordinarily understood as that process by which information is transmitted. Thus, the earlier-presented model serves not to redefine these concepts, but rather to integrate them. In other words, it is possible to see the history of humankind as being both a record-keeper of its artifacts, practices, and beliefs and, at the same time, a changing process of interaction. While acknowledging that human beings are capable of having a past which produces the present and is always forwarded to the future, we simultaneously may analytically separate (1) the organization of any one 'moment' in the past or present (culture) from (2) the process which brought forth the moment and delivers it to the future (communication). However, it should be clear that while, for purposes of analysis, one may separate the two phenomena, in practice, their lives are inextricably bound in dialectic fashion. By the very force of its presence, the structure must inevitably affect the system.

All the papers in these volumes, in one way or another, are attempts to arrive at an understanding of some portion of this order and/or process. However, as the papers were competitively selected from those presented at a multi-disciplinary, open-format conference, they are not intended to represent evenly all areas germane to the study of social structure and system. Instead, there were two major emphases in the selection process: first, that a paper include interesting theory and/or data not typically available in standard social-science texts, and, second, that there be represented a good deal of highly contemporary culture and communication issues.

*   *   *

This second emphasis on contemporary problems is probably best served through the material offered in this first volume, *Studies in Mass Communication and Technology.* Unfortunately, little research has been directed to studying concretely the relative effectiveness of the mass media in comparison to interpersonal interaction (e.g., formal education, family relations, traditional religion, peer affiliation) in terms of their respective roles in the process of acculturation. Yet, whether or not the mass media have come to be *the* most powerful body of acculturative agents in the 20th century, it is understood that their role in this regard is strong and extensive. Volume One, then, explores both structural (institutional and artifactual) and systemic or behavioral functions of mass communication and related technological issues.

The first section, International Communication, consists of institutional analyses of world-wide political economy in relation to information technology, as well as comparative accounts of mass-media industry/government relations. In the Institutions section which follows, regulational, public-policy-setting, and organizational perspectives on mass-media industry are offered.

The third division, Mass Media Content, provides analyses of mass-media artifacts in addition to methodological criticism concerning the sociological interpretation of such events. Behavior and Acculturation, the section which follows, is an investigation of the interpersonal functions and social ramifications of people's interaction with the mass media.

Lastly, the fifth section, Technology, focuses specifically on how the development, distibution, and application of certain industrial arts have shaped human socialization.

REFERENCES

BRIDWHISTELL, R. L. (1970). *"Kinesics and Context: Essays on Body Motion Communication."* Philadelphia: University of Pennsylvania Press.

FIRTH, R. W. (1951). *"Elements of Social Organization."* London: Watts.

PART I

INTERNATIONAL COMMUNICATION

1

Euro-American Conflicts in the Sphere of Transborder Data Flow (TDF)

JÖRG BECKER
Marburg University
Federal Republic of Germany

In 1978 and 1980, two very important analyses of international information policy appeared independently of each other: the 1978 French report prepared by a special Presidential Commission under the title, "L'informatisation de la Société," by Nora and Minc, and the 1980 MacBride Report, "Many Voices, One World," from Unesco. The two reports are the result of very differing historic, national and international impulses and motivation.

The Nora and Minc Report deals primarily with scientific and technical information in high media technology, with a discussion of the dovetailing of "telecommunication" and "informatics" under the term "telematics." It refers to decentralized application possibilities for telematics in a strongly centralized society and the consequences of this for a national French computer industry. It sees French sovereignty threatened by U.S. dominance of the computer market (hardware and software). To minimize job losses and be able to create and expand independently it recommends the development of a national French computer industry and collective European efforts in the field. The French government policy has conceded high political, economic, and financial priority to telematics. At present it spends annually the equivalent of approximately 700 million U.S. dollars for the improvement of information technology, 360 million U.S. dollars to support the major French computer manufacturer, 235 million U.S. dollars for the development of computer peripherals and 175 million U.S. dollars for the components industry (Clayton, 1980, p. 28). French government policy and the Nora and Minc Report represent the logical continuance of what Servan Schreiber (1968, p. 173) had called for:

[The European governments cannot afford] to leave the Americans in possession of the field in the world of computers. . . . A consequent European policy must consist of uniting all available forces . . . of the German, French, and Dutch industry . . . it is only a market of these dimensions which would still make it possible for a computer industry to take up by 1980 the contest with the American companies. . . . No industrial sector will ever be able to be independent if we do not begin with the computers. If there is a struggle for the future, it will be fought on the field of data processing.

Unlike the Nora and Minc Report, the MacBride Report is chiefly concerned with the mass media in terms of the North-South conflict. (Statements and recommendations on the subject of high-media technology and informatics were considered at a relatively late stage by the MacBride Commission.) The Report concentrates on Third World dependence on the mass media of industrial countries. It calls for radical rethinking, laying greater emphasis on social factors of communication than on the purely technological. It recommends the development of communication infrastructures within the Third World countries, as well as their regional and horizontal cooperation, with the aim of reducing their dependence on the industrial countries. The isolated liberalistic perspective, aware only of the concept of freedom of the press, without integrating this in a structural analysis of political dependencies, is abandoned in the MacBride Report in favor of a comprehensive international democratization concept for media policy. The main demand is the dismantling of prevailing concentration, versatility, and reciprocity in information flow, with the participation of those affected. The realization of this demand in the MacBride Report constitutes the necessary prerequisite for the free flow of information.[1] In relation to the North-South conflict, the MacBride Report states:

The available data demonstrate that the industrial countries dominate more than 95% of the computer industry. The unequality on this sector is more inclined to increase than to diminish, given that every new step in the direction of still more finely developed technology consolidates the advantages of a very small number of countries. . . . To be really free, the flow of information must be two-sided, it should not move in one direction only. . . . A situation of dependence still exists in many parts of the world. . . . This flow of information is neither free nor balanced. This substantiated criticism is the basis for the current endeavour to achieve a new world communication order (International Commission for the Study of Communication Problems, 1980, p. 129).

The MacBride Report is the result of about ten years' debate on the decolonialization of the media in the Third World. The central roles in this debate are played by individual countries of the Third World, the Non-

---

[1]For a critical analysis of the MacBride Report, see Hamelink (1980).

Aligned Movement, critical social scientists in Western industrial countries, UNESCO, COPUOS of the UN, and the ITU.

In the case of the conflicts dealt with by Servan Schreiber and the Nora and Minc Report (which was summed up by Eger, 1978, as 'The Coming Information War'), the central roles in this debate are taken by the French government, engineering experts and lawyers, the OECD, the European Council, and the Commission of the European Community.

These two debates have been conducted, hitherto, largely in parallel, without any analytical connection, and without the experts involved on both spheres of conflict adopting a broader, more comprehensive perspective. If an attempt is made to relate the two debates, it becomes apparent that the varied patterns of argument and strategies correspond to something of an international role-game between the Third World, the USA, and Europe. In other words, the European-American conflict on questions of transborder data flow (TDF) repeats the conflict over mass media between the Third World and the industrial nations; only this time Europe plays the part of the Third World.

According to the definition of the Intergovernmental Bureau of Informatics, TDF means the "movement across national borders of data and information for processing and storage in computer systems" (Transnational Data Report, 1980, p. 41). TDF occurs primarily in three sectors: broadcasting across borders, earth resource satellites, and computer-to-computer communications. The latter sector is of particular importance in the European-American conflict. If hardware and software are considered separately from computer-to-computer-communications, the European-American situation can be seen as follows.

During the 1970s, the export of computers and related equipments contributed to growth for the U.S. foreign trade balance. At a level of 3.4 billion U.S. dollars, computer exports by the U.S. in 1978 had tripled over the level of 1970. In 1979 50% of 4.1 billion U.S. dollars exports went to the European Community, of which 72% was to Great Britain, France, and the Federal Republic of Germany. As opposed to this, the U.S. imports computers primarily from Canada, France and Japan, for a total amount of only 700 million U.S. dollars. (Zycherman, 1980). As an example of a single country in Europe, Austria's dependence on foreign computer technology means that IBM dominates the Austrian market, with 66%, followed by a wide margin by Univac, with 9%, Honeywell Bull, with 8%, and Siemens Data, with 6% (Schmalke and Signitzer, 1980, p. 286). The world market leader, IBM, dominates the overall European market (55%), the Federal Republic (61%), France (55%), Great Britain (40%), and Japan (36%) (Schmalke and Signitzer, 1980, p. 288).

The West European computer market is most definitely a growth market. If the increase registered in this market is measured in terms of on-line interactive searches per annum, the following are the growth rates in western Europe: 1972, +400%; 1973, +50%; 1974, +200%; 1975, +40%; 1976, +155%; 1977, +66%, over that of the previous year. Since the West European computer market is young in comparison to that of the U.S., the growth rates for alpha-numerical on-line interactive searches are not quite as large: 1972, +35%; 1973, +135%; 1974, +90%; 1975, +63%; 1976, +35%, as compared to the previous year.[2] The growth of the computer market in Western Europe as measured by the number of terminals, is expected to grow from 625,000 in 1979 to 1,720,000 in 1983 and 3,960,000 in 1987 (Benedetti, 1980, p. 10).

Growth comparisons between the computer market in the U.S. and Western Europe do arrive at differing forecasts in the time-lag of the two growth curves, in the size of the gap, and even as to whether the two curves move towards or away from each other, but they say nothing on the penetration of Western European hosts by U.S. data bases. The U.S. continues to be the major world provider of data bases, particularly in terms of volume. There are said to be over 55 million records (citations) in on-line bibliographic data bases, over 80% of them provided by U.S. originated data bases.[3] (For these reasons, the little data available on TDF covers only the tip of an iceberg, since it does not include the computer-to-computer-communications within a country and with U.S. data exclusively.)

Although no public figures are available for the software sector, (i.e., for the intensity and quality of TDF between the U.S. and Western Europe),[4] it must be assumed that by far the overwhelming amount of data flow consists of the movement of raw data from Europe to the U.S., while it is processed and interpreted data which flows from the U.S. to Europe. It is to be assumed further that this data flow largely involves an exchange of information between the headquarters of TNC's and their subsidiaries. Moreover, scarcely any personal data is transferred and private business networks are by far of greater significance than those of state or public authorities.

In summary, the Euro-American TDF can and must be described as unbalanced, one-sided, and non-reciprocal. Its main actors are the US' TNC's, to which, as in the debate over a New International Information Order (NIIO), the entire structure of the military-industrial-communications complex in the U.S. may be related.

In the course of debates concerning NIIO, the Third World accused the industrial countries of information and media *imperialism*, which met

---

[2] Confidential files from the companies, EUSIDIC, and Martha Williams.

[3] Confidential files from PA International Management Consultants.

[4] The only valid data can be found in the report "Data Communications in Western Europe in the 1980s," by Logica Ltd., for the Eurodata Foundation in London. Although the costs for the first volume amounts to $41,000. U.S., the figures are not available for public use.

with the joint defensive front of the U.S. and Europe.[5] Whereas the industrial countries rejected the demand for decolonialization of the mass media in the Third World (as raised by the 1973 Conference of the Non-Aligned Movement in Algiers, for example), describing this as verbal coterie and communist conspiracy, in the TDF debate in relation to the USA. The language then applied by the Third World is now being heard from the European side, with similar analytical considerations being raised. A few examples can serve *pars pro toto:*

Simone Veil (1980, p. 12), President of the European Parliament:

> This phenomenon conceals obvious risks of a new *imperialism.* . . . We shall have to watch out together for the dangers which may be presented by a society in which a system of communication of information, both sophisticated and highly standardized, may become its vital axis. (emphasis added)

Hermann Kronz (1980, p. 30), collaborator of the European Commission in Luxemburg:

> The flow of publically available data between the USA and Europa at present runs only from West to East. It is absolutely essential that this one-way traffic soon develop into a *two-way* movement. (emphasis added)

A study prepared for the Austrian Federal Ministry for Science and Research comments on the market policy of IBM in Austria:

> Thanks to the excessive sales prices charged in Austria, the initial investments of the parent company are already completely amortized within the 3rd or 4th year. This means, however, that in the form of excessive list prices Austria pays the sort of *colonial surcharge* otherwise only ever seriously expected from developing countries (Schmolke and Signitzer, 1980, p. 287)—(emphasis added.)

Peter Canisius, German Documentation Center:

> [We must first concentrate our forces] in order to be better able to meet an . . . *international challenge* coming from across the water (Kirchner, 1981, p. 15) (emphasis added.)

The language used by the Europeans against the U.S. is somewhat more cautious than that of the Third World against the industrial countries; it is also inconsistent in its theoretical deductions and it does not prevail in all Western European countries. Nonetheless, the European reproaches against the U.S. are not limited to the general accusation of imperialism, but also appeal to the principle of non-intervention, and to the concept of *sovereignty*, which also plays a central role in the arguments of the Non-Aligned Movement. For example, Louis Joinet, Secretary General of the French Com-

---

[5]Cf. my article on the parallel between the U.S. and the German position towards the Media Declaration (Becker, 1981).

mission for Data Processing and Liberties, stated:

> Information has an economic value, and the ability to store and process certain types of data may well give one country political and technological advantage over other countries. This, in turn, may lead to a loss of *national sovereignty* through supranational data flows (Zycherman, 1980, p. 17)—(emphasis added.)

The study of "The Vulnerability of a Computerized Society" prepared by the Swedish Defense Ministry includes the statement:

> Since Sweden is dependent on *international* data transmission circuits passing through several countries, we are also dependent on the political situation in other countries. . . . The growing international data flow involves security and vulnerability problems of other dimensions than those existing under purely *national* conditions. (*Transnational Data Report*, 1978, p. 17)—(emphasis added.)

The reference made to the concept of sovereignty is of particular interest. Specifically, one must consider that prevailing Western thought on the law of nations has always subordinated this to individual human and civic rights, as was again made very clear in the UNESCO debate on the Media Declaration of 1978. The examples presented here, in the form of the two concepts "information imperialism" and "national sovereignty," could be supplemented without any difficulty by examples from all other conflict areas within the North-South debate, and could be equally well applied to the "information war" between Europe and the U.S. This is illustrated particularly in considering such problems as rights of access, technology transfer, economic dependence, cultural domination, economic protection, and "free" flow of information.

These anti-U.S. European positions can, to a certain extent, be dismissed as verbal radicalism not followed by deeds. As justifiable as this objection may be in part, it nonetheless overlooks that this language is the expression of a specific political culture in Western Europe, which traditionally places a taboo on Communist-stigmatized criticism of the U.S. This criticism of U.S. TDF-dominance has hitherto reflected a mistrust, best described as populist in nature, scarcely systematic, but decidedly heterogenous. It feeds, on the one hand, on a nationalistic, narrow-minded, conservative anti-Americanism—on a pessimistic cultural rejection of advancing technology, as well as on a weariness with civilization. On the other hand, it also draws on a social democratic/socialist-oriented criticism of the growing power of the TNCs or the position of smaller, more neutral countries in Europe, such as Sweden and Austria. A serious threat to U.S. dominance can only be expected to arise, however, if these still heterogenous positions in Western Europe and the power groups behind them join ranks. This could happen if, as in Canada (Robinson, 1980, pp. 18-19), TDF in Western Europe exercises a yet far more unfavorable effect on the foreign trade balance, if an increasing loss of jobs makes itself felt in Europe.

In European political action as well as verbal reaction to the U.S., parallels can be drawn with the attitude of the Third World towards the industrial countries in the mass media debate. Since it was always the strategic intention of the Non-Aligned Movement and the Third World, in relation to the industrial countries, to sanction its position on the mass media on the juristic level of international law—which has always been attacked by the industrial countries as state intervention against freedom of the press—they deliberately brought these debates before the forum of UNESCO. The Third World had an even greater interest in bringing its demands before the World Administrative Radio Conference (WARC) of the International Telecommunication Union (ITU), since ITU resolutions are of an immediately binding, legal character. In contrast, the industrial countries have treated UNESCO resolutions as nothing more than non-binding recommendations, or have tried to shift the mass media debate to less political UN institutions such as the UNDP. The strategic behavior of the main characters involved in the "information war" between the U.S. and Europe has been very similar. In their national legislation on the data protection of natural persons (and, in certain Scandinavian countries, of juristic persons, as well), and in supranational legislation (such as in the regulation of data protection by the Council of Europe), the Europeans chose the path of legal codification. In response to this, the U.S. is attempting to shift the debates out of the European Council (where the U.S. enjoys observer status only) to the OECD, which is qualified to make recommendations only and is far more technologically-oriented and less political than the European Council.

The development of independent national mass media systems in the Third World (as expressed in numerous government-sponsored *national development plans* for the mass media) corresponds to the expansion planned centrally in Western Europe with massive government support for independent, national data networks for scientific and technical information and documentation. Thus, for example, the development of the West German Information and Documentation Program of 1974 was clearly the product of national economic considerations and was motivated by the fear of foreign competition: "The inadequate utilization of existing information resources endangers national efficiency and the ability to compete, thus impeding scientific, economic and social progress." (Federal Republic of Germany, 1976, p. 9). The VIth Research Report from the Federal Government in Bonn makes it apparent that state R&D costs in the information and documentation sector have more than doubled, from 49 million DM in 1975 to 102 million DM in 1980.[6]

In the course of the mass media debate, individual countries in the

---

[6] Deutscher Bundestag: *Bundesbericht Forschung VI*, Bonn 1979 (Drucksache 8/3024), p. 44.

Third World have developed a *protectionist policy*, in relation to the industrial countries, for their national sovereignty and cultural identity. This has been effected by the restriction of entry permits for Western journalists, by the complete ban on the import of U.S. entertainment films in post revolutionary Iran, or by the legally-backed shift of U.S. soap-operas on Haitian TV from prime-time to the late evening. As demonstrated by the review shown in Table 1.1. Japan and the European Community most certainly implement a protectionist policy in relation to the U.S. in the sector of standardization and fee policy for data processing and data services, although the European governments are eager to deny this fact. As the most

TABLE 1.1   Selected Impediments to U.S.-Trade in Services

Type of Action	Details on the Type of Action	Description of Action or Practices	Industry	Country
Restrictive actions related to NTB codes—technical barriers to trade (standards/cert.)	Provisions to ensure that technical regulations, standards and certification systems are not prepared, adopted or applied with view to creating obstacles to international trade	Restrictions on the use/uses of dedicated telecommunication lines	Data processing and data base services vendors and users MNCs	EC, Japan
Restrictive actions related to NTB codes—technical barriers to trade (standards/cert.)	Provisions to ensure that technical regulations, standards and certification systems are not prepared, adopted or applied with view to creating obstacles to international trade	Telecommunication policies which limit or deny the availability of dedicated telecommunication lines	Data processing and data base services vendors and users MNCs	EC, Japan
Restrictive actions related to NTB codes—technical barriers to trade (standards/cert.)	Provisions to ensure that technical regulations, standards and certification systems are not prepared, adopted or applied with view to creating obstacles to international trade	Various arbitrary and discriminatory practices designed to pressure or force users desiring dedicated lines to use usage sensitive services	Data processing and data base services vendors and users MNCs	EC, Japan
Restrictive actions related to trade in services	Discriminatory taxation on services provided by non-resident companies	Discriminatory charges for telecommunication services	Data processing and data base services vendors and users MNCs	EC, Japan
Restrictive actions related to trade in services	Discriminatory taxation on services provided by non-resident companies	Discriminatory charges for telecommunication services predicated on considerations other than costs	Data processing and data base services vendors and users MNCs	EC, Japan

Source: US Trade Representative, 17 June 1980, quoted from *Transnational Data Report*, Vol. III, 7/1980, pp. 22-23.

promising strategy against mass-media penetration from industrial countries, the Third World has chosen the path of regional and *horizontal cooperation*. Examples include the Press Agencies Pool of the Non-Aligned Movement, the news agency of the OAU and the Latin-American Working Council for National Information Systems (ASIN).

These forms of horizontal cooperation correspond in the Euro-American "information war" to the development of the European data network EURO-NET DIANE, implemented in 1979 and mainly financed by public funds from the governments of the European Community.[7] EURONET DIANE is intended not only to reduce the dependence of European users on the U.S. American suppliers of information; with its public subsidies and thus cheaper access fees for European users, it also represents opposition to the purely commercially-run and expensive access fees charged by the U.S. data banks. Since U.S. hosts are not permitted on EURONET DIANE, but U.S. data bases are nonetheless offered via EURONET DIANE, it could transpire that European users of EURONET have a cheaper access to U.S. data than North American citizens. A mechanism of this kind could lead to considerable loss in revenue for Lockheed or Systems Development Corporation (Ettel, 1979).

The seesaw position occupied by Western Europe in international information policy, caught as it is between the dominance of the U.S. and the maintenance of the Third World in its dependent situation, is indicated in Figure 1.1. Since the U.S.–Western Europe dyad is structurally similar to the Western Europe–Third World dyad, the overall triad (U.S.–Western Europe–Third World) will only remain stable in the interests of the overlapping TNCs for as long as Western Europe maintains its seesaw function. Departure from the narrow framework of international information policy

---

[7]The following 16 hosts are connected with EURONET DIANE:

BLAISE	British Library
CATED	French building association
CILEA	Lombardy University interfaculty computing centre
CISI	International Informatics Company
DATACENTRALEN	Danish Government host service
DIMDI	German institute for medical information
ECHO	European Commission Host Organisation
ENQUIRY SERVICE	(Online directory of services)
EPO	European Patents Office
FIZ-Technik	German Technical Information Centre
GID	German information and documentation association
INKA	German Energy, Physics, Mathematics Centre
IRS	Information Retrieval Service of European Space Agency
JRC	EEC Joint Research Centre
SPIDEL	French Société pour l'Informatique
TELESYSTEMES	French host service

FIGURE 1.1. The Nature of Transborder Data Flow

UNITED
STATES

PREDOMINANT FLOW OF RAW DATA
TO BE PROCESSED

PREDOMINANT FLOW OF TECHNOLOGY
AND MEDIA PRODUCTS

PREDOMINANT DIRECTION OF INFORMATION

OTHER
FIRST WORLD
COUNTRIES

TECHNOLOGY AND MEDIA PRODUCTS

RETRIEVAL OF INFORMATION

RAW DATA

TECHNOLOGY AND MEDIA PRODUCTS

RETRIEVAL OF INFORMATION

RAW DATA

THIRD
WORLD

Source: Rein Turn (Chairman): *Transborder Data Flows.* Concerns in Privacy Protection and Free Flow of Information. Report of the AFIPS Panel on Transborder Data Flow. Vol. I, Washington: American Federation of Information Processing Societies 1979, p. 5.

and relation of this triad to more far-reaching political considerations would appear to suggest the following plausible assessment. The period following 1945 is to be characterized less by a global loss of power for the U.S. than by the growth of Western European power. Two peculiarities with reference to Western Europe will work in the *long term* to loosen the symbiotic relationship within the North Atlantic treaty system.

On the one hand, it is in Western European interests to at least minimize the atomic armament race, since an atomic war would have far more devastating effects on Western Europe than on the U.S. The present hesitation shown by many Western European politicians in the implementation of the NATO double resolution, the refusal of certain NATO countries to permit the stationing of neutron bombs, and the increasing Western European trade with the Eastern European states, could all be indicators of independent

Western-European interests in the sphere of security policy.

Secondly, Western Europe has been aware of its dependence on the Near East for energy supplies. Since Western Europe's dependence for energy is greater than that of the U.S., and since it touches on Western Europe's relationship to the Third World, Western Europe's interests in the energy sector are different from those of the U.S.

Whether Western European policy in relation to the U.S. on the question of TDF (rejection of a dependency position, sovereignty claims, agreements under international law as to the quantity and quality of TDF, development of national data networks, protectionism and regional cooperation within Western Europe) should reveal itself as qualitatively novel, and in the long term as part of an uncoupling process from the USA, will depend considerably on international development, outlined above, in the security and energy sectors. Also, the U.S.–Western Europe dyad will be much affected by Europe's relationship to the Third World, in which differing positions from those of the U.S. are to be determined. It is precisely on the services sector, to which the TDF is to be counted, that a bitter struggle is already under way between the U.S. and Western Europe for Third World markets. While the national control of TDF in the U.S.–Western Europe–Third World triad may in fact develop, it can be determined that the competition of the transnational electronic oligopoly has already led to sharpened concentration movements, both in the U.S. and in Europe. On the one hand, Siemens bought up share holdings in Advanced Micro Devises Corporation, reached agreement on technology exchange with Intel Corporation, acquired the companies Litronix and Microwave Semiconductor Corporation, and bought shares in American Microsystems and Amdahl Corporation. On the other hand, this European breakthrough into the U.S. market led to a comprehensive buying up and support action for the U.S. semiconductor producers by such powerful corporations as Exxon, Standard Oil, and Honeywell (Rechtziegler, 1980).

Against this background, the respective national control over TDF either by the U.S. or Western Europe must be qualified considerably, since the transnational ownership situation of the respective TNC's means that these have access to both U.S. and Western-European data bank systems. This may be illustrated by the following.

The U.S. data bank Bibliographic Retrieval Service, with Lockheed, and SDC, the world's three largest data banks, was recently purchased by Indian Head, Inc. Indian Head belongs to the German-Dutch industrial conglomerate Thyssen-Bornemisza, which also bought out Predicasts, a U.S. firm which in turn holds a share in the Swiss host service Datastar (Who owns whom? 1980).

The Thyssen-Bornemisza group also owns the Information Handling Service in Denver and the Seibt-Verlag in the Federal Republic of Germany.

Access is planned to the data bases offered from the Thyssen-Bornemisza group via EURONET (Datenbasis-Verleger, 1981).

As long as national governments do nothing to alter the flexibility, the concentration tendencies, and the cartel-like agreements made between the TNC's, clear limits will continue to be set on all forms of state policy aimed at the maintenance and expansion of an autonomous national economic, including the case of TDF.

REFERENCES

BECKER, J. (1981). The Federal Republic of Germany's policy after the Unesco-Media-Declaration of November 1978. In E. Jahn and Y. Sakamoto (Eds.), "Armaments, Communication, Food, International Division of Labour." Frankfurt, Germany: Campus. (Proceedings of the International Peace Research Association, Eighth General Conference, 1980.)

BENEDETTI, M. (1980). A million Europeans use transmissions every weekday. *Transnational Data Report 3* (No. 5), 10.

CLAYTON, R. (1980). "Information Technology," Ed. by Cabinet Office. Advisory Council for Applied Research and Development. London: Her Majesty's Stationery Office.

Datenbasis-Verleger drängen auf den europäischen Markt. (1981). *Börsenblatt für den Deutschen Buchhandel* (Jan. 6), 54.

EGER, J.M. (1978). The coming information war. *Washington Post* (Jan. 15).

ETTEL, W. (1979). "Informationskrieg" und seine Hintergründe." *Nachrichten für Dokumentation 2*, 63–68.

Federal Republic of Germany. (1976). "The Programme of the Federal Government for the Promotion of Information and Documentation (I & D Programme) 1974-1977," Ed. by the Federal Minister for Research and Technology. Bonn, Germany.

HAMELINK, C., (Ed.) (1980). "Communication in the Eighties: A Reader on the MacBride Report," Rome, Italy: IDOC International.

International Commission for the Study of Communication Problems. (1980). "Many Voices, One World." (MacBride Report.) Paris, Unesco.

KIRCHNER, W. (1981). "DIMDI, Euronet und Infoline." (Radio RIAS Berlin manuscript, March 5.)

KRONZ, H. (1980). Informationstechnologie im Europäischen Raum. In T. Bartel (Ed.), "Gefährdet die Informationstechnologie unsere Freiheit?" (Jahrestagung 1979 der Deutschen Vereinigung für Datenschutz.) Munich, Germany: Oldenbourg.

RECHTZIEGLER, E. (1980). Mikroelektronik, internationaler Konkurrenzkampf und ökonomische Expansion. *IPW Berichte 11*, 9–17.

ROBINSON, P. (1980). Some economic dimensions of TDF. *Transnational Data Report 3* (No. 3–4), 18–19.

SCHMOLKE, M., and SIGNITZER, B. (1980). Österreich im internationalen Mediensystem. In "Auftrag des Bundesministeriums für Wissenschaft und Forschung." (First version, mimeo.) Salzburg, Austria.

SCHREIBER, J.-J. S. (1968). "Die amerikanische Herausforderung." Hamburg, Germany: Hoffmann & Campe.

Transnational Data Report. (1978). *1* (No. 5), 17.

Transnational Data Report. (1980). *3* (No. 3/4), 41.

VEIL, S. (1980). *Transnational Data Report 3* (No. 7), 12.

Who owns whom? (1980). *Euronet Diane News* (No. 21), 3.

ZYCHERMAN, J. (1980). Data protection laws must not become non-tariff barriers. *Transnational Data Report 2* (No. 8), 17.

2

Irresponsible Information and Stagflation:
An Overlooked Relationship Between
Communication and Economics

RENÉ-JEAN RAVAULT
Département des Communications
Université du Québec à Montréal
Montréal, Québec H3C 3P8, Canada

INTRODUCTION

The purpose of this paper is to discuss the contribution of the study of national and international communication practices to the explanation of stagflation in the countries belonging to the core area of capitalism. Understanding stagflation is becoming increasingly crucial, yet most economists remain quite puzzled by this phenomenon. Indeed, if stagflation can be defined as *the combination of increasing inflation with increasing unemployment and economic stagnation,* its understanding and, consequently, its remedies have not yet been found. Previous failures in attempting to deal with stagflation suggest that the explanation cannot be found at a microeconomic level involving economic factors only. Consequently, the contention of this paper is that much of the explanation of stagflation can be found at a macroeconomic level involving all aspects of international relationships. Not only classical aspects of economic exchanges, but also economy of information, language, and culture have to be taken into account.

The author's purpose is to demonstrate that where a "hard" discipline such as economics has failed, a multi-disciplinary approach, with emphasis on communication (a rather new and "soft" discipline dealing mainly with people, information, language, and culture), can make a substantial contribution to the understanding and eventual solution of this monumental problem.

IRRESPONSIBLE MASS MEDIA, OVER-CONSUMPTION,
AND RAMPANT INFLATION

After finally 'discovering' advertising and marketing handbooks, and after seriously promoting Galbraith's analyses of the role of advertising in *The Affluent Society* (1958), *The New Industrial State* (1967), and, above all, "The Unseemly Economics of Opulence" (1960), some macro-economists belonging to neo-Marxist schools are finally unveiling the "Blindspot of Western Marxism" (Smythe, 1977) and, by the same token, the "Blindspots of Economics" (Smythe, 1980). This "blindspot" of both Western Marxism and Economics, of course, is the economic function of the mass media. Dallas W. Smythe, one of these neo-Marxist scholars, goes so far as to see the function served by the advertisement industry as the *sole* economic function of mass communication in capitalist societies (Smythe, 1981, p. 263). For Smythe, the unique economic and social function of the mass media is the one which has been the daily practice of advertisers and businessmen for at least fifty years and which finally has been brought to the attention of Canadian scholars by the *Report of the Special Senate Committee on Mass Media* (Davey, 1970) and by Jacques de Guise (1971) in his article: "L'industrie des Média ou le Marché des Auditoires." De Guise claims that the mass media are bringing audiences with specific needs and specific buying power to advertisers. Smythe's argument urges even more strongly that advertisements are not "just" important, but that the rest of media content is a "free lunch" which has no function but to promote advertisement through the creation and maintaining of a proper ambiance and ideological context.

This consideration of (non-advertisement) media content as a "free lunch" has also been made by several American scholars (Brown, 1971, 1979; Tuchman, 1974; Powers, 1977; Barnouw, 1978).

These authors insist that the main function of the media in English-speaking North America is to promote, organize, and accelerate consumption to the point of making this activity the dominant characteristic of the North American lifestyle. To achieve this end, advertisements are presented within a context that "excites, stimulates, and titillates an audience" (Bensman and Lilienfield, 1971), while simultaneously avoiding anything that might threaten the audience's present values or worldview (see Epstein, 1973). Thus, the mass media gratify both consumers and advertisers in the same stroke.

In addition, as Smythe and others have observed, this "gratifying" and "confirming" function of the mass media/advertisement system occurs in all private, profit-seeking mass-communication institutions (e.g., film, record, and print industries). To be profitable, all mass-media products have to follow this recipe: in order to create and maintain an atmosphere favorable to consumption, a milieu in which no basic issue is raised, no question asked, no problem posed—a milieu in which all potential customers are made to feel quite comfortable and secure. The issue of monoculturalism and unilingualism may illustrate this point.

In order to respect certain strong values as well as to avoid international competition in mass-communication products, almost no foreign mass-culture products are imported into the United States (although some foreign products from England and from countries belonging to the former white British Commonwealth do enter the U.S.). This Anglo-American (more or less) spontaneous practice of cultural protectionism vis-à-vis foreign-made "entertainment" accounts for the way Anglo-American countries are informed about the rest of the world. Indeed, when foreign news is presented to Americans, it requires translation, filtering, and sterilization through the highly protective mechanisms of American international press agencies such as UPI, AP, and their British counterpart, Reuters. As Gunter (1979, Summary, p. 1) states:

> The United States has been a massive supplier of media products to the rest of the world, but it uses very few foreign media products itself. International news reaches the U.S. largely through AP and UPI. The U.S. TV system is the second most "closed" to foreign programming in the world.

This closedness of Anglo-American countries to foreign mass-media products is aggravated by the combination of factors related, on the one hand, to organizational, technological, and financial constraints within mass-communication institutions and, on the other hand, to cultural, linguistic, and educational weaknesses of the domestic audiences. For instance, since it is getting more and more expensive to send and maintain foreign correspondents overseas, many mass media organizations have cut the number and, sometimes, the quality of their correspondents abroad.

This deterioration of the quality of foreign correspondants has been analyzed in "De notre correspondant au bar du Hilton" ("From our correspondent at the Hilton's bar") by Jean-Louis Servan-Schreiber (1972). In this humorously titled chapter, Servan-Schreiber points out that foreign correspondents' inability to speak the language of the country to which they are assigned, as well as their lack of sensitivity to the subtle and sometimes obvious cultural differences of "alien" civilizations, literally "excommunicate" them from the foreigners about whom they have to report, and force them to rely almost exclusively upon their colleagues who have been on the scene for only a few more days or hours.

Furthermore, the use of electronic technologies has not increased the quality and frequency of international news in the U.S., as Epstein (1974, p. 51) puts it:

> The high cost of transmitting stories electronically also affects the distribution of stories over time as well as space. Since none of the network newsprograms are given sufficient budgetary allocations to transmit film stories regularly back

to New York from overseas bureaus by satellite relays, all but momentous foreign news stories must be shipped back by airplane, which means that they seldom can be shown to an American audience on the day they happen.

It seems that in this reduction process in quality, quantity, and ubiquity of foreign news, the main constraint comes from how newsbrokers see their audiences. The masses are often (and properly) considered to be ignorant of foreign languages, cultures, and affairs. According to Epstein, this conception leads Anglo-American newsbrokers to over-simplify and over-dramatize news from overseas. The following example given by Epstein is alarming, since it deals with Western Europe, an issue with which U.S. viewers might be expected to be more familiar:

> One assignment editor explained that in choosing European stories, "the first rule is that overseas news must hold some interest for American viewers." Since it is generally assumed that the audience is not familiar with European news makers or politics, the stories routinely selected by assignment editors (without special commissions from producers) are limited to certain forms of visual action which presumably can be understood without any further frame of reference. These include demonstrations, conflicts between uniformed authorities and protestors, and natural disasters (Epstein, 1973, p. 247).

If this quotation from Epstein supports the cynical and pessimistic judgment that "civilizations have the communication institutions they deserve," it correctly underlines the point that not only mass media, but people and, consequently, the ways people have been formed and informed through their education, are ultimately responsible for this ignorance. Indeed, both the defendants and critics of the establishment indirectly acknowledge this point. The defendants of mass-communication industries typically assert that through audience research (e.g., Nielsen polls in the U.S.A., B.B.M. in Canada) the mass media are trying to deliver what their audiences want. Critics of capitalistic information systems also affirm that the mass media under capitalism contribute significantly to maintaining the **status quo**. Neo-Marxist critics frequently point out that the content of mass media, with the pretense of "objectivity", never carries issues or material which challenge dominant ideology. Indeed, if we return to the area of language, culture, and foreign affairs, it becomes obvious that the "established vision of the world" taught to Anglo-Americans through formal education leaves little room for the learning of foreign languages and cultures. It is almost as if educational institutions, like mass-communication institutions, were profit-oriented (which indeed, more and more, they are) and consequently, it is almost as if these highly-respected institutions were doing their best to gratify their customers by removing alien influences which might conflict with the cherished world-views. Indeed, American education seems to be increasingly preoccupied with fun and leisure, so that only during "spare time" is science and technology taught—and then, almost always over instruction in human affairs.

As Carey (1975) points out, Anglo-American education is characterized by a strong "isolation of science from culture: science provides culture-free truth where culture provides ethnocentric error."

Consequently, the American educational system, with its emphasis upon empiricism, provides a vision of science and technology which is supposedly value- and culture-free. The emphasis is on materialism—on the study of the relationship of human beings with their physical environment. The study of human relationships and, particularly, studies of relationships involving people belonging to different cultures and civilizations, are at best peripheral, particularly during periods of economic crisis. Indeed, even in fields where knowledge of interpersonal and intercultural interaction is relevant, such as international marketing, American handbooks do not emphasize or even note the paramount importance of foreign language skills.

English, after having established itself as the international language of business, is increasingly the international language of science and research. This situation, in turn, seems to have hidden many language and cultural issues away from the research of scholars whose first and only language is English. Furthermore, after having de facto excommunicated non-English speaking researchers from their international meetings, Anglo-American scholars seem to have succeeded also in imposing their own cultural bias, the "imperialism of empiricism," upon the field of international and inter-cultural communication research. Acculturation to a specific scientific culture is quite challenging for a foreign researcher, but, for an American scholar, such a culturally- and linguistically-protected atmosphere is probably no more threatening and consequently no more stimulating than watching highly-gratifying mass media products such as *Star Trek, Star Wars*, and *Jesus Christ Super Star*, in which God himself, his human creatures and their own creatures, the robots, speak English, and only extraterrestrial monsters speak strange languages. And, even then, some get rid of their monster's stigma as soon as they start speaking English e.g.: "*E.T.* phone . . . home . . ."

However, if this linguistically- and culturally-comforting function of Anglo-American institutions has not been noticed by the new-Marxist critics of capitalist societies, the ethnocentric function certainly contributes to the creation and maintenance of an atmosphere in which consumption is the privileged way of life. Other cultures, languages, and civilizations could value other ways of life which might be less materialistic and less consumption-oriented and, consequently have to be kept away.

But liberal critics such as Galbraith, as well as neo-Marxists such as Smythe, are going even a step further in pointing out that the function of the "free lunch" (non-advertising media content) is not only to stimulate and sometimes create consumption but also (and more and more aggressively) to urge audiences to borrow money in order to consume much more than they can afford.

It can be deduced from the more or less neo-Marxist analysis of the economic role of mass-communication industries at a national level that they are irresponsible to the extent that they only contribute to the organization and stimulation of *consumption*, while neglecting to play any direct and significant role in the organization and stimulation of *production*.

An analysis of the function of Anglo-American mass-communication systems will show that the system may very well work and progress. As Galbraith's theory contends, such a system can work very efficiently and even prosper to the extent that, through the stimulation of over-consumption and credit to consumers, it creates and maintains an artificially-inflated demand which has to be met by an ever-increasing production. As a matter of fact, the main resentment Galbraith has against this system is not that it is doomed in the long run, but rather that it is a "barbarous" system, since its purpose is not the improvement of human condition but rather the growth of the system **per se.** Indeed, this Galbraithian analysis of Western capitalism as a kind of "vicious circle" in which the artificial stimulation of consumption increases the demand for goods and services which in turn increases the production of these goods and services has led many observers to consider the consumption-production relationship as a whole. Many people speak of a "consumption-oriented economy" or of a "production-oriented economy" to describe the economic system of Western materialistic societies. However, even if it cannot be challenged that, at a *global* level, consumption has a tendency to generate production and vice versa, it is the main contention of this paper that within the *international division of labor,* formation and information institutions have been, and still are, playing a significant role in the way countries belonging to the first world are becoming specialized. While Anglo-American countries which, according to Smythe, are constituting the core-area of capitalism and are becoming more and more specialized in the production of audiences and consequently of consumers and borrowers, the countries belonging to the periphery of capitalism, such as Japan, those of North Western Europe, and some newly industrialized countries are becoming more and more specialized in the production of goods and services for exportation towards Anglo-American domestic markets. In other words, education and mass-communication institutions are contributing to the acceleration of consumption in Anglo-American countries and to the acceleration of production of goods and services within the countries belonging to the periphery of capitalism.

While most scholars interested in the relationship of international communication to international economy have been dealing mainly with North–South or First World–Third World issues, one can justifiably address the international division of labor *within* the First World. Neo-Marxists studying the relationship between international communication and international economy have a strong tendency to consider the First World as a monolithic block vis-à-vis the Third World, while establishment economists tend to consider the U.S. economy as if it were still enjoying "splendid isolation." However, even within a relatively "isolated" economy, a system which places the emphasis upon increasing government spending and the stimulation of consumer demand for goods and services has to cope with some form of inflation. Furthermore, when a model emphasizing over-consumption is applied to an "open" system having to compete with the rest of the world, it becomes obvious that it has to rely more and more on imports in order to meet a demand which has been artificially exacerbated through mass-media advertising.

Thus, the neo-Marxists, through their analysis of "the blind-spot-of-economics," have contributed an explanation as to why ever-increasing imports and inflation have become a substantial part of capitalist economic systems. It is in this way that it can be said the commercial media are playing an irresponsible role in the economy of their nations. This neo-Marxist denunciation of commercial media as being economically irresponsible is enhanced by the traditional Marxist-Leninist understanding of the role of the press as a socioeconomic organizer. However, as is argued in the next part of this paper, it would be naïve and dangerous to believe that all the countries belonging to the Western world have irresponsible media, while only socialist countries have responsible media, and that there is no continuum between these two poles. Indeed, there are many subtle combinations of these two extreme forms at work in many countries of the First World belonging to the periphery of capitalism and with which Anglo-American countries are economically competing in an ever increasing fashion.

RESPONSIBLE MASS MEDIA, OVER-PRODUCTION, AND RELATIVE DEFLATION

Will (1976) and Flichy (1980) have argued that during the 17th, 18th, and 19th centuries, the press (which was not yet a totally *mass* medium) played a very important role in the information and formation of producers of goods and services and in the very organization of the materialistic production process. This period, they argue, coincided with the ascending power of the "Puritan Bourgeois" (see Weber 1930). But, at the transition between the 19th and 20th centuries, as technology, specialization, and Taylorism progressed in capitalist industry, all the workers participating in the production process no longer needed to be informed about everything relevant to the production process. According to Will and Flichy, in the core area of capitalism the role of the media and of most learning institutions shifted from the formation of a few knowledgeable and wise producers to the shaping of a mass of insatiable consumers.

However, if this shift from the organization of production towards the organization of consumption characterized the changing function of the mass media in the most industrially-developed countries at the beginning of the 20th century, it did not spread uniformly over the globe. For instance, Lenin's Russia went quite the opposite route. Indeed, if the "popularization" of mass-media products in the core area of capitalism was characterized by a shifting from the Bourgeois Puritan's organization of production towards the organization of mass consumption, the Marxist press in pre-revolutionary Russia (while addressing itself to larger and larger number of militants of the clandestine Communist party) was emphasizing a kind of proletariat puritan's organization of the revolution and the planned economic development of the U.S.S.R. As Lenin himself insisted at the very beginning of the 20th century:

> A newspaper is not only a collective propagandist and collective agitator, but also a collective organizer. In this respect it can be compared to the scaffolding erected around a building in construction; it marks the contours of the structure and facilitates communication between the builders, permitting them to distribute the work and to view the common results achieved by their organized labour (Lenin, 1902, p. 202).

Most historians in the Western World, while paying attention to the propaganda and agitation function of the Marxist press, have overlooked this crucial difference in the economic function of the press. It seems that the political and ideological differences between the mass media of the "Free World" and the press of "socialist dictatorships" have been over-emphasized, while the difference between the function of stimulation of consumption (considered by neo-Marxist writers as "irresponsible") and the function of organization of production (considered in socialist countries as "responsible") has been omitted.[1] Indeed, it is only recently that neo-Marxist critics in the U.S. and Canada have refocused attention upon the irresponsible function of the mass media in the core area of capitalism, without necessarily proposing the Socialist press as a model to follow.

However, this point of view is not so foreign to many countries of the Western World belonging to the periphery area of capitalism. Most North-Western European nations, and Japan, have demonstrated a particular sense of responsibility within their information and formation institutions.

People speaking on behalf of either the U.S. government or major American private corporations have a tendency to believe that all the Western World shares the American key concepts of communication (e.g., "freedom of information," "international free flow of information"). Consequently, they also believe that, sooner or later, communication systems of the rest of the "Free World" are going to end up under the exclusive control of private

---

[1]This is particularly the case in American handbooks in international journalism. (See e.g., Siebert et al., 1956; Markham, 1967, as well as the French manual by Cayrol, 1973.)

enterprise. However, despite these visions, most countries of the Western World (including English-speaking countries such as England and Canada) have maintained, developed, and improved the existence of public broad-casting systems. But while certain American critics as well as unconditional supporters of the free-enterprise system have insisted upon the political dangers of such "public" mass-communication systems (e.g., such networks' sole protection and endorsement of the empowered), the potential functions of economic mobilization and economic organizaton that such systems *can* fulfill have been overlooked.

Governments in countries where there is some form of public broad-casting have not all been equally irresponsible. On the contrary, some, especially during the last thirty years, have been quite responsible on this matter. To avoid what, on the "private" side of the alternative, seems to be the constraints imposed by selfish and very short term profit-seeking mass-communication entrepreneurs and what, on the "public" side of the alter-native, seem to be the constraints imposed by megalomaniac politicians, the concept of "responsible information" which should satisfy "everyone's right to be properly informed" has been elaborated, developed, and has taken a noticeable impetus within the most economically advanced countries of North-Western Europe as well as Japan.

However, if these concepts of "right for everyone to proper information" and "responsible information" can be considered everywhere as a creative compromise between the so-called "irresponsible" information system pro-vided by private mass-communication enterprises and the alleged "govern-mental propaganda" of the publicly owned media networks, it must be pointed out that these rather new concepts are not implemented in the same fashion and at identical levels in all of these countries. For instance, while, in most countries of North-Western Europe and in Canada, these concepts have been applied mainly to political, social, and cultural issues, in Japan, they seem to have been applied mostly to the area of national and international economy.

In Western Europe, Canada, and, probably, Mexico, the general tend-ency has been to follow the policies established in 1949 by the West-German states of Bavaria and Hesse and widely publicized in 1963 by Pope John XXIII's Encyclical letter, and, in 1964, by his successor, Pope Paul VI's declaration, according to which

> The right to be properly informed is a universal, inviolable, and unalterable modern man's right since it is grounded within human nature. It is both a passive and an active right since it consists in the right to look for information as well as the right for everyone to receive it.[2]

---

[2] Pope Paul VI, declaration to the members of a United Nations special seminar on freedom of information, Rome, The Vatican, April 1964.

Indeed, these concepts of "responsible information" and "right for everyone to proper information" clearly come from political and ideological dilemmas pertaining to European history. Amazingly promoted world-wide by two recent Catholic Popes, they are establishing a bridge between the old puritan and bourgeois' Protestant ethic and some aspects of the Marxist-Leninist understanding of the concept of mass information which has been recently revitalized in the West through important UNESCO and United Nations' debates. From the puritan and bourgeois' Protestant ethic, the concept of "responsible information" keeps the idea of a "useful" and "proper" information but, instead of being accessible only to a few "puritan bourgeois" it begs for general "public access." And, in order to be truly accessible to everyone, these concepts, in a fashion which can be considered as being located midway between the Marxist-Leninist dogmatic interpretation of news and the American cult for "hard" and "genuine" facts, insist upon the point that "information has to be presented in a proper context through which everyone can give a proper meaning to facts" (Balle, 1973, p. 204).

More specifically, in most of North-Western Europe, the social orientation of these concepts originates from the right of *everyone* to have *equal* access to proper information. Their political orientation derives from an assumption that dogmatism and ideological dominance is avoided when all political factions are provided with some access to the media. For example, Jean Schwoebel, a *Le Monde* journalist, argues that in order to be free from governmental intervention, information institutions should avoid being publicly owned, and in order to be free from any indirect but insidious constraints from the ruling classes information institutions should also avoid being managed by private entrepreneurs (Balle, 1973, p. 204). According to Schwoebel (1968), the solution to this dilemma is, of course, *Le Monde's* original system of self-management and self-financing. *Le Monde's* journalists, with the help of an elected administrator, are independent owner-managers of their institution. However, when one reads *Le Monde*, one realizes that a solid formation through a long education is needed. Not all French persons are equally able to understand this possibly "elitist" paper. But instead of diminishing the quality of their "elite" newspapers to the lowest common denominator to make them profitable in the short term, several countries of the First World have made noticeable collective investments in order to upgrade the level, quality, and quantity of their national educational systems. According to many observers who have recently studied Japan, (for example, see Vogel, 1979 and Servan-Schreiber 1980, p. 304) it is there that the highest educated proportion of a country may be found. Since many of Japan's mass-media consumers *are* highly educated, it is not surprising that Japan also has the largest circulation of education and information-oriented media (Kato, 1978). In Japan, the educational function of the media, largely fulfilled by public radio and television networks, is also shared by private radio and TV networks, as well as by the newspaper industry. Although it would be difficult to argue that the dominant understanding of the function of the press in Japan is the legitimate offspring of a marriage between the puritan bourgeois Protestant ethic and the Marxist-Leninist theory of the press successively consecrated by two recent Catholic Popes, it remains nevertheless, as Merrill et al. (1970, p. 259) point out, that "the Japanese press is free from government control and influence, and it has progressed rapidly under a combination of 'libertarian' and 'social responsibility' theory of the press." It can be added that the "social responsibility" theory which is applied through the presentation of education and information-oriented contents in most mass media seems to be more important in this country than the "libertarian" theory of the press. Indeed, while Anglo-American mass communication industries are obsessed with showing substantial profits even in the short term, Japanese media and, especially, the most important newspapers, according to Merrill et. al. (1970, pp. 255-256), are very often, if not always, in the red.

It becomes obvious that the concept of "sound business practice" as related to the economy of information has a meaning in Japan which is almost diametrically opposed to the one it seems to have in the core area of capitalism. Again, in Anglo-American countries, it is supposed to be a "sound business practice" to make information media profitable through the selling of audiences to advertisers. Therefore, in the countries belonging to the core area of capitalism, mass-communiction products are considered as gratifying conveniences able to advertise advertisements and their function is to do little or nothing else.

However, in Japan and some other countries, it seems that the main function of mass-communication products is to inform, if necessary at a cost, the productive economic agents of the nation (instead of the consumers.) In Japan, mass-communication products are not considered as conveniences to be consumed in a passive fashion by their audiences. On the contrary, mass-communication products are considered as crucial ingredients of a creative process in which almost all persons involved in the production of tangible goods and services participate. Thus, Japanese mass-communication products are considered as investments which, instead of being directly profitable, can be immediately costly but ultimately "profitable". While in countries belonging to the core area of capitalism, entrepreneurs owning large and diversified consortiums combining media enterprises with non-communi- cation industries are often using the rapidly-generated profits of their com- munication enterprises to balance deficits suffered by their other enterprises, in Japan the high cost of proper information is largely compensated by the benefits generated by the selling of better and more appropriate tangible goods and services.

But if it can be said, in a neo-Marxist way, that Japanese mass media are more responsible than their Anglo-American counterparts, it must also be added, in a somewhat neo-Marxist fashion, that they contribute to the information of a much larger number of people involved in the production process than the elitist media specialized in economy in the core area of capitalism.

While in Anglo-American countries, the understanding of the production process is reserved for a few, in Japan, a greater number of workers are involved, through clear participation policies, with many aspects of the conception, elaboration, production, and marketing of goods and services. Their formation lasts longer and is more intensive and their knowledge acquired through education is kept up to date through the mass media (Merrill et al., 1970, pp. 255–257).

Given the above discussion of Japan, it becomes clear that Smythe's analysis of the economic function of the mass media can account for the aspects of stagflation in the core area of capitalism which are the by-products of the economic relationship between Anglo-American countries and their most dynamic overseas competitors. Furthermore, it can be added that those factors related to the economic information of the Japanese workers, combined with the previously-addressed Japanese working conditions (see How Japan does it, 1981), contribute to the explanation of the present economic situation.

Finally, the fact that Japanese workers do not have much time available for "leisure" (which, according to Smythe, is fulfilled in the West by collective and individual consumption or information for consumption through the media) diminishes their need and demand for consumption and, consequently allows them to save and invest money in productive enterprises instead of borrowing for media-stimulated overconsumption.

However, if this neo-Marxist analysis of the economy of the mass media unveils important blind spots and consequently suggests some interesting lines of action in order to improve the function, role, and organization of both formation and information systems and institutions in Anglo-American countries, it nevertheless misses a subtle but crucial point which is related to the function of the international traffic of languages and mass-communication products. Indeed, if it can be logically deduced that Anglo-American mass-communication products are used by their audiences as commodities for final consumption, while in Japan (most notably) such products are used by audiences as resources or ingredients for decision-making and creation of tangible goods and services, Smythe's analysis does not go so far as to demonstrate that non-Anglo-American audiences exposed to Anglo-American mass-communication commodities can use these products to make decisions and create tangible goods and services for exportation to Anglo-American domestic markets.

Although Smythe comes very close to making such a statement, his neo-Marxist ideal as well as his English-Canadian cultural and linguistic background (within which Harold Innis' theories on communication and impe-rialism constitute an important part) keeps him from clearly seeing the consequences his neo-Marxist approach could have upon the explanation of the present international economic situation.

INTERCULTURAL INFORMATION AND INTERNATIONAL COMPETITION, THE BLIND SPOTS OF BLIND SPOTS SPOTTERS

Although Smythe is certainly the neo-Marxist whose argumentation is closest to the rationale upon which this paper is based, it is almost by accident that he mentions that importers of foreign-cultural products can use those prod-ucts to improve their economic situation, especially through the export of tangible goods and services towards the country from which they import cultural products. When Smythe analyzes the recent "re-opening" of China to Anglo-American linguistic and cultural "imperialism," for example, it is only after having lamented that "No socialist justification can be found for competing in market research, product and package design, mass media advertising techniques with Western Consciousness Industry" (Smythe, 1981, p. 247) that he adds, "the best that could be said for China's recent policy on foreign trade and 'technology' is that it will increase the possibilities of a favorable balance of trade." Smythe's utopian and more Proudhonian than Marxist socialism forces him to see this period of the history of China as one of the revisionist "zigs zags of China's struggles toward socialism (Smythe, 1981, p. 247), instead of seeing that, perhaps, the Chinese have realized that the best way to fight fire is with fire. Getting their new inspiration from their Asian neighbors, such as Japan, Hong Kong, Taïwan, and South Korea, the Chinese seem to have decided that the best way to fight Western mul-tinational capitalism is with Asian international capitalism. Indeed, through this new and voluntary "re-opening" of China, the People's Republic of China may have decided to turn around the American dream of coca-colonization of one billion Chinese consumers into an American nightmare in which one billion Chinese producers join the workers of Japan, Hong Kong, Taïwan, and South Korea in the economic invasion of the domestic markets of the Western World.

If avoidance of this dialectic evolution of international economic strat-egies is a function of Smythe's remaining blind spots, first it must be ac-knowledged, before scrutinizing these remaining blind spots, that Smythe's continuing blind-spot spotting, as it were, has always been of seminal im-portance in mass-communication research and particularly to the develop-ment of this thesis.

If we turn to the functionalist schools and the work of Shils and Janowitz (1966, p. 409) while studying the impact of the Allied propaganda upon the

Wehrmacht in World War II, we may note that the Nazis employed the Allied propaganda efforts "as a point of departure for strengthening the unpolitical resolve of their men." This finding is very applicable to current concerns in transnational and intercultural communication.

As Shills and Janowitz explain:

> [The Nazis] had the legend of the effectiveness of Allied propaganda in World War I as a warning from which to "conclude" that if the Germans failed to be tricked by propaganda this time, success was assured. A typical instance of this attitude was contained in a captured order issued by an officer in command of the garrison of Boulogne on September 11, 1944, in which he appealed to his men not to be misled by Allied propaganda. The German order claimed that the propaganda attack in the form of leaflets was in itself an expression of the weakness of the Allied offensive, which was in desperate need of the port for communications . . .
>
> The Nazis realized that it would be impossible to suppress the flood of Allied leaflets, and therefore sought to clearly label them as such and to employ them as a point of departure for counterpropaganda (Shils and Janowitz, 1966, pp. 409-410).

Shils and Janowitz conclude that:

> it seems necessary, therefore, to reconsider the potentialities of propaganda in the context of all the other variables which influence behavior. The erroneous views concerning the omnipotence of propaganda must be given up and their place must be taken by much more differenciated views as to the possibilities of certain kinds of propaganda under different sets of conditions (Shils and Janowitz, 1966, p.419).

When this analysis is applied to transnational and intercultural communications since World War II, we can see that (especially within those countries belonging to the periphery of capitalism) First World, Anglo-American mass-communication products are used as contextual information about Anglo-American domestic markets. Like Schils and Janowitz with respect to Germany, Lasswell, George, and other mass media content-analysts have demonstrated that, during World War II, "mass communications of opponents, allies and neutrals" (George, 1959, p. vii) were used as "a principal source of information" (Lasswell, 1966). In peace time, when warfare is replaced by international economic competition, it seems obvious that the most successful competitors are using (probably unconsciously) foreign mass-communication products as contextual information, allowing them to better understand foreign consumers' needs, dreams, values, attitudes, and so on. Since I have documented this point in detail (see Ravault, 1980, a, b, c, d), I will note here that Japan has become the first world importer of American motion pictures in 1980 and that the Japanese seem to have a very peculiar

style of watching foreign movies. As Anderson and Richie (1959, p. 147) have
observed:

> At a foreign-film showing in one of the smarter theaters hardly anyone will enter
> the auditorium during the middle of a picture . . .
>
> While waiting they usually buy a program, much thicker than its European
> equivalent and containing information not only about the stars but about the
> director and cameraman as well. The story, in full detail, is also always in-
> cluded. . . One can walk through the lobby and find nearly everyone immersed
> in the program reading the full details of what they are going to witness in a
> few minutes.
>
> In addition to buying the film's program, some will come armed with the
> complete dialogue script, usually published some time before the film opens
> and widely available. The original language is on one page with the Japanese
> translation facing it. These scripts are particularly popular with those studying
> English and it is not uncommon for students to sit through two or three showings,
> using the film as an English text.

To conclude this crucial point, it can be added that observers of the
Japanese press have noted that, contrary to most readers in Anglo-American
countries, Japanese are very fond of detailed news on foreign issues (see
Merrill et al., 1970, p. 258).

Finally, in addition to its own system of surveillance of foreign environments, Japan is one of the largest importers of informative and enter-
taining mass-communication products from Anglo-American countries. Thus,
it becomes important to explore further the fact that Anglo-American irresponsible (entertainment) media products might be used in a responsible
fashion (education) by competing nations on the periphery of capitalism.

Smythe, as a neo-Marxist, has remaining blind spots which prevent him
from accepting, and consequently seeing, this crucial consequence of the
application of his own approach to the understanding of international communications and economy. Many, such as Smythe, prefer to denounce the
lack of humanity which characterizes materialistic capitalism rather than
pointing out the dialectical contradictions of this dominant economic system.
Smythe and others have a tendency to overestimate the power of American-
based multinational companies and to overlook their gradual takeover by
Japanese, German, and other foreign multinational companies. There is also
sometimes a tendency to criticize capitalism independent of its variations
among nations. The Marxist tendency to systematically look at class conflicts
and avoid looking at international and intercultural conflicts sometimes causes
scholars to overlook the important dialectic contradictions within the capitalist system resulting from international specialization of labor. Indeed, some
countries are becoming producers of goods and services while others are
becoming consumers of these foreign-made goods and services. This tend-

ency to overestimate the importance of nationalism, cultures, and languages is reinforced by what may be attributed to scholars' unilingual backgrounds in English. To a certain extent, it seems that ethnocentrism leads to belief that capitalism is somehow an Anglo-American invention. According to most textbooks, international trade was developed around the Mediterranean shores many centuries before England became a country. China and Japan seem to have been important commercial powers long before America was discovered. Therefore it seems to be a typical neo-Marxist, English-speaking bias to assume that international capitalism grew with the diffusion of the English language and Anglo-American mass culture.

Such scholarly ethnocentrism can be pointed to in other related ways. If, for instance, English-Canadian communication scholars are very worried about the penetration of American culture into Canada, it is interesting to note that *Quebecers* do not seem any longer to be similarly concerned. In general, the unilingual scholars seem to underestimate the strength of cultural screens. Finally, scholars such as Smythe, Mattelart, Schiller and Nordenstreng deal exclusively with the study of international communications between the First and Third Worlds. However, when these men (who tend to consider the First World as a monolithic block) generalize their findings from the study of these very specific North-South relationships to international communication theory, they have a tendency to neglect crucial differences which have little to do with communications.

Yet, as noted earlier, if these remaining blind spots preempt Smythe and others from recognizing that Anglo-American irresponsible mass-communication products could be used in a responsible fashion by countries which import them, it must be acknowledged that Smythe's work, and especially his neo-Marxist interpretaion of the economic function of mass communications in Anglo-American countries, helps us to better understand the process of stagflation in these countries.

CONCLUSION

One part of the solution to the stagflation in which Anglo-American countries are sinking would be to copy the Japanese communication model. Mass communication should be considered as an investment in the economic information of the nation's productive activities rather than as a profitable business through which audiences are sold to advertisers for the stimulation of overconsumption. Also, a much greater consideration must be given to foreign news (see Perkins, 1979). Foreign languages should be taught at all educational levels as Senator J. William Fulbright (1979) recommended. Ethnic and linguistic minorities should be protected and exploited for their cultural and linguistic backgrounds, and finally foreign mass-culture products should be imported in a significant fashion.

However, for the sake of Smythe's international socialism, the present administration in the United States does not seem to understand the situation in this fashion and is very far from taking the appropriate steps to correct it. Knowing that the publication and diffusion of Marx's *Das Kapital* among capitalist circles slowed down the socialist revolutionary process rather than accelerating it, this is probably why Smythe does not want to reveal the internal contradictions of transnational capitalism.

Indeed the actions presently taken by Ronald Reagan are not likely to go against Anglo-American mass-media imperialism which again is used by foreign economic competitors as contextual intelligence. In a new era of deregulation, the Federal government is not likely to conceive of regulating mass-media industries to make them more responsible. Returning to the WASP ethic, the U.S. government is returning to the English language- and culture-dominated philosophy of the "melting pot." And finally, to face up to the "*world challenge*," America seems to be willing to restore protectionism and go back to the "splendid isolation."

However, it is obvious that if America slows down its imports, economic difficulties will rise at unacceptable levels in other capitalist countries. Crises will result and socialism may triumph whatever the strength of U.S. military capabilities.

REFERENCES

ANDERSON, J.L., and RICHIE, D. (1959). "Japanese Film: Art and Industry." Rutland, Vermont: C.E. Tuttle.

BALLE, F. (1973). "Institutions et Publics des Moyens d'Information, presse—radiodiffusion—télévision." Paris: Montchrestien.

BARNOUW, E. (1978). "The Sponsor, Notes on a Modern Potentate." Oxford, England: Oxford University Press.

BENSMAN, J., and LILIENFIELD, R. (1971). The journalistic attitude. *In* B. Rosenberg and D.M. White (Eds.), "Mass Culture Revisited." New York: Van Nostrand Reinhold.

BROWN, L. (1971). "Televi$ion, the Business Behind the Box." New York: Harcourt Brace Jovanovitch.

BROWN, L. (1979). "Keeping Your Eye on Television." New York: Pilgrim Press.

CAREY, J.W. (1975). A cultural approach to communication. *Communication* 2 (No. 2), 1–22.

CAYROL, R. (1973). "La Presse Ecrite et Audio-Visuelle." Paris: Presses Universitaires de France.

DAVEY, K. (1970). "Report of the Special Senate Committee on Mass Media," Vol. 1–3. Ottawa, Canada: Queen's Printer for Canada.

DE GUISE, J. (1971). L'industrie des Média ou le Marché des Auditoires. *Recherches Socio-graphiques 12* (No. 1).

EPSTEIN, E.J. (1973). "News from Nowhere, Television and the News." New York: Random House.

EPSTEIN, E.J. (1974). News from nowhere. *In* G. Tuchman (Ed.), "The TV Establishment, Programming for Power and Profit." Englewood Cliffs, N.J.: Prentice Hall.

FLICHY, P. (1980). Les Industries de l'Imaginaire, pour une analyse économique des média." Grenoble, France: Presses Universitaires de Grenoble, Institut National de l'Audio Visuel.

FULBRIGHT, J.W. (1979). We're tongue-tied. *Newsweek* (July 30).

GALBRAITH, J.K. (1958). "The Affluent Society." Boston, MA: Houghton-Mifflin.

GALBRAITH, J.K. (1960). The unseemly economic of opulence. *In* C.H. Sandage and V. Fryburger (Eds.), "The Role of Advertising," pp. 66–73. Homewood, IL: Richard D. Irwin.

GALBRAITH, J.K. (1967). "The New Industrial State." Boston, MA: Houghton Mifflin.

GEORGE, A.L. (1959). "Propaganda Analysis, A Study of Inferences Made from Nazi Propaganda in World War II." New York: Row Peterson and Co.

GUNTER, J.F. (1979). "The United States and the Debate on World Information Order." Washington, DC: Academy for Educational Development.

How Japan does it, the world's toughest competitor. (1981). *Time 117* (No. 13) (March 30).

KATO, H. (1978). "Les Politiques de la Communication au Japon." (Communication Policies in Japan). Paris: UNESCO.

LASSWELL, H.D. (1966). "Language of Politics, Studies in Quantitative Semantics." Cambridge, MA: MIT Press.

LENIN, V.I. (1902). "What is to be done?" Peking, China: Foreign Languages Press. (1975).

MARKHAM, J.W. (1967). "Voices of the Red Giants, Communications in Russia and China." Ames, IO: Iowa State University Press.

MERRILL, J.C., BRYAN, C.R., and ALISKY, M. (1970). "The Foreign Press, a Survey of the World's Journalism." Baton Rouge, LA: Louisiana State University Press.

PERKINS, J.A. (1979). "Strenth Through Wisdom, A Critique of U.S. Capability, A Report to the President from the President's Commission on Foreign Language and International Studies." Washington, DC: Government Printing Office.

POWERS, R. (1977). "The News' Casters, the News Business as Show Business." New York: St. Martin's Press.

RAVAULT, R.-J. (1980a). De l'Exploitation des "Despotes Culturels" par les Télépectateurs. *In* A. Méar, (Ed.), "Recherches Québécoises sur la Télévision," pp. 167–177. Laval, Québec: Albert Saint-Martin.

RAVAULT, R.-J. (1980b). "De l'Exploitation Economiques des 'Seigneurs de la Culture de Masse; par leurs 'Vassaux'." (Paper presented at the Congrès de fondation de l'Association Canadienne de Communication, Montréal, Québec, le 31 mai, 1980.)

RAVAULT, R.-J. (1980c). "International Expansion of Anglo-American Communications and Economic Recession in Anglo-American Countries." (Paper presented at the XXX International Conference on Communication, I.C.A., Acapulco, Mexico, May 18–23, 1980.)

RAVAULT, R.-J. (1980d). "Some Possible Economic Dysfunctions of the Anglo-American Practice of International Communications." Unpublished dissertation, University of Iowa.

SCHWOEBEL, J. (1968). "La Presse, Le Pouvoir et l'Argent." Paris: Seuil.

SERVAN-SCHREIBER, J.-J. (1980). "Le Défi Mondial." Montréal, Quebec: Select.

SERVAN-SCHREIBER, J.L. (1972). "Le Pouvoir d'Informer, qui le détient, comment il s'exerce, ce qu'il sera demain." Paris: Robert Laffont.

SHILS, E.A., and JANOWITZ, M. (1966). Cohesion and desintegration in the Wehrmacht in World War II. *In* B. Berelson and M. Janowitz (Eds.), "Reader in Public Opinion and Communications," 2nd ed., New York: Free Press.

SIEBERT, F.S. PETERSON, T. and SCHRAMM, W. (1956). "Four Theories of the Press." Urbana, IL: University of Illinois Press.

SMYTHE, D.W. (1977). Communications: Blindspot of western Marxism. *Canadian Journal of Political and Social Theory 1* (No. 3), 1–28.

SMYTHE, D.W. (1980). Communications: Blindspot of economics. *In* W.H. Melody, L. Salter, and P. Heyer (Eds.), "Culture, Communication, and Dependency: The Tradition of H. A. Innis," pp. 111–125. Norwood, NJ: Ablex.

SMYTHE, D.W. (1981). "Dependency Road: Communications, Capitalism, Consciousness, and Canada." Norwood, NJ: Ablex.

TUCHMAN, G. (Ed.) (1974). "The TV Establishment, Programming for Power and Profit." Englewood Cliffs, NJ: Prentice-Hall.

VOGEL, E. (1979). "Japan as Number One: Lessons for America." Cambridge, MA: Harvard University Press.

WEBER, M. (1930). "The Protestant Ethic and the Spirit of Capitalism." London: George Allan and Unwin.

WILL, N. (1976). "Essai sur la presse et le capital." Paris: Union Générale d'Editions.

3

Estimating the Impact of Imported versus National Television Programming in Brazil

JOSEPH D. STRAUBHAAR

Office of Research
U.S. International Communication Agency
1750 Pennsylvania Avenue NW
Washington, D.C. 20547

This paper assesses the impact of imported television programs upon the audiences of one major developing country, Brazil. This impact is estimated by the proportion of audience hours spent watching imported versus national programming. Although the number of imported programs broadcast in Brazil continues to increase, the relative proportion of the audience watching them has declined, indicating, perhaps, a decline in their impact.

This paper examines briefly the literature on the flow of television programs and compares several means of measuring the flow of imported television programs and estimating its impact. After describing the most appropriate measure, the impact of imported versus nationally-produced programs is examined for São Paulo, Brazil, 1963-1977.

MEASURING THE FLOW OF IMPORTED TELEVISION PROGRAMS

The flow of television programs into other cultures has been intriguing, among issues of cultural dependence and diffusion, partially because it can be measured. The goal of measurement is, of course, to give insight into the impact of imported programs on local viewers and their cultures.

In early non-quantitative studies, Schiller (1971) and Wells (1972) saw imported programs overwhelming most countries, particularly in Latin America. In the first quantitative analysis, Nordenstreng and Varis (1974) found that many Latin American countries imported much of their television programming from the U.S.

Breaking down the overall flow of programs, Beltran and Fox de Cardona (1979, p. 59), Read (1976), and Tunstall (1977) found a strong current of news material and television entertainment programs from U.S. commercial suppliers to Latin America. However, Tunstall (1977, pp. 38-42) concluded that the flow had declined from a high point that it reached during the mid-1960s. Pool (1977, p. 143) also saw a decrease in the outward flow of American programs as national and regional centers of production in the developing world increased.

In making such evaluations, the choice of measurement is critical. Different measures will give varying impressions of the impact of imports. For example, in Brazil there was fierce and partisan debate between commercial broadcasters and critics from academia and government. Commercial broadcasters examined only the proportions of imported and nationally-produced programs in evening prime-time, when audiences were larger and the proportion of nationally-produced programs was much higher. Academic critics looked at the entire broadcast day and found much lower proportions of national programs. The issue was heated because the research results seemed likely to affect formation of government policy toward broadcasters.

The two sides in this controversy represent the basic approaches to measuring the flow of programs. The first and simplest is the measure used by the Brazilian academic and governmental critics, the relative proportion of imported to domestically-produced programs in an entire sample week. The other is to emphasize the viewing times with largest audiences, either by examining only prime-time, as the Brazilian networks did, or by examining the whole broadcast week but weighting programs broadcast at different times by their audience sizes.

The first measure was used in the pioneering study by Nordenstreng and Varis (1974), who reported that the percentage of imports in Latin American television broadcasting varied from 30% in Argentina and Colombia to 50% in Mexico and Chile to 65-70% in Uruguay and virtually 100% in the Dominican Republic. Most imports came from the U.S.[1]

A study in São Paulo, Brazil, by the Grupo de Mídia (1978, p. 7) covering the period 1960 to 1978 concluded that imported programs dominate much of the television broadcast day in Brazil. They estimated that the percentage of broadcast time in sample weeks filled by imports rose steadily from 19% in 1960 to 49% in 1978.

The weakness of this measure is that it does not discriminate between the importance of imported programs broadcast at different times. There is no recognition that a television program broadcast at 8 p.m. reaches more

---

[1]The completeness of the data available to Nordenstreng and Varis varied, since the data were drawn from voluntary responses to questionnaires. The data on Brazil were apparently not complete enough to report.

people and has greater exposure or probable impact than a program broadcast at 1 p.m.

Controversy erupted over the appropriateness of this measure in 1974. A University of Brasilia study estimated that 57% of total broadcast time in a sample week in Brasília was occupied by imports (*O Estado de São Paulo*, Sept. 1, 1974). That figure formed the basis for a sharp denunciation of commercial television by the Minister of Communications, Quandt de Oliveira.

A new measure of imported programs' impact was introduced when the principal Brazilian commercial network, TV Globo, defended its performance. It cited its own figures, which showed that, in its programming "between six in the evening and eleven at night, 80 percent of the programs are Brazilian, created and produced in Brazil."[2]

Marco Antônio Dias (1975), of the University of Brasilia, criticized TV Globo's measurement: "In [the TV Globo statement], it is recognized that in relation to total programming, only 53.6% is constituted of national material, which is to say 46.4% is admittedly of foreign products."

WEIGHTING BROADCAST HOURS BY THEIR AUDIENCE

The TV Globo calculation is based on the premise that what really counts are the prime-time hours, 6-11 p.m.[3] This is sensible in that it allows for the differential impact of broadcast times, but Dias' critique, that the entire broadcast day must be taken into account, is also important. Specifically, there *are* appreciable audiences at all hours to be considered, but some sort of weighting must be given to reflect the number of people watching at any given time.

A weighted estimated of audience impact was created for this study. This method consisted of taking every program of every station in a sample week, determining its type or category (nationally-produced *telenovela*, imported feature film, etc.) and multiplying the number of minutes of its duration by the total audience estimated by the major audience rating research company, the Instituto Brasileiro de Opinião Publica e Estatística (IBOPE), to have been watching at that time on that day. That weighted figure is then added to the total for that type of program on that particular station and for the total of all stations. By adding all national productions and all imports together, the probable impact of imported vs. national programs can be estimated. I refer to the weighted measure as the percentage

---

[2] Programming Bulletin, *Rede Globo de Televisão*, 1974; *Visão*, Dec. 16, 1974).

[3] Another TV Globo analysis (1979) used the same premise when it discussed TV Globo's accomplishments in nationalizing its programming by analysing the ten most popular programs nationwide.

TABLE 3.1   Import Percentage Of Audience Hours Contrasted To Import Percentage Of Total Hours Broadcast In São Paulo

Year	Audience Hours	Hours Broadcast
1963	36%	34%
1965	48	34
1967	38	39
1969	43	49
1971	47	48
1973	37	42
1975	41	53
1977	42	53

Sources: IBOPE reports for October in months given, *O Estado de São Paulo* television program listings combined with weighting factors.

of total audience hours, as opposed to the total broadcast hours measure used by Nordenstreng and Varis (1974) and Dias (1975). It insures that an American feature film broadcast to an audience of 35 million at 8 p.m. on TV Globo will be estimated to have had greater probable impact than the same film broadcast to an audience of 5 million at 2 p.m.

Comparing these two measures shows that the probable impact of a certain type of program on the audience, as estimated by the number of audience hours spent watching it, is not necessarily the same as the amount of the broadcast day that it occupied. This study shows that imported programs occupied 34% of all television broadcast hours in a sample week in October 1963.[4] At the same time, São Paulo audiences spent 36% of their viewing time, or audience hours, watching imports. That figure indicates that imports probably had slightly more effect than their slightly smaller proportion of total broadcast hours would indicate. By 1977, however, imports occupied 53% of total broadcast hours in a sample week but attracted only 42% of audience hours (Table 1). While more audience hours indicate greater probable impact, more broadcast hours do not necessarily do so.

ESTIMATING IMPACT OF IMPORTED TELEVISION PROGRAMS

Throughout this study, a program's percentage of total audience hours is used as the best estimate of its probable impact on the audience. The phrase

---

[4] It has been established by a number of studies that one week periods can provide reliable samples of program content (Nordenstreng and Varis, 1974; Dias, 1975; Grupo de Mídia, 1978). I selected weeks in October on the advice of experts from the major Brazilian audience research firm, IBOPE, as being the most stable, representative month.

"probable impact" specifically indicates an estimate of relatively greater probability of impact based on relatively higher real exposure to the audience.

The impact of individual programs or program types could be better estimated in experimental settings where actual behavior or attitude change after exposure would be measured. Some excellent work has been done, for example, in estimating the impact of television violence upon audiences (Gerbner *et al.*, 1977). However, to estimate the impact of imported programs on the Brazilian audience as a whole, aggregate indicators were used: program listings from newspapers and stations, and audience ratings.

By this study's estimate, the probable impact or audience exposure of imported programs peaked in the 1960s and early 1970s, leveled off in the mid- and late 1970s and will probably decrease in the future. The audience hours accounted for by imported television programs leveled off at a point (42% in 1975-1977) below their peak points (48% in 1965 and 47% in 1971); the contrasting percentage of broadcast hours filled with imported programs rose steadily, if irregularly, from 1963 to 1977.

The difference between imported programs' proportions of audience hours and broadcast hours indicates that many of the imports are essentially fillers. The major Brazilian broadcasters produce most of their own prime-time programming and use imported programs to expand their broadcast schedules into early morning and late evening hours (Grupo de Mídia, 1978) because they are relatively inexpensive (Raoul, 1975).

This Brazilian experience supports the predictions of Pool (1977) and Tunstall (1977) that audiences will prefer programing produced in their own countries or cultures when it is available, and that the primary dilemma for producing national programs is economic. When audiences are small, nationally-produced programming may be limited by resources despite strong demand or preference for it. In Brazil, audiences are very large and generate enough advertiser interest and revenue to support extensive national programming.

The study by the Grupo de Mídia (1978, p. 15) showed lower estimates of audience exposure to imported programs. They found that "weekly audience exposure" to foreign-produced programs went from 25% of all viewing time (in a sample week in São Paulo) in 1960, to 34% in 1968, 32% in 1972, and 39% in 1978. Although their estimate is generally comparable to that of the present study, they estimate audience exposure, or probable impact, of imported programs to have been somewhat lower in the early 1960s and somewhat higher in the late 1970s.

This difference is important. The Grupo de Mídia study indicates that probable impact of imports may well be increasing (from 32% in 1972 to 39% in 1978). This direction of change differs from the plateau and slight decline (from 47% in 1971 to 42% in 1975 and 1977) that this study found.

If aggregate indicators conflict, it is important to examine the likelihood of specific kinds of imported and nationally-produced programs increasing or decreasing in popularity and probable impact. Disaggregating the overall proportion of imported versus national television programs allowed examination of the patterns for individual program types.

DISTINGUISHING IMPORTED PROGRAMS
FROM NATIONAL PRODUCTIONS

In order to calculate broadcast hours and audience hours devoted to various kinds of imported and nationally-produced programs, care was needed to define categories. It was very important to have the finest possible breakdowns between kinds of imported and domestic programs. For instance, many Brazilians criticize what they see as a constant theme of violence running through imported cartoons, live adventure or superhero series, and police or detective-type series.[5] Others wonder if the kinds of violence typical of various kinds of imported programs can be equated: "Is the violence of the cat Tom hitting the mouse Jerry with a club, or vice versa, the same as a group of criminals beating up Baretta?"[6]

I found it important to distinguish carefully between different kinds of programs, such as adult-oriented police adventure shows, child-oriented superhero adventure shows, and cartoons, to see which are vehicles for which values. Although there was only very limited data available about what programs had actually been broadcast,[7] I was able to get relatively satisfactory breadowns or categorizations for the different imported and nationally-produced programs. There were several categories of imported and nationally-produced programs which were easily defined. Others were compromises between ideal distinctions and those that could be made reliably clear.

IMPORTED TELEVISION PROGRAMS

An examination of the kinds of programs imported into Brazil clearly showed that they were far from uniform in character. They were directed at different

---

[5] Raquel Moreno, *Folha de São Paulo*, Nov. 18, 1979.

[6] Marcos Santarita, *Jornal do Brasil*, May 20, 1977.

[7] The only consistently available data base for analyzing program schedules turned out to be the daily schedules in the newspaper *O Estado de São Paulo* archives. Those provided only program titles. Brazilian informants helped identify the kind of program that the title represented but that was all that could reliably be uncovered about the nature of the programs.

audiences and stressed different themes. Since their impacts were likely to be quite different, I divided them in four categories.[8]

1. *Series*, such as "Bonanza" or "Kojak"
2. *Children's programs*, such as animated cartoons, series, or other programs primarily aimed at children, such as "Flipper" or "Wild Kingdom"
3. *Feature films*
4. *All other imports*, such as musical programs, sports, and documentaries

The proportions of total São Paulo audience hours drawn to these various kinds of imported programs, and their probable impacts, varied considerably (Table 2). Imported series programs peaked in audience hours in 1965 (34%), while the audience hours of feature films peaked later in 1975 (19%). Imports directed at children peaked in audience hours in 1971 (25%).

Over the whole 1963-1977 period, it seems that imported feature films and series not aimed specifically at children shared the same basic audience.

TABLE 3.2   The Audience Impact of Imported Programs: Audience Hours Drawn by Program Types on Major São Paulo Stations, 1963-1977

	1963	1965	1967	1969	1971	1973	1975	1977
Series (except children's)	25%	34%	15%	16%	11%	4%	9%	17%
Children's Programs	4	3	10	12	25	16	12	12
Feature Films	7	3	7	13	10	16	19	13
All Imports inc. others (total)	36	48	38	43	47	37	41	42
All National Programs	64	52	62	57	53	63	59	58
	100%	100%	100%	100%	100%	100%	100%	100%

Sources: IBOPE reports for October in years given, *O Estado de São Paulo* television program listings combined with weighting factors explained earlier.

---

[8] Programs were assigned to these categories by several criteria. Imported series and feature films were generally identified by the generic Brazilian term *filmes*. Series could be distinguished by their time span, i.e. an hour or less, and a continuing title and plot line. *Filmes* of one and one half or two hours were nearly always feature films. Both series and feature films could be assumed to be of foreign origin unless they were specifically identified as domestic or national productions. A 1973 sample of 1,297 feature films shown on Brazilian television showed that only six (0.5%) were Brazilian productions, 878 (67%) were American, 262 (20%) were British, 93 (7%) were Italian, and 58 (5%) were French (*Movimento*, Feb. 28, 1977). For series, the American proportion was higher and the national or Brazilian proportion lower, just as in most countries of the world (Read, 1976, p. 71).

They seem to have substituted for each other.[9] Together they accounted for a considerable part of all the hours spent watching television in São Paulo.

Demographic breakdowns of audience ratings for imported series and feature films revealed that the upper socio-economic groups watched them most. In the largest cities, some minor stations broadcast imports in prime time to meet this demand.

Imported programming for children followed the overall pattern for imported programs. Audience hours for it climbed during the 1960s, peaked in 1971 (25%), and declined to a plateau in 1975-1977 (12%). The relatively great probable impact of imported children's programs produced considerable concern from Brazilian television critics.[10]

NATIONAL PRODUCTIONS WITH IMPORTED SEGMENTS

There are also many programs which are produced domestically but contain foreign-produced segments or imported elements such as film footage or music. Making the proper allowance for such imported segments' impact proved difficult.[11]

1. *Variety shows,* which include elements of music, comedy, news, interviews and games
2. *Music programs*
3. *Comedies*
4. *News* shows, usually modeled on the American newscast style of short items read by an announcer and integrated with filmed actuality footage
5. *Public affairs* interviews or documentaries
6. *Sports,* primarily Brazilian soccer games but also including some coverage of international soccer, racing and other sports events
7. *Children's entertainment programs*
8. *Educational programs*

After careful analysis of selected examples of these program types, it

---

[9] A correlation of series' audience hours with feature film's, 1963-1977, shows a strong negative $r = -.82$, which indicates that the two types of programming tended to be substituted for each other. Although I find it useful to consider this strong negative correlation, the reader should be aware that the low number of pairs ($n = 8$) gives it no statistical significance.

[10] Violence on imported American programs was of particular continuing concern to Brazilian academic and press critics. (Cf., Straubhaar, 1980; Pfromm Neto, 1978; *Veja*, "As criancas bionicas" (The Bionic Children), March 23, 1977.)

[11] I intended to complement statistical analysis of probable impact with data about the amount of imported elements in Brazilian-produced programming. Unfortunately, it was impossible to reliably separate out foreign-produced segments in Brazilian national productions, using program schedules.

seemed valid to assume that music shows, variety shows, sports, and comedies were predominantly national in origin, although imported music, filmed musical performances, and foreign soccer games were occasionally included. News programs, educational programs, and documentaries more often contained imported material (Dias, 1975). However, they also were predominantly national or domestic in their origins, and identifying foreign material was difficult. Only Brazilian children's programming was so loaded with foreign film segments that it required a statistical adjustment to account for them.[12] Nevertheless, for all these program types, the reader should allow for a certain proportion of imported program elements absorbed in Brazilian productions which do not appear in my statistics.[13]

Of these Brazilian-produced programs, variety programs and news had the greatest probable impact. Variety programs (both studio-produced and live *shows de auditório*) declined in popularity in the mid-1970s, as they were pushed out of prime time by nationally-produced *telenovelas* (Table 3). The one popular variety show of the mid-1970s ("Fantástico") did have a large proportion of foreign news and documentary items within it. As a whole, the genre had, according to Sodré (1972, p.36) an "American" form, "the music hall style show," but "with a national content: Brazilian personality types, situations, allusions and games."

Television news in Brazil followed the American format in presentation and used considerable material from U.S. and European news services. In the 1970s, however, the major network, TV Globo, began to maintain its own overseas correspondents and other networks also tried to substitute for imported news and documentary footage when economically possible.

Brazilian music and comedy programs did not have great impact, in terms of audience hours. They were, however, always well represented among the top ten programs.

EXCLUSIVELY BRAZILIAN PRODUCTIONS

There are several Brazilian programming forms which seldom, if ever, included foreign film segments. Those were:

---

[12] In 1963-1967, the newspaper program listings showed programs which were usually one half to two thirds composed of foreign cartoons and series for children. For such programs, I made an estimate of the percentage of their content that was probably foreign and added that on to the total figure for imported children's programming for that station. After 1969, imported cartoons and children's series were usually identified by name in the program listings, although some "Brazilian" shows continued to contain imported cartoon or series segments.

[13] A 1974 University of Brasília study estimated that foreign segments might constitute as much as 37% of what seemed to be "national," domestic production (*O Estado de São Paulo*, Sept. 1, 1974). This study monitored actual broadcasts in Brasilia and recorded the time occupied by imports and by Brazilian productions in a sample week. Unfortunately, this study was done only once, in 1974. The figure of 37% is a high estimate, according to television experts I interviewed, who thought the percentage might well be lower in other years.

TABLE 3.3   Percentage Of Total Audience Hours For Brazilian-Produced Program Types
On The Major São Paulo Television Stations

	1963	1965	1967	1969	1971	1973	1975	1977
Telenovelas	2%	12%	13%	18%	17%	22%	20%	22%
Variety, Shows de Auditório	11	4	9	12	18	14	11	5
Music	7	8	9	7	3	4	2	3
Sports	4	9	9	5	1	3	2	3
News	9	6	8	6	8	8	11	10
Public Affairs	12[1]	2	1	1	1	3	2	3
Comedy	3	3	5	6	3	4	2	3
Children's	1	3	2	2	0.1	4	2	4
Educational	3	0.3	0.3	0	1.5	1	2	3
Feature Films or Drama	6	0.3	0.1	0.1	0.5	1	4	1
All Others	6	6	7	2	1	1	1	2
Total Braz. Productions	64%	52%[2]	62%[2]	57%[2]	53%	63%	59%	58%

[1] In 1963, "public affairs" included a great deal of electoral campaign material not found in following years.

[2] Total figure does not reflect rounding for individual program categories.

Sources: IBOPE reports for October in months given, *O Estado de São Paulo* television program listings.

1. *Telenovelas* ("soap opera" style serials of 8-9 months duration, unlike continuing U.S. programs, broadcast in evening prime time)
2. *Brazilian-produced plays* or *feature films,* clearly labeled as such
3. An *"other"* category which included the daytime game shows, women's interview programs, and religious programs

By the 1970s, Brazilian television critics considered *telenovelas* to be the most important genre. *Telenovelas* had the greatest probable impact, in terms of audience hours, of all nationally-produced programs. They attracted more audience hours than either foreign series or feature films but not more than the two combined (Tables 2, 3). Unlike imported series, *telenovelas* consistently had many more audience hours than broadcast hours, indicating their dominance of prime time hours and audience preference.

Brazilian-produced theatre for television and feature films had a marginal impact in terms of audience hours, but often were important in setting trends for other productions. Brazilian-produced series in 1978-1980 were developed out of dramatic special pilot films.

Daytime programming for women and children became increasingly significant in the late 1970s, since any expansion in Brazilian daytime programming meant a decrease in the number of imported films and cartoons broadcast then. Of particular note were daytime news, talk shows, and *telenovelas* aimed at women, and educational *telenovelas* aimed at children.

CONCLUSIONS

Starting with television broadcast schedules and audience ratings, there are two useful measures of the flow of imported television programs and their impact on national audiences and cultures: the proportion of total broadcast hours occupied by imported programs, and the proportion of audience hours actually spent watching imported programs. There are sizeable differences between the estimates produced by these two measures, since the second reflects a weighting of the first by the size of audience drawn by various programs.

In this Brazilian case study, a measure of broadcast hours between 1963 and 1977 shows the proportion of broadcast time occupied by imported programs to be steadily increasing. The weighted measure, audience hours, shows that the proportion of time spent watching imported programs rose until 1971, peaked then, and declined slightly to a plateau in 1975-1977. The two measures clearly indicate differing trends in the probable impact of imported programs.

Although impact is difficult to assess without longitudinal studies under controlled conditions, a reasonable inference can be made that greater exposure to imported programs reflects a greater probability of impact. Therefore, audience hours reflect more closely than broadcast hours the probable impact of imported programs upon national audiences and cultures.

In Brazil, the probable impact of imported programs, in terms of audience hours, has stabilized and apparently declined somewhat.

REFERENCES

BELTRÁN, L.R., and FOX DE CARDONA, E. (1979). Latin America and the United States: Flaws in the free flow of information. *In* K. Nordenstreng and H.I. Schiller (Eds.), National Sovereignty and International Communication," pp. 33–64. Norwood, NJ: Ablex.

DIAS, M.A. (1975). "Responsibilidade Cultural da Radiodifusão." (The Cultural Responsibility of Broadcasting.) Simpôsio sobre Radiodifusao, Associacão Brasileira de Teleducação. (mimeo.)

GERBNER, G., ELEEY, M.F., JACKSON-BEECK, M., JEFFRIES-FOX, S., and SIGNORIELLI, N. (1977). TV violence profile no. 8: The highlights. *Journal of Communication* 27 (no. 2), 171–180.

Grupo de Midia. (1978). "O Efeito Homogenizador (ou Alienante?) da TV na Cultura Brasileira."

(The Homogenizing (or Alienating?) Effect of TV on Brazilian Culture.) (III Ciclo de Estudos do Grupo de Atendimento, "Propaganda nos paises em Desenvolvimento," Sao Paulo.)

NORDENSTRENG, K., and VARIS, T. (1974). "Television Traffic—A One-Way Street." Paris: Unesco. (Reports and Papers on Mass Communication, No. 70.)

PFROMM NETO, S. (1978). "Efeitos de Violencia Televisada sobre Criancas." (Effects of Televised Violence on Children.) (Paper for I Simpôsio Nacional sobre Televisão e Crianca.) *Cadernos de Comunicacão Proál 4.*

POOL, I. DE S. (1977). The changing flow of television. *Journal of Communication 27* (No. 2), 139–149.

RAOUL, J.S. (1975). "O Desenvolvimento da Televisão no Brasil." (The Development of Television in Brazil.) (Suplemento do Centenario, O Estado de São Paulo, Oc. 4.)

READ, W.H. (1976). "America's Mass Media Merchants." Baltimore, MD: Johns Hopkins University Press.

SCHILLER, H.I. (1971). "Mass Communications and American Empire." Boston, MA: Beacon Press.

SODRE, M. (1972). "A Comunicação do Grotesco: Um Ensaio sobre Cultura de Massa no Brasil." (Communication of the Grotesque: An Essay on Mass Culture in Brazil.) Petropolis, Brazil: Editora Vozes.

STRAUBHAAR, J. (1980). "Television Violence in Brazil: The Impact of Imported American Programs, Brazilian Industry and the Brazilian Government on Society." (Paper presented at Northeast Conference on Latin American Studies, Dartmouth.)

TUNSTALL, J. (1977). "The Media are American." New York: Columbia University Press.

TV GLOBO. (1979). "Brazil: Country, People, Television." Rio de Janeiro, Brazil: TV Globo.

WELLS, A. (1972). "Picture Tube Imperialism?" Maryknoll, NY: Orbis Books.

4

The Mass Media and National Integration in Nigeria

ADELUMOLA OGUNADE
School of Journalism
Southern Illinois University
Carbondale, Illinois 62901

In multi-ethnic nations struggling toward national cohesion among disparate ethnic groups, it is not unusual during crises to accuse the mass media of promoting and exacerbating ethnic differences. The mass media allegedly exaggerate ethnic disputes, arouse hatred and fears by false news and invented threats, and whip the people on both sides into a lather of ethnic frenzy. It was in this context that the Nigerian military leaders assembled at Aburi to preserve the territorial unity of Nigeria and save the nation from a civil war. They discussed the role of the mass media in the crisis.

The military leaders agreed that the irresponsible performance of government information media fueled the crisis. This was not the first time that Nigerian mass media, particularly the newspapers, were blamed for the breakdown of law and order. The commissions which probed the shooting of striking miners at Enugu in 1949 (Report of the Commission of Inquiry, 1950) and the inter-tribal rioting in Kano in 1953 (Report of the Kano Disturbance, 1953) condemned the press in similar terms.

The important role played by communication in development has been studied extensively, while relatively little attention has been paid to the role of communication in fostering national integration. Yet, in Nigeria, as in most African nations, "we cannot really talk of modernization in any significant way in the absence of national integration" (Dudley, 1975, p. 29). With few exceptions, most African states have yet to employ consciously the mass media to create national unity rather than disparate ethnic groups.

The purposeful use of the mass media to foster national cohesion raises a number of questions:

1. What is national integration?
2. Who or what influences the content of nation-building messages?
3. How are the mass media to be used to promote national integration?
4. What are the implications for mass media construction, representation, and contextualization of reality? For training of mass media
   personnel? For government ownership of the mass media?

DEFINING NATIONAL INTEGRATION

The concept of national integration may be hard to define. For Smock and
Bentsi-Enchill (1975, p. 5), national integration "requires that identification
with national community supersede in certain situations more limited ethnic
loyalties." Coleman and Rosberg (1964, p. 9) define integration as the "progressive reduction of cultural and regional tensions and discontinuities . . .
in the process of creating a homogeneous political community." For Binder
(1964, p. 630), integration involves the creation of "a cultural-ideological
consensus of a very high degree of comprehensiveness." Etzioni (1965, p.
4) has argued that a community is integrated when (a) it has effective control
over the use of the means of violence; (b) it has a center of decision making
affecting significantly the allocation of resources and rewards; and (c) it is a
dominant focus of political identification for a large majority of politically
aware citizens.

Doro and Stultz (1970, p. 172) posit two different dimensions of integration: (a) territorial or horizontal, and (b) political or vertical. They claim
that national integration in Africa usually refers to the process of achieving
territorial integration—"subsuming the parochial loyalties of culture, region,
language, and ethnic and tribal groups to the over-riding interests of the
national community." There is no doubt that loyalty to the nation, rather
than to an ethnic group, is the common denominator.

Through its newly adopted 1979 Constitution, Nigeria has taken national
integration from the theoretical to the pragmatic. Discrimination on the
grounds of place of origin, sex, religion, status, or ethnic or linguistic association or tie is prohibited, while national integration is promoted by the
Nigerian Constitution's encouraging free mobility throughout the Federation, full residence rights for all citizens, and intermarriage across regional,
religious, ethnic, and linguistic groups; the role to be specifically played by
the mass media in this process is ill-defined.

MASS MEDIA IDEOLOGY

Neher and Condon (1975, p. 221) are undoubtedly right when they contend
that "mobilization of a national consciousness, to supersede regional and

ethnic consciousness, is partially a function of communication." The utilization of mass communication to foster national integration necessarily includes the creation and diffusion of symbols, slogans, myths, etc., consonant with the ideological orientation of the dominant political culture. Indeed, the use of the mass media to influence attitudes and behavior is feasible only within the context of a widely understood and accepted ideology.

Ideology structures people's perception and thought process by systematically excluding certain realities and shaping others. Clearly, a nation's mass-media ideology is a reflection of the national ideology, in general. However, since few African nations are truly "ideological" states, it is not surprising that they share a singular incapacity to recognize the relationship between effective communication and national ideology. Effective communication depends on the expansion and modernization of channels of communication. Efforts to modernize and expand the mass media without parallel efforts to ideologize and indigenize their contents are wasteful.

Historically, in nations where no ideology was formally adopted, the mass media synthesized one by conceptualizing the eclectic offerings of diverse policy-makers. This was possible because of the high caliber of the mass-media personnel and their intuitive ability. Unfortunately, most of the mass-media personnel in developing nations lack these qualities. It is not realistic to expect, for example, that mass-media personnel who have internalized foreign professional norms and values would be enthusiastic in promoting national integration in a one-party political culture. It is simply not sufficient to improve the technical proficiency of media personnel without ideological education. National integration cannot be championed enthusiastically by media personnel having values and aspirations which undercut those of the society in which they work.

INTEGRATION AND NIGERIAN MASS MEDIA

Deciding what the mass media should do for society carries with it the need to envisage the kind of society desired. Prior to the adoption of the 1979 Constitution, the ideal Nigerian society was never really defined. The absence of a coherent political and social philosophy left the mass media without ideological orientation or Constitutional directives. Consequently, the mass media, used and abused for selfish ends, did not look beyond the horizons of ethnicity and work for Nigerian unity.

Nigerian politicians, when threatened, were not above appealing to ethnic loyalties nor using the mass media to further selfish ends. While the politicians kindled the fire of tribalism for their personal ends, journalists irresponsibly, perhaps illegally, helped fan it into a wildfire, causing disintegration. A major proportion of the political commentary and cartoons in the government newspapers, for example, consisted of ethnic slurs and stereotypes depicting opponents as cannibals, uncultured, and enemies of national unity.[1]

At the root of the media's inability to promote national integration is the problem of ownership. Government ownership of the mass media in Nigeria offers important opportunities for promoting national integration, as well as imposing inherent dangers. In the past the opportunities were largely ignored while the dangers were exploited. In ethnically heterogeneous societies the mass media cannot rise above the ethnic interests of their diverse owners, be they governments, political parties, corporate bodies, or private individuals (see Schramm, 1964, p. 106).

As Nigerian military leaders at Aburi recognized and several studies have confirmed (Grant, 1975; Hydle, 1972; Okonkwot, 1976), government and party newspapers and broadcast stations were at the forefront of the divisive ethnic rivalry which culminated in the civil war. In this context, ownership has an ominous dimension. Yet this problem was never seriously addressed by the framers of the 1979 Constitution. Given the media's less than laudable role in the First Republic, a situation in which the Federal and State governments enjoy absolute constitutional monopoly of the broadcast media and own all the major newspapers, this is not in the nation's interest. The current government stranglehold on the mass media effectively minimizes the media's ability to perform their constitutional role.

If, as Section 21 of the 1979 Constitution stipulates, the mass media are "at all times to be free to uphold the . . . responsibility and accountability of the Government to the people," a formula that reduces government ownership of the mass media and guarantees their constitutional protection and editorial independence is urgently needed.

Ownership alone does not explain the limitations of the Nigerian mass media as agents of national integration. Their history, content, and limited circulation, and the professional caliber of the staff, are also significant. We shall consider how these factors have hampered the mass media in Nigerianization of the diverse ethnic groups that make up the country. Focus is on the widely used print and broadcast media.

RADIO

No medium of mass communication in Nigeria is more ethnicized and politicized than radio. Introduced at a time when Nigeria's Constitution was evolving under great strains of regionalism rooted in tribalism, radio was strongly affected by ethnic and political considerations. This resulted in rival

---

[1] See the resume of articles of abuse printed in the *Nigerian Morning Post*, July 25, 1964.

broadcasting services and the singular failure of radio to become a force for national integration. With the feuding politicians, backed by ethnic-based regional establishments, unable to agree "about the role of broadcasting in Nigeria's life generally" (Ume-Nwagbo, 1979, p. 826), it was not surprising that radio accentuated ethnic and linguistic identity at the expense of a national one.

Ethnicization of radio is usually justified by the aphorism, "Unity in Diversity." Certainly, there is much to be said in favor of this aphorism in a multi-ethnic society. But without a unifying ideology, there are dangers in over-emphasizing diverse ethnic heritages. This becomes dangerous in an atmosphere of intense ethnic rivalry, in which radio becomes less a medium of communication and more a weapon of ethnically based political power. An ethnically based system of multiple owners, multiple stations, and multiple services without national ideological direction necessarily limits the realization of the full potential of radio for national integration.

Since 1954, broadcasting has expanded in step with the ethno-political divisions of the country. This may be appropriate, insofar as it satisfies the pressures exerted by the ethnically defined states. However, with pressures for further ethnic divisions in the nation, ethnic parochialism may be given a shot in the arm. The opportunity for radio to minimize the centrifugal tendencies of disparate ethnic groups and to promote a modern national sentiment will be greatly reduced.

One of the most crucial problems facing African countries is how to transform inherited colonial bureaucracies into ones responsive to the aspirations and needs of the people. This problem is particularly acute insofar as the "media institutional forms developed in the Third World grew as extensions and imitations of those in industrialized societies" (Golding, 1979, p. 294). The implications of this for national integration are far-reaching. Because they are extensions or limitations, the African mass media are often manipulated according to foreign models and criteria. As Golding (1979, p. 295) put it, "Institutional transfer involved far more than organizational replication, it meant the wholesale acquisition of modes of practice, standards and assumptions."

In Nigeria's case, the existence of radio as a replication of the BBC hampers the communication process and prompted Ugboajah (1979, p. 40) to observe:

> Nigerian society to date has made little impact on the broadcasting media and, conversely, they have done little to appropriately shape the psychological processes, overt behaviors, and normative cultures of the rural people who comprise most of the population. Much of the problem stems from the fact that the Nigerian pattern of broadcasting is derived from the BBC. The granting of Nigeria's independence in 1960 and the replacement of foreign nationals by Nigerians . . . did little to change the system. Today, by and large, Nigerian

broadcasting system is maintained by Nigerians whose thinking has been shaped by the British system . . . this British system has proven counter-productive.

Though a strong indictment of the management of Nigeria's broadcast media, Ugboajah's position is shared by Katz (1977, p. 120), who argues that the media must "be more indigenous, not just in programming, but in *style*." It is problematic that, in a nation where more than 200 languages are spoken, mass media can be available in the vast majority of the Nigerian languages. For those who do not understand English or Hausa or Yoruba, Nigerian mass media hardly exist, except for the broadcasting of music. Even then, much of the music that is broadcast is foreign.

Radio is very important, since it is the most widely used mass-communication medium in Nigeria. Present-day facilities and services enable the voices of the federal and state governments to reach out to the entire population. But the opportunities presented are greatly diminished by their routine use to publicize government programs and achievements.

NEWSPAPERS

The newspaper has yet to become an integrating force in Nigeria. Historically, Nigerian newspapers were polemical party sheets, irreverent and increasingly living up to their reputation of being free "to poison the springs of goodwill and foul the well of trust, to impregnate the body politic with envy, hatred and malice.[2] Beginning with the press war between the *West African Pilot* and the Daily Service in the 1940s, most of the newspapers have used their pages to promote ethnically divisive political rivalry. This tradition has survived the attainment of independence.

The post-independence period has witnessed the proliferation of government-owned newspapers. As with the development of broadcasting, the establishment of newspapers has kept pace with the ethno-political division of the country. Eager government officials consider the newspaper as a propaganda organ and a symbol of government viability. As a medium for Nigerianizing the populace, newspapers are ineffective, because their readership seldom cuts across ethnic barriers and their content is largely confined to reifying government policies and condemning government critics.

It is also relevant that government papers seem protected from prosecution. Though Section 50(2) of the Criminal Code makes it an offense "to promote feelings of ill-will and hostility between the different classes of the population," no government paper has been prosecuted under this section. Yet much of what appeared in government newspapers in the period before

---

[2] Legislative Council Debates, Nigeria, March 18, 1946.

the 1966 military takeover clearly generated feelings of ill-will between different ethnic groups.

CONCLUSION

In his study of the fundamental processes of nation-building, Mazrui (1972, p. 278) said that the crisis of national integration "arises because different clusters of citizens do not accept each other as compatriots. The sense of a shared nationality has yet to be forged." Promoting a sense of shared nationality is one of the roles the mass media can perform, even though most African states are yet consciously to employ the mass media for this end. To be relevant and effective in any political culture, the mass media must construct and represent social reality in the context of the dominant ideology. When the ideology of a multi-ethnic state is not clear or is not understood, the contradictions of the society are reflected in its mass media's conflicting constructions and representations of social reality. This is hardly conducive to the promotion of a sense of shared nationality.

In "non-ideological" Nigeria, the ethnicized and politicized mass media are yet to become vigorous advocates of national integration. The factors of hegemonic government ownership, historical legacy, discordant professional values, content, etc., severely limit their effectiveness. To play a positive role in the building of a democratic and socially just society based on ethnic harmony, the mass media need to be unchained as a first step. The critical need is to devise an arrangement which accommodates government interests in the mass media and at the same time enhances the media's ability to perform their constitutional mandate.

REFERENCES

BINDER, L. (1964). National integration and political development. *American Political Review* 58, 622–631.

COLEMAN, J.S., and ROSEBERG, C.G., (Eds.) (1964). "Political Parties and National Integration in Tropical Africa." Los Angeles, CA: University of California Press.

DORO, M.E., and STULTZ, N.M. (Eds.) (1970). "Governing in Black Africa." Englewood Cliffs, NJ: Prentice-Hall.

DUDLEY, B.J. (1975). Military government and national integration in Nigeria. *In* O.B. Smock and K. Bentsi-Enchill (Eds.), "The Search for National Integration In Africa." New York: Free Press.

ETZIONI, A. (1965). "Political Unification." New York: Holt, Rinehart and Winston.

GOLDING, P. (1979). Media professionalism in the Third World: The transfer of an ideology. *In* J. Curran, M. Gurevitch, and J. Wollacott (Eds.), "Mass Communication and Society." Beverly Hills, CA: Sage.

GRANT, M.A. (1975). "The Nigerian Press and Politics Since Independence." Unpublished dissertation, University of London.

HYDLE, L.H. (1972). "The Press and Politics in Nigeria." Unpublished dissertation, Columbia University.

KATZ, E. (1977). Can authentic cultures survive new media. *Journal of Communications 27* (No. 2), 113–121.

MAZRUI, A.A. (1972). "Cultural Engineering and Nation-Building in East Africa." Evanston, IL: Northwestern University Press.

NEHER, W.W., and CONDON, J.C. (1975). The mass media and nation-building in Kenya and Tanzania. *In* D.B. Smock and K. Bentsi-Enchill (Eds.), "The Search for National Integration in Africa." New York: Free Press.

OKONKWOR, R.C. (1976). "The Press and Nigerian Nationalism, 1859–1960." Unpublished dissertation, University of Minnesota.

"Report of the Commission of Inquiry into the Disorders in the Eastern Provinces of Nigeria." (1950). London.

"Report of the Kano Disturbances, 16th, 17th, 18th, 19th May 1953." (1953). Kaduna.

SCHRAMM W. (1964). "Mass Media and National Development." Stanford, CA: Stanford University Press.

SMOCK, D.B. and BENTSI-ENCHILL, K. (Eds.) (1975). "The Search for National Integration in Africa." New York: Free Press.

UGBOAJAH, F.O. (1979). Development indigenous communication in Nigeria. *Journal of Communication 29* (No. 4), 40–45.

UME-NWAGBO, E.N. (1979). Politics and ethnicity in the rise of broadcasting in Nigeria, 1932–62. *Journalism Quarterly 56*, 816–821.

5

Mass Non-Communication in Developing Nations—An Overview Based on Mass Communications Research Prior to the Mid-Seventies

OLUFOLAJI A. FADEYIBI
School of Communications and Theatre
Temple University,
Philadelphia, Pennsylvania 19122

Governments of many developing countries are fascinated by such catchy slogans as "mass media for social change" and "mass media for national development." They are impressed by data showing high positive correlations between economic growth and mass media availability. Consequently, many government leaders in the developing nations equate modernization with Westernization, where Westernization = radio + television + newspapers.

These governments invest large sums of money in transmitters, broadcasting stations, and newspaper facilities. To facilitate the exposure of the masses to the media, some governments build community listening centers where, according to Franklin (1949, pp. 3-4):

> The receiver is often not properly looked after. Speaker horns get out of alignment, sets get wheezy and so on. Listeners soon lose interest under such conditions. . . Even when the receiver is regularly and properly operated in a welfare hall, the hall usually has appalling acoustic properties and is crowded with children who want to shout, women who want to dance and scream out gossip across the hall, youths who just want to hear a loud noise "from the box" and a few serious listeners who would like to shoot everybody else in sight.

Nonetheless, two decades or more after independence from colonial rule, many African leaders and governments are still wondering why, in spite of efforts to provide radio sets and listening centers, the mass media have not been the panacea, the magic wand, intended. They wonder why the masses remain largely ignorant of govenment policies and goals. They wonder why the mass media have not educated the masses and why their countries have not become modernized—just like America. In short, they wonder why the mass media have not changed their people's attitudes and behaviors.

On the basis of the foregoing, it is the contention of this paper that (a) the mass media have failed to function in the service of change, because the emphasis has been placed more on the physio-technical rather than audience factors, and (2) the mass media have failed because they have been called upon to function as the sole agents of change, something they cannot do.

Many developing countries continue to take their audiences and audience effects for granted. They think that media facilities create exposure and that exposure leads to change. As Davison (1959, p. 360) notes:

> The communicator's audience is not a passive recipient—it cannot be regarded as a lump of clay to be molded by the master propagandist. Rather, the audience is made up of individuals who demand something from the communications to which they are exposed, and who select those that are likely to be useful to them. In other words, they must get something from the manipulator if he is to get something from them.

This explains why, to a certain extent, the mass media have not fulfilled expectations in developing nations. There is no transaction between the communicator and the audience. No need-ascertainment surveys are carried out. The earlier "hypodermic needle" mass-communication effects concept is still very much alive. In Sydney Head's (1974, p. 321) words:

> Officials of some governments still tend to regard broadcasting as a one-way medium. They see it as a means of issuing directives, orders, fiats, or edicts, rather than (as) a means of establishing dialogue. They see it as a way of imposing conformity, rather than as a means of developing consensus; as a weapon of propaganda, rather than as an avenue of enlightenment. Such officials use the national broadcasting service as a personal megaphone, rather than as a device for responding to the wants and needs of those at the receiving end.

Uses and gratifications research tells us that the mass audience is not a tabula rasa and that mass communication does not take place in a vacuum. Communications in developing countries often take audience effects for granted because the masses are largely uneducated. However, illiteracy does *not* mean inability to think and have attitudes.

To the extent, therefore, that media messages are not related to audience needs, the audiences remain largely apathetic to government's objectives. The governments interpret this to mean insufficient and inadequate information. Consequently, they increase the flow of information by heavily loading the channels of communication. The masses remain uninformed despite the increased flow. Hyman and Sheatsley (1947, p. 413) have noted that the most difficult barriers to information dissemination are psychological:

> To assume a perfect correspondence between the nature and amount of material presented in an information campaign and its absorption by the public, is to take a naive view, for the very nature and degree of public exposure to the material is determined to a large extent by certain psychological characteristics of people themselves.

They then discuss the psychological barriers of chronic "know-nothings," and the role of interest in information campaigns. In a May 1946 National Opinion Research Council (NORC) survey, they tried to determine public knowledge of the report of the Anglo-American Committee on Palestine. In their report, they wrote:

> If all persons provided equal targets for exposure, and the sole determinant of public knowledge were the magnitude of the given information, there would be no reason for the same individuals always to show a relative lack of knowledge. *Instead, there is something about the uninformed which makes them harder to reach, no matter what the level or nature of the information* (Hyman and Sheatsley, 1947, p. 413).

Hyman and Sheatsley also measured the public's interest toward different issues. On the basis of their analysis, they concluded that "The widest possible dissemination of material may be ineffective if it is not geared to the public's interest" (Hyman and Sheatsley, 1947, p. 415).

The implications of these findings for developing nations are that increasing communication flow is not the only solution to creating audience awareness, and that, because communication in many developing nations is not geared to audience interests, it fails to sensitize the masses to issues their governments consider to be of national significance. Mass-media communication in these countries tends to be manipulative rather than collaborative. Few surveys of audience interests are conducted, and feedback is usually not solicited. Consequently, in the midst of massive information flow, apathy and ignorance reign supreme.

Beyond the failure to relate mass-mediated messages to audience needs, mass-communication research also indicates that the mass media are not as potent or insidious as they were once supposed to be.

In developing nations, the success of a mass-communication campaign is often determined by the degree to which it converts people to new points of view or by the extent to which it changes attitudes and behavior.

Klapper (1960, p. 8) has summed up the immediate impact of mass communication:

> Mass communication ordinarily does not serve as a necessary and sufficent cause of audence effects, but rather functions among and through a nexus of mediating

factors and influences. . . . On such occasions as mass communication does function in the service of change, one of two conditions is likely to exist. Either (a) the mediating factors will be found to be inoperative and the effect of the media will be found to be direct; or (b) the mediating factors which normally favor reinforcement, will be found to be themselves impelling toward change.

Klapper (1960, p. 17) reports on studies by Lazarsfeld, Berelson, and Gaudet on the effects of the 1940 presidential campaign on residents of Erie County in Ohio, and by Berelson, Lazarsfeld, and McPhee on the decision-making processes of voters in Elmira, New York during the 1948 presidential campaign. In the Erie County study, it was reported that only 5% of the respondents were "converted," and in the Elmira study, only 3% crossed party lines. The researchers therefore concluded that media "exposure crystallizes and reinforces more that it converts."

Yet the mass media are employed for precisely this role of conversion in most developing countries. In both the Erie County and Elmira studies, face-to-face or interpersonal communication was found to be more effective in changing attitudes and opinions than the mass media. Traditional communication in developing countries is based on personal interaction. However, in their reliance upon the Western mass media, developing nations have, in the main, ignored the use of their more potent and traditional modes—modes that are very functional even in the highly-developed U.S.

In that mass-mediated messages in developing countries often seek to change deeply-rooted attitudes and traditions, past research on cognitive consistency (see #9 and #10) may also be used to understand the failures of "modernization." Specifically, it might be argued that, in the face of dissonant information, audience members may employ certain psychological defense mechanisms which serve to work against changes advocated through the mass media. The following may illustrate this point.

In spite of mass-media campaign on the feasibility, adaptability, and profitability of mechanized agriculture, subsistence farming is still the rule in many developing countries. Developed nations, Western mass-media researchers, and some leaders of emerging nations find it very difficult to understand the stiff resistance of uneducated and rural peoples to innovation. However, as Shalaby (1972) points out, African agriculture is "a highly integrated way of life . . . involving emotional expression, family ties, religious sentiments, social interaction, and established habits of behaviour." Subsistence agriculture is the raison d'etre of the polygamous system—harnessing the services of wives and children on the farm. To accept mechanized farming would be to break ties with the land, disrupt the family structure, and, more importantly, accept and support the end of a tradition. So, even if the communication literally "gets across" to the people, it is stiffly resisted or ignored.

In summary, then, we see that for many governments of developing countries media availability is taken for media effect. Mass-mediated messages in these contexts are usually not based on audience needs but on the communicator's intent. Also the masses (whose attitudes the messages are designed to change) are the most resistant and least susceptible to change.

It is suggested, then, that increased emphasis be devoted to audience factors. Even then, developing nations still face many other problems. For example, Head (1974, pp. 350-351) speaks to the issue of language:

> The fragmentation of its potential national audience into separate linguistic groups drastically lowers the efficiency of a broadcasting system. So severe is this fragmentation in Africa that many countries have adopted a European language as the standard, which automatically cuts off access to most of the broadcasting service for most of the population . . . Either way, government leaders face a dilemma; whether to allow broadcast languages to proliferate for the sake of perserving traditional cultures, winning the loyalty of minority groups, and reaching a maximum audience at the risk of encouraging tribalism and separatism; or whether to standardize on a single broadcast language for the sake of emphasizing nationhood.

The case is even more serious for newspapers. It is estimated, for example, that illiterates outnumber literates ten to one in all independent countries in Africa. It is also estimated that about 80% of the African populations live in rural areas. "What these people have in common," said Murden (1976, p. 6), speaking of the underdeveloped nations, are "their problems and their history of misery. They are poor; they are diseased; they can neither read nor write; they die young; they are increasing by more than a million a month."

Thus, for the masses of most developing nations, newspapers are out of reach; television sets are out of sight. Little wonder then that the language and literacy problems have transformed the mass media in developing nations into what are now referred to as the "elite media." As a result, people who need them least have the greatest access to them. Feedback, if any, is thus retrieved from the active audience—the elite society. Programming is designed by the elite; supposedly for the masses, but with the elite audience in mind. Quite appropriately, therefore, some writers have referred to the inert and uneducated masses in developing nations as aliens in their own countries.

It would appear that education may be the key to mass-media participation in developing nations. To be meaningful, the education has to be two-pronged so as to inform not only members of the audience, but also to educate communicators to the options available in reaching their audience. The masses need to be educated through formal and informal adult-education classes. If appropriate, they need to be convinced that there are newer and better ways of doing things, and that occasions arise when tradition should give way innovation. However, the mass media cannot educate an inert mass.

Those responsible for the mass media need to be aware of the necessity of tailoring programming to audience needs. They need to be convinced of the necessity of opening feedback channels in order to facilitate collaborative rather than manipulative communication. Above all, they should be willing to conduct audience and media research. Money spent on research is not wasted. The result in terms of creating awareness, increasing motivation, and delivering the goods could be immense.

An issue raised earlier questioned whether or not government emphasis on the provision of the physical facilities—radio, television sets, and newspapers—had been wrongly focused. This emphasis may be due, in part, to media statisticians who relate national development to the status of media development in a nation, so that units of technology become the index of development. Schramm and Carter, for instance, reported correlations of .72 and .74, respectively, between a scale of economic development and other scales representing the development of mass-media receiving and propagating systems in 100 countries (Schramm, 1964, p. 47). Lerner (1964, p. 63), in his studies in the Middle East, found high correlations among four of his measures—urbanization, literacy, media participation, and political participation in 54 countries.

Such aggregation of data falsifies reality and ignores the many previously-noted psychological hurdles that mass-mediated messages have to encounter before reaching and influencing their audiences. Availability of Western mass-media channels is not development per se; it is their use or abuse, much more than their presence, that makes the difference between development and stagnation.

Beltran (1969) states that social communication entails "a general integration of social dialogue between the forgotten many and remembered few for the mutual benefit of all." Most governments of developing countries, having now provided the infra-structural base of the mass media should now devote increasing attention to the social impediments to productive communication. Much of this attention must be a consideration of past research and a dedication to future inquiry.

REFERENCES

BELTRAN, L.R. (1969). Communication and modernization: The case of Latin America. (Paper presented at the Eleventh World Conference on the Society for International Development, New Delhi.)

DAVISON, W.P. (1959). On the effects of communication. *Public Opinion Quarterly 23*, 343–360.

FRANKLIN, H. (1949). Report on the development of broadcasting to Africans in Central Africa. *In* S.W. Head (Ed.),"Broadcasting in Africa: A Continental Survey of Radio and Television." Philadelphia, PA: Temple University Press, p. 349.

HEAD, S.W. (1974). "Broadcasting in Africa: A Continental Survey of Radio and Television." Philadelphia, PA: Temple University Press.

HYMAN, H.H., and SHEATSLEY, P.B. (1947). Some reasons why information campaigns fail. *Public Opinion Quarterly 11*, 412–423.

KLAPPER, J.T. (1960). "The Effects of Mass Communication." Glencoe, IL.: Free Press.

LERNER, D. (1964). "The Passing of Traditional Society: Modernizing the Middle East." New York: Free Press.

MURDEN, F.D. (1956). "Underdeveloped Lands: 'Revolution of Rising Expectations,' " New York: Foreign Policy Association. (Headline Series, No. 119.)

SCHRAMM, W. (1964). "Mass Media and National Development." Stanford, CA: Stanford University Press.

SHALABY, M. (1972). Rural reconstruction in Egypt. Quoted in F.O. Ugboajah, "Traditional-Urban Media Model: Stock-Taking for African Development." *Gazette, International Journal of Mass Communication Studies 18* (No. 2), 81.

6

Public Broadcasting in Britain and the United States: A Comparative Analysis

NORMAN A. FELSENTHAL
Department of Radio–Television–Film
Temple University
Philadelphia, Pennsylvania 19122

In Britain, non-commercial broadcasting is embodied in the British Broadcasting Corporation, a mammoth and revered institution that was chartered in 1927 and held a government-sanctioned monopoly on all broadcasting in the United Kingdom until 1954. The BBC monopoly was broken in 1954 when Churchill's post-war government created the Independent Television Authority and allowed competition from a commercially supported television channel. The BBC monopolized radio until 1972, and even today the 28 on-air Independent Local Radio stations (or ILRs) are no real competition for the BBC's four national networks and 20 local stations.

Currently, the BBC splits its TV audience evenly with independent television and captures over 80% of the radio audience. This is in marked contrast to public television in the United States, which generally averages less than 3% of the audience and may surge to 10% for a popular and heavily promoted program. The contrast in radio is even greater, since American public radio is generally drowned out by its commercial cousins and seldom gathers more than 1 to 2% of the listeners.

The dominance of public broadcasting in Britain and of commercial broadcasting in the United States is in some ways a historical accident. American broadcasting preceded the British by only two years, and both systems were initially privately owned. American radio exploded with the Roaring Twenties and the business-oriented philosophy of the period. The British were startled by the direction their American counterparts seemed to be taking. Instead of following the American lead, the British pulled back, reorganized the privately held British Broadcasting Company into a government-chartered British Broadcasting Corporation, and proceeded cautiously under the watchful eye of a puritanical John Reith, the first Director-General.

American public broadcasting in the form of university-owned radio stations was almost buried in the avalanche of commercial expansionism. Noncommercial broadcasting limped through the 1930s and 1940s, received some recognition from the Federal Communications Commission in the 1952 Sixth Report and Order, but lacked any real stature until passage of the Public Broadcasting Act of 1967.

"The attempt in the United States," said British television producer Jeremy Issacs (1980), "was to graft a very weak public service system on a very strong and healthy commercial system." He also noted that in Britain broadcasting is run by broadcasters, while in America broadcasting is run by businessmen.

Another difference between the British and American systems is one of control. BBC programming is highly centralized, with virtually all of the programming decisions and most of the production originating in London. Programs on the two television channels and four radio networks are carried to all corners of the country, although regional centers do supply localized news and weather segments. The American system places control in the hands of the individual television stations through a complicated process known as the Station Programming Cooperative, and PBS is much more of a distribution system than a national network with production capabilities.

Both systems have been accused of "elitism," although the charge is heard less frequently in Britain today than 20 years ago. Both systems feel an obligation to provide specialized programming for minority audiences— Hispanics, Blacks, children, and the elderly in the United States; immigrants, children, the elderly, and the Scottish and Welsh nationalists in Britain.

In terms of television programming, both systems are dependent on outside sources for their most popular programs. American public television has been roundly criticized for its dependence on British imports, particularly the costume dramas presented on *Masterpiece Theater* and other high visibility programs. PBS officials insist that British imports make up less than 14% of the programming, although they admit that these imports do fill a much larger percentage of prime time.

American television programs are very popular on the BBC, but these programs come not from PBS but from the commercial networks. *Dallas*, for example, is a top-rated show in Britain as well as in the United States. The British deplore violence in their own programming but eagerly purchase "high energy" action adventure series such as *Starsky and Hutch* from American producers. The BBC is directed by its Board of Governors to limit the number of programs it obtains from non-British sources to 14% of all programming aired, and almost all of this comes from the United States. Some

PBS series, including *The Best of Families* and *The Adams Chronicles*, have appeared on the BBC, but the American public-television contribution to British programming has been minuscule.

The British have perfected the televised costume drama to a high art. One reason is the strong sense of history that permeates the British psyche. Another is the huge number of dramatic programs—some 400 each year—produced by the BBC drama group.

"The advantage of a big production house," says Shaun Sutton (1980), head of drama for BBC television, "is the opportunity to experiment and take chances. Small production houses can afford to fail." Sutton also notes that most of the people active in television drama in Britain come from the theater, not from film as in the United States. British actors do not command the high salaries that prevail in the U.S. The cost for a one hour drama in Britain is only 20 to 30% of the cost for a similar American production.

If British and American public broadcasting have one thing in common, it is the financial crisis under which both systems operate. Principal funding for BBC operations comes from a mandatory license fee imposed on each television household. This fee, currently £34 for households with color receivers and £12 for homes with a black and white set, is fixed by Parliament and is something of a political football, despite ardent claims by the British that the government does not influence BBC's operation. In fact, the BBC takes its begging bowl to Parliament each year in much the same way that the Corporation for Public Broadcasting approaches Congress. Prime Minister Thatcher's Conservative government has steadfastly refused to raise the fee despite pleas that the BBC license has not kept even with inflation, that severe cuts in programming and other services are imminent, and that public opinion polls indicate that 73% of the licensees would be willing to pay up to £50 a year.

Consequently, the BBC has been forced to become entrepreneurial, generating income from a variety of sources including the sale of programs in 92 countries; the sale of books, records, posters, and other publications; the public display of costumes from well-known BBC productions such as *Elizabeth R* and *The Six Wives of Henry VIII*, and the publication of a *TV Guide*-listing of radio and television programs, *Radio Times*. This publication has the largest circulation of any periodical in Britain, some four to five million copies weekly, and earns its parent a profit of about £2,000,000 yearly.

Almost all of the expensive dramatic series now produced by the BBC are funded jointly under a coproduction agreement with Time-Life or some other distribution company. This need for financial support through coproduction is distasteful to the British and something they would never do in better times. Obviously, it influences the decision-making process, and the BBC has admittedly lost some of its independence in the search for "salable" productions. American public television stations dependent on corporate underwriting are not unfamiliar with the need to choose noncontroversial topics and even to compromise ideas in order to secure financial support.

Education is one other area in which the BBC is both similar and dissimilar from its American counterpart. The British have always given a substantial portion of their broadcast day to curricular-related programming, both on radio and on television. American public broadcasting actually began as educational broadcasting, but curricular-related programming—programming directly related to school and university coursework—has never achieved a very high level of success. Some attempts have been made to offer college courses over television, sometimes with specially prepared tele-lectures and at other times with previously produced program series such as *Civilization* and *The Ascent of Man*.

In contrast, the British have had remarkable success with an entirely different concept, the Open University. The Open University was established in 1969 as a totally independent degree-granting institution for intellectually talented adults who did not have an opportunity to pursue a traditional university education.

"The intent," said Robert Rowland (1980), head of the BBC-Open University Project, "was to create a university of the second chance, not the second rate." Academic standards are on a par with Oxford and Cambridge, and only one in three applicants is accepted for enrollment. The BBC role in this unique partnership is to produce and air the radio and television programs that are a vital part of each Open University course.

A typical course consists of 32 texts, 32 TV programs, 32 radio programs, a variable number of audio cassettes, and home experimentation kits when appropriate. Transmission of these programs is by open circuit broadcasting during the early morning and early evening hours and on the weekends. About 70,000 students are enrolled in Open University courses, and another 40,000 have completed the equivalent of a four-year university program and received their degrees. Even the Open University, with a yearly budget of £43 million, is not immune from financial stringency. Some Open University courses are being coproduced, and the BBC currently has coproduction contracts with the University of California, the University of Hawaii, and Miami-Dade County Community College.

The impact of the Open University has been profound, not only in Britain, but also in the United States. American universities recognize that their traditional base of students—the 18- to 22-year old—is shrinking and that older, nontraditional students constitute a market for college classes.

Walter H. Annenberg's recent gift of $150 million to the Corporation for Public Broadcasting was, to some degree, inspired by the success of the Open University. Annenberg, formerly American ambassador to Britain, has pledged $10 million each year for a fifteen year period to support the creation of televised university-level courses for adults. These courses will be developed and administered jointly by public broadcasting professionals and by academics from existing institutions of higher education. No American equivalent of the British Open University will be created, because the large number and the geographic distribution of American colleges and universities make such an institution unnecessary.

In addition to noting its different history, production system, and funding process, it should also be mentioned that British public broadcasting has been successful in two areas that differ substantially from the U.S. system. First, the British produce a critically acclaimed product that is salable throughout the world. American public television does not enjoy the same worldwide distribution. Although Hollywood and the commercial U.S. networks have supplied so many films and programs to non-American audiences that they have been accused, with considerable justification, of cultural imperialism, the rest of the world rarely gets to see the "other kind" of American media product.

Secondly, the British have demonstrated the tremendous educational potential inherent in radio and television. Although the American system was founded as an educational network, this pursuit has been abandoned for up-scale audiences and corporate underwriters. Of course, the Annenberg grant may help public broadcasting refocus on this original goal while continuing to serve a multitude of audience needs with diverse and creative programming.

REFERENCES

ISSACS, J. (1980). (Lecture to the British Mass Media Seminar, London, July 17.)
ROWLAND, R. (1980). (Lecture to the British Mass Media Seminar, London, July 21.)
SUTTON, S. (1980). (Lecture to the British Mass Media Seminar, London, July 10.)

PART II

Institutions

7

The Museum as a Communicator of Culture

THOMAS NEWMAN
The Metropolitan Museum of Art
New York, New York 10028

The museum occupies a key position as a communicator and therefore as a producer of culture. Surprisingly, few attempts have been made to discuss the social role of museums from this perspective. Perhaps it is because the museum has traditionally been considered a storehouse for the artifacts of culture, rather than an active creator of culture, that its communication function has been overlooked.

When considered as a communicator of culture, the museum can be studied much like other communication institutions. For example, it is possible to analyze the museum as an organization to see how it operates day to day. This would entail an examination of the museum's internal structure, its explicit goals, and its professional ideologies. Another approach might be to look at the museum's relationship to, and effect on, organizations and institutions within the larger social system and culture as a whole. Furthermore, any of these topics could be approached from a historical perspective, tracing their origins and developments over time.

This discussion is not an in-depth study of any one of these areas but is more an overview of some of the questions and other issues which are relevant to an examination of the role of the museum as a communicator of culture. While most of the following discussion is specific to art museums, many of the issues raised are applicable to science museums, theme parks, history museums, and a variety of related institutions, as well.

There are several conflicting strains running through the ideology of the museum, but there is general consensus that it is the function of the museum to select and preserve the artifacts of culture. Its prestige drives primarily from its skill in evaluating what to preserve. This selection process is an active force in the creation of culture, having consequences that can be seen as a form of "agenda-setting" (McCombs and Shaw, 1972), a term borrowed from studies of the sociology of news. "Agenda-setting" refers to the process by which the mass communicator's "agenda" of concerns and priorities, as indicated by the relative amounts of attention and prominence given to the issues or items selected for communication, shapes the audience's "agenda" of concerns and priorities. It would seem that this concept can provide useful insights in a wider context of the communication of culture.

For example, the effect of museum purchases on the art market and the interaction between exhibition and prices has been quite thoroughly discussed in the popular press and seems to conform to the "agenda-setting" model. Less easily quantifiable effects such as influences on the priorities of other museums and related institutions, like universities and art galleries, or on collectors, teachers, critics, and working artists, have not been subject to the same attention. Nor has the influence of individuals, galleries, or other institutions on the "agenda" of museums been examined systematically. In this regard, the influence of corporate and government patronage would appear to be a fertile area of exploration.

Thus, an analysis of the role of the museum requires an understanding of how museums communicate with other organizations and groups which together form an extensive system. One of the factors that would have to be examined in such an analysis would be the evolution of the field of art history and the corresponding professionalization of art museums. Among the key issues in this evolution is the invention of the concept of "objectivity," and here there are parallels with the myths of objective journalism and objective science. Just as news reporting is supposed to reflect objectively but not create events in the real world, the museum is supposed to reflect objectively standards of taste and quality that are somehow "given." Thus, the museum professional, according to official ideology, is supposed to be able to remain aloof from the hurley-burley of marketplace and fashion, serving the greater interests of scholarship and research.

However, while journalists and museum professionals may think of themselves as objective arbiters and neutral reflectors of the culture, it seems there is ample evidence from the study of mass communication to suggest that their selectivity inevitably reinforces those aspects of the cuture upon which their imprimatur is placed, while other aspects of the culture not so blessed are weakened and delegitimized.

As is often the case in complex organizations, museums have a variety of goals, not all of which are well-integrated and some of which may even be contradictory. While the myth of objectivity and the corresponding stance of the museum professional as an outside reflector of culture is an important aspect of the museum's ideology, there is a contradictory belief that ac-knowledges the museum's active role. According to this variant of the dom-inant ideology, one of the functions of the museum is to define and enforce standards of quality, setting as a goal the overall elevation of public taste and aesthetic awareness. There is in the museum a real ambivalence between these roles.

Linda Nochlin (1972, p.9) has traced this internal contradiction back to the opening of the Louvre to the public following the French Revolution, concluding that "the museum may be said to have suffered from schizophrenia from the start." The institution was conceived as an instrument for democratic education, "a means of spreading historical and esthetic knowledge among an ever-broadening segment of society, allowing to all a share of the cultural manna which had formerly been the food of a privileged few." At the same time, the museum set art apart from the social structure for weekend worship at "the shrine of an elitist religion."

The Louvre is generally regarded as the first great public museum. It is not so well known that, ten years before the Louvre opened its doors to the masses, the real birth of the popular museum took place in Philadelphia about the year 1782 (Sellers, 1980). In that year an extraordinary man, Charles Willson Peale, with a vision far ahead of his time, built a skylight gallery for his collection of portraits so that he might display them to advantage. At that time Peale was one of the foremost American painters, as well as an accomplished radical politician, inventor, naturalist, and a man with numerous avocations. As this gallery grew in popularity, Peale began calling it a museum. On a charming ticket that he printed in 1788—he was by this time charging admission—he exhorted visitors to gaze upon "wonderful works of nature and curious works of art" (Sellers, 1980, p.36). His museum contained an eclectic assortment of his own and his sons' portraits and trompe-l'oeil paintings, scientifically-classified animal and mineral specimens displayed in life-like settings (dioramas), mechanical inventions, artifacts of other cultures (particularly fine examples of Native American material culture), a few freaks of nature (which Peale was prevailed upon to exhibit despite his reluctance), and, eventually, the painstakingly reconstructed skeleton of a mammoth. This last, the excavation of which Peale commemorated in a large painting, illustrated Peale's extremely advanced ideas about natural science. For example, he refused to mix bones from different sites, which had always been done before and which had resulted in some rather fanciful reconstructions. Instead, Peale made plaster casts of existing bones to fill in symmetrical gaps in the structure, a procedure that led to a remarkably accurate skeleton.

Peale lived in a time when the boundaries between art and science were less firm than they are now. He considered the study of nature and the study of painting to serve the same end. All his exhibits afforded "a moral sentiment to the visitors to the Museum," and he explicitly regarded his displays as educational. As he must have repeated often in his continual struggle to raise funds for his museum, "if it should be immensely rich in the numbers and value of articles, unless they are systematically arranged, and the proper modes of seeing and using them attended to, the advantage of such a store will be of little account to the public" (Sellers, 1980, p.111). Although Peale's Museum collapsed after his death (some of the collections were purchased by P.T. Barnum), his Rousseauian educational philosophy had an indelible effect on the growth of the American museum.

I would suggest that it was, in part, Peale's curious blend of popular enrichment and pedagogy that led to the inclusion of explicit goals for social change in the ideology of modern American museums. Only later in the evolution of the museum did the ideology of professionalism and objectivity arise, with a resulting emphasis on preservation of the collection. It has only recently become apparent that these goals have never been integrated. As long as only a small number of well-behaved visitors came to museums, these goals did not conflict. However, the swelling tide of admissions to museums, and the broadening interest in the museum by people previously uninitiated in the proper rules of museum behavior, have led to what are euphemistically called "security problems." It has become apparent that paintings and sculpture on view are at risk. The role of the museum educator, whose traditional job has been to provide both indoctrination and information—to initiate new members to the museum audience and to encourage those already involved to assume an ever-deeper commitment—has become more vital. Yet the educator's success brings even more diverse audiences to the museum and opens further the rift between the museum's twin goals of preserving the works of art and exhibiting them.

It is perhaps not well understood that the attempt to mix social change with objective professionalism has some curious outcomes, due, it seems, to the different models of communication from which each goal derives. Educators, in the tradition of Peale, hope to raise the level of public taste by communicating directly to the mass audience. Curators, by contrast, tend to function according to a model of communication that is based on professional networks for diffusion of knowledge. It resembles the diffusion of influence model perhaps best illustrated by Kadushin (1974) in his study of elite journals. Kadushin found that ideas which first appear in intellectual journals "trickle down" through less elite publications, finally appearing in the popular press. This model of professional communication is related to Crane's (1976) analysis of systems of reward. Museum curators rise in status and gain rewards not so much from reaching a large or diverse public, but rather through recognition by their peers within their specialized fields. Their relevant audience is their fellow professionals—curators and professors of art history. Educators tend not to have such a well-developed system of professional communication, and therefore their relevant audiences are their public and their administrative supervisors.

It is in the interest of the professional curator to maintain the "trickle down" model of communication and, in fact, to create a steep pyramid through which the museum's influence can trickle. This maintains the professional's control of key points of leverage on the culture while allowing those who set the original agenda to distance themselves from, and take no interest in, popularizations of their work. However, since the mid-1960s, changing policies of government and corporate patronage for the arts have contributed to a shift in the priorities assigned to exhibition and preservation, and hence have encouraged a movement toward flattening the pyramid in favor of a model that more closely resembles mass communication.

Government funding for museums for both the National Endowment for the Arts and the National Ednowment for the Humanities has tended to ignore the trickle-down model of communication, and to coopt the professionals by offering them positions on peer review panels. These agencies have followed a decidely populist path, encouraging audience-building projects and making decisions in part on the basis of obvious political needs for geographical and presumably other kinds of diversity (Newman, 1975).

In addition to the influence of government funding policies, the constraints of corporate patronage has helped to further erode the hegemony of the curatorial model of communication. In the traveling museum exhibit corporations found a vehicle for enhancing their own public image as responsible and charitable participants in the world of culture. As stated recently by David Finn (1981, p.56), whose public relations firm Ruder and Finn is closely identified with the development of these exhibitions:

> The overall goal of such sponsorship is thought to be the prestige a company might gain by associating itself with the creativity and quest for excellence represented by the arts. The Philip Morris advertising series, which has been described as a landmark in the field of corporate sponsorship, states it clearly: "it takes art to make a country great. . . . It also takes art to make a company great."

For corporations, larger shows seemed more attractive than smaller ones, and exhibits with maximum appeal to national and international audiences were organized to take advantage of this new source of patronage. A totally new scale of exhibit became possible, and with it a new scale of communications activities, including extensive mass-market merchandising and television tie-ins. The resulting phenomenon was the blockbuster exhibition.

It is apparent that blockbuster exhibitions are a sign of the museum's move toward communication with mass audiences. As such, big traveling loan shows, which appear to be virtuoso preformances by curators, are in fact educational efforts which curators have had to support despite less than proportionate reward within their own professional circles. The combination of blockbuster exhibitions with a populist system of government funding has certainly put museums on an entirely new course, away from the curator's pyramid and toward mass communication.

Curators, in the meanwhile, have developed their own new technology for displays to counterbalance the temporary blockbuster shows. Their new device is a triumph of art history, of professionalism, and of the traditional steep pyramid model of communication. In its most pure form, it is called the study-storage collection, but many recent installations of permanent galleries are consistent with this elitist, scholarly approach. The distinguishing characteristic of this new approach is that the entire collection, or as much of it as possible, is put on view, usually in a fairly didactic arrangement with extensive labels. These installations differ markedly in design from the slick, streamlined blockbuster shows. Where the blockbuster is spare, emphasizing unique objects and masterworks, and is set up to handle large crowds and keep them moving, the study installation is vast, exhaustive, and set up to accomodate stationary, contemplative viewers.

These installations are very much what curators consider appropriate educational activities of museums. For the curator, only the original object is a truly legitimate object of study, and it is in the presentation of original works of art that the museum fulfills its central educational role. This is the one thing that the museum, and the museum alone, can do. The stereotype of curatorial insistence on the original art work runs exactly counter to museums' use of the mass-communication media. No matter how well-made, a film or a television image is a form of reproduction. Curators traditionally dislike reproductions, or at best consider them irrelevant. Although there are many notable exceptions, it seems there is a curatorial point of view that suggests one uses the mass media only to draw crowds, and distinctions about how this is accomplished are quite outside their range and interest, assuming the facts are correct and good taste is preserved, if that is not a contradiction in terms when utilizing a mass medium.

Educators have different traditions going back to Peale and tend to view the mass media as a means of addressing the goals for social change that the museum has espoused. They feel that the media are a way to awaken sensitivity among people whose aesthetic sense is dormant (and who, therefore, do not come to museums.) For this, the original object may be quite irrelevant, in that the educators' intended audience lacks a strategy for appreciating art. There are skills that can be taught prior to bringing people into the museum that, of themselves, are important, uplifting, enriching, and satisfying; and these same skills serve the uninitiated well when and if they do arrive prior to the first museum visit. There is also concern that the museum may have little choice in the matter of its relationship to the mass audience. If the museum itself does not control its communications through the mass media, others will exploit its image of legitimacy, its accumulated expertise, and its collection, offering in return as little as possible.

It is consistent with an educational perspective for the museum to become increasingly concerned with its complete communication system, with maintaining the integrity of the museum's information from its source through to its ultimate audience. This implies that the museum would have to regulate more closely, and thus become more directly involved in, the production and distribution of mass media content related to the museum's resources. The rise of museum publishing in recent years is an indicator of the growing strength of this educational point of view. Its advocates also point to the happy coincidence that financially-strapped museums might be able to take in some revenue from their communications activities if they participate in the production and dissemination of their educational messages. There is, they say, money to be made by flattening the pyramid.

Most curators would probably agree that these educational communications activities are desirable, but, in a time of intense competition for scarce resources, things could look pretty gloomy for the scholarly, curatorial approach which is apparently being driven into eclipse by the mass-media, blockbuster loan shows, and revenue-producing publishing. However, a compromise solution might be at hand in the form of the new communication technologies.

The first of the new media to attract widespread attention have been the various pay-television services. New opportunities in this field came to the attention of many museum professionals with the publication of *Keeping Pace With the New Television* (Mahony et al., 1980), a follow-up study to the Carnegie Commission's 1979 evaluation of the public television system, *A Public Trust* (Carnegie Corporation of New York, 1979). The Pace Report, as it has come to be known, recommended that PBS establish a cultural pay-cable TV service to bring performing and visual arts to the traditional elite audience. While PBS attempts to launch such a plan, commercial broadcasters and entrepreneurial organizations are moving ahead with their own advertiser-supported cable TV services to reach the "up-scale" audiences cultural programming may attract.

Videodisc holds vast potential as a museum medium of communication in several distinct modes — exhibition adjuncts, archival storage, and a relatively inexpensive, high-quality form of electronic publishing (Newman, 1981). Videotext and viewdata will probably have a role in museum communication, as well, although it is not clear exactly how or when.

The common feature in all these newer technologies is that they enable communications to be directed toward audiences that are much smaller than those dictated by the economic structure of mass-network TV. Furthermore, the paying audience for the newer media would seem to resemble the traditional museum audience, or at least the audience that has emerged in the last two decades. This audience is thought to be a likely supporter of museum-oriented programming, although they are not the group most excluded from participation in high culture that educators have sought to reach in periods of raised social consciousness.

It would seem, therefore, that narrowcasting may hold potential for museums to integrate the curatorial and educational approaches. Specialized programming would allow the museum to address its elite audience, reaffirming the trickle-down pyramidal model for communication that is consonant with the traditional curatorial, scholarly approach. At the same time, the narrowcast audience will be large enough to meet the educator's outreach requirements; much as educators wish to raise everyone's level of aesthetic awareness, they have come to understand that their effectiveness is blunted by the consraints of communicating to a diverse mass audience.

While the newer communication technologies may allow for some resolution of the contradiction between the museum's different goals, the problem of integrating the goals cannot be solved until museum professionals come to grips with the implications of the museum's role as a communicator of culture. The promise of these new technologies should not lead one to assume that there can be a technological solution to a problem that involves a conflict among goals, functions, and ideologies.

Likewise, the current increase in attention being paid to technological innovation should not distract from the fact that it is still the museum's foremost and unique responsibility to preserve the artifacts of culture. In our pluralistic and rapidly-changing society, this function has become all the more crucial. However, it should be obvious that for the museum to survive and carry out its responsibility it must have the support of the public — it must have a supportive social climate in which there is consensus about the need for cultural preservation. The best way to bring about this consensus is to communicate adequately to the public the significance of these cultural artifacts and the important role the museum plays in our society. Thus the museum's two apparently contradictory goals of preservation and exhibition, as manifested in the conflict between the ideologies of curatorship and education, need not be seen as antithetical, but rather as mutually reinforcing.

REFERENCES

Carnegie Corporation of New York. (1979). "A Public Trust: The Report of the Carnegie Commission on the Future of Public Broadcasting." New York: Bantam Books.

CRANE, D. (1976). Reward systems in art, science, and religion. In R. Peterson (Ed.), "The Production of Culture." Beverly Hills, CA: Sage

FINN, D. (1981). A sound footing for corporate support. *Museum News* 59 (No. 4), 56.

KADUSHIN, C. (1974). "The American Intellectual Elite." Boston, MA: Little Brown.

MAHONY, S., DEMARTINO, N., and STENGEL, R. (1980). "Keeping Pace With the New Television." New York: Carnegie Corporation.

MCCOMBS, M.E., and SHAW, D.L. (1972). The agenda-setting function of mass media. *Public Opinion Quarterly* 36, 176–187.

NEWMAN, T. (1975). "Art and Money: Decision-Making at the National Endowment for the Arts." Master's Thesis, University of Pennsylvania.

NEWMAN, T. (1981). Video discs: The emerging picture. *Museum News* 59 (No. 4), 28–33.

NOCHLIN, L. (1972). Museums and radicals: A history of emergencies. In B. O'Doherty (Ed.), "Museums in Crisis." New York: George Braziller.

SELLERS, C.C. (1980). "Mr. Peale's Museum." New York: W.W. Norton.

8

Unconventional Programs on Commercial Television: An Organizational Perspective

JOSEPH TUROW
Department of Communications
Purdue University
West Lafayette, Indiana 47906

That American commercial network television is unadventuresome and derivative has become a truism among critics, practitioners, and academics (see, for example, Barnouw, 1975; Brown, 1971; and Shanks, 1976). Possibly as a consequence of this viewpoint, research and writing on production of television content has tended to focus on the constraints which yield predictable content (e.g., Baldwin and Lewis, 1972; Cantor, 1972; Melody, 1973; Tuchman, 1974; and Turow, 1978). Left virtually unopened has been an entire research area relating to the possibilities of programming change within the commercial television system. The purpose of this paper is not to challenge the notion that much of American commercial television is patterned and derivative. Rather, it is to explore the organizational and interorganizational conditions which foster those rare instances when unconventional programs are conceived, produced, scheduled, and aired.

Unconventional television programs may be defined as those programs understood within the TV industry as departing strongly from the current norm. A large body of literature has grown around the study of innovation in non-symbol producing organizations (see, for example, Burns and Stalker, 1961; Johnson, 1970; Khadwalla, 1977; National Industrial Conference Board, 1967; March and Simon, 1958; Marquis, 1976; Panel on Invention and In-

*Many thanks go to Patricia Buzzanell of Purdue University for her hard-working help during the preliminary stages of this project. Thanks are due to Paul Rosenthal, Mardi Gregory, and other members of the Communication Studies Program at UCLA for their friendliness and support during the interviewing stage. A major portion of this investigation was funded by the Purdue Research Foundation.

novation, 1967; Rogers and Rogers, 1967; Rothberg, 1976; Schon, 1966; Steele, 1975; Wainright and Gerlach, 1968; and Young, 1970). Though only a small number of articles even mentions the concept of *mass media* innovation (see Crane, 1976; DiMaggio and Hirsch, 1976; Hirsch, 1972; Peterson, 1976; and Peterson and Berger, (1972), the two bodies of literature, taken together, do provide a useful framework for developing hypotheses about the conditions that foster unconventional television programs. Both note that innovations are risky and unlikely to be developed during relatively stable organizational and environmental conditions that encourage the status quo, e.g., when competition is not a problem or when market (i.e., distributor or consumer) dissatisfaction might ensue if accepted approaches are abrogated (Hirsch, 1972, pp. 741–42; Young, 1970, p. 53; Rogers and Rogers, 1967, pp. 70–71). On the other hand, the writings stress that a firm is much more likely to produce innovative products when it or its environment experiences tension-inducing changes (see, for example, Panel on Invention and Innovation, 1967, pp. 3 and 48).

These studies also agree that audience force is not the primary motivation of innovation. While consumers ultimately play an important part in accepting or rejecting innovations, the most important factors in a firm's environment which induce tensions toward innovation include aggressive competition (that may ignite a fear of falling behind); changing technology, particularly as it relates to product and technique obsolescence; changing demands by distributors; and changing government policy (Rogers and Rogers, 1967, pp. 156–163; Rothberg, 1976; DiMaggio and Hirsch, 1976). Developments *within* a firm which are cited as encouraging innovation include executives' desire to eliminate excess capacity (Rothberg, 1976), and the desire by a newly-appointed individual to accumulate or exhibit power by taking risks and succeeding.

Of course, a production firm is ordinarily dependent upon outlets for the presentation of its innovations to consumers. Outlet receptivity to innovation concerns television production firms where three commercial networks purchase most of the programs created by these firms (Cantor, 1980). Therefore, it is important to point out that although the factors just mentioned suggest reasons for the generation of program innovation within TV production firms, they need only be rephrased slightly to predict situations under which the television networks would search for, and accept, innovations from those producers. That is, it is likely that tension-inducing changes that affect neworks, production firms, or the relationships between the two, will have crucial consequences for the inception, development, and release of innovations.

When product innovation is crucial to a firm's survival, the firm often implements mechanisms to promote innovation. Often, special departments are formed to facilitate this task. In the television industry the three commercial networks have program development departments to help production firms design new shows. Marquis (1976) states that such institutional responses to routine demands for innovation generally result in a certain level of innovation that is conventional for *that* firm in *that* industry. Unconventional innovations are produced in response to what, for that firm, is an extraordinary (i.e., unpredicted and nonroutine) problem.

Other factors related to innovation are the size of the firm and the degree to which the firm is in the mainstream of its industry. Marquis implies, and Johnson (1970, p. 42) explicitly states, that large organizations tend to take a lot longer to consider and implement unconventional suggestions than they do to consider and implement mundane ones. Rogers and Rogers (1976, p. 144) argue that one important reason for this difference is an inflexibility and a hesitancy to take risks that often develops among the executives who control the routine channels by which policy is made. They suggest that unusual ideas which find acceptance often have been moved through the organization by atypical agents, connections, and procedures. In the same vein, Marquis [in agreement with Perrow (1980) and Downs (1967)], points out that relatively unestablished organizations have been more likely to come up with unconventional innovations than have large mainstream firms. The reason, he suggests, is that "technical people within [the mainstream of] industry are apt to be preoccupied by short-term concerns . . . cost cutting, quality control, expanding the product line, and the like" (p. 15). The staff of unestablished firms, with no large product lines to protect and expand, is more likely to concentrate on unusual problems and during possibilities.

Applying these ideas from the literature on innovation to the television industry leads to six hypotheses about the genesis of unconventional programs:

1. Unconventional shows tend to be produced by companies, and sold to networks that lag in the ratings or experience extraordinary changes in their competitive environment.
2. Unlike the conventional shows, most unconventional shows tend to be developed by firms not comfortably engaged in the ongoing production of other programs.
3. Since it is unestablished firms and firms in competitive trouble which are the most willing to risk innovation, it is likely to be the *coming together* of an unestablished production firm with a network experiencing extraordinary problems or changes that most favors the development and airing of unconventional shows.
4. In large organizations (like the networks), unconventional shows tend to be championed by newly placed executives, or by those wanting to risk their current positions to move to more powerful ones as a direct result of their involvement in the programs.
5. Unconventional programs, more often than conventional shows, are

conceptualized outside the normal channels of typical production firm/network program development.

6. Unconventional programs, because they are perceived as risky from the start, take a much longer time to move from the concept-generating stage to the production and airing stage.

The purpose of this investigation was to determine if these hypotheses are supportable and to explore other organizational and interorganizational factors relevant to the development of unconventional shows.

THE METHOD

This research entails 2 comparative analyses of the genesis of three "conventional" series and three series described as unconventional. An analysis of reviews and articles in *Variety* determined the shows selected. Specifically, the analysis showed 26 series and specials that fell into the "unconventional" category, and three of those series—"Rowan and Martin's Laugh In," "All in the Family," and "United States"—were selected for study. Each of these was then paired with a conventional series that appeared around the same time, on the network—"Kraft Music Hall," "Arnie," and "Facts of Life," respectively. The pairing of these shows highlights the point that a network can accept both conventional and unconventional programs for airing in the same season.

The genesis of each show was traced by reviewing articles in the popular and trade press and, more importantly, by interviewing people involved in the shows' creation and airing. The executive producer of every show (as listed in its *Variety* review) was contacted and interviewed, using an open-ended question format with specific probes. The goal of the interview was to understand the sequence of events that led to the program's first airing and to specify that sequence as far as possible in terms of the people involved, the decisions made, the reasons for those decisions, and the time between them. In the process, names of key production, network, and (in the case of "Kraft Music Hall") advertising personnel involved in the show's development were elicited. Many were contacted and questioned. In all, 32 people in Los Angeles and New York were interviewed.[1] Several were involved in more than one program. The interviews typically lasted about 20 minutes,

---

[1]The author gratefully acknowledges the following people who consented to interviews: Marvin Antonowsky, Jimmy Baker, Frank Barton, Al Burton, Dick Clair, Sam Cohn, Michael Dann, Ed Friendly, Larry Gelbart, Paul Keyes, Dianne Kirgo, Perry Lafferty, Norman Lear, Gary Markowitz, Dick Martin, Jerry Mayer, Glen Padnick, David Panich, Marty Ragaway, John Rich, George Schlatter, William Self, Stuart Sheslow, Danny Simon, Gary Smith, Ben Starr, Russ Stonam, David Swift, Grant Tinker, Sid Vinedge, Dighby Wolfe, and Robert Wood.

though some were longer and a few were shorter. They were transcribed and compared—for each show, then across different shows—to determine if the hypotheses were supported.[2]

THE COMPARATIVE CASE STUDY

The comparative case study upheld the hypotheses, though not without qualification. The findings are best conveyed and explained by describing the organizational processes in context—that is, by comparing and contrasting the geneses of the conventional and unconventional shows.

The Conventional Series

Distilling the essential details about "Kraft Music Hall," "Arnie," and "Facts of Life" that bear upon the hypotheses of this study highlights the three different kinds of organizations that have traditionally brought viable program ideas to the commercial networks—advertising agencies, established production firms, and the networks themselves. For various reasons (see Turow, 1980), the ad-agency route is now very rarely used to generate network series programs. However, in the fall of 1967, when "Kraft Music Hall" made its debut, it was traveled somewhat more often.

Actually, while the specific format of Kraft Food's program was new in 1967, the title was not. From the 1930s through the 1960s, the Kraft name has been associated with a number of radio and television series. In the 1966–67 season Kraft decided to sponsor an episodic drama called "Road West." Ratings were poor. By the middle of the year, it was clear to many in the TV industry that Kraft would be interested in sponsoring a new program. Consequently, various television industry executives passed through Kraft's advertising agency, J. Walter Thompson (JWT) in New York, trying to pitch their ideas to Bill Highland, head of the television department.

One of these people was Lester Gotlieb, a notable New York figure in the then-powerful G.A.C. talent agency. Gotlieb suggested to Highland that Kraft use the "Music Hall" title in a prestigious weekly series using G.A.C. talent. Two G.A.C. clients, Gary Smith and Dwight Hemlon, would be

---

[2]One finding, expected in organizational research (see, for example, Spencer and Dale, 1979), should be noted. For certain shows, different sources presented somewhat different versions of the same events. In some cases, factual contradictions arose. In others, there were different opinions about the meaning of events. It is significant, perhaps, that most of these conflicts related to the successful unconventional shows "Laugh In" and "All in the Family." Despite these problems, the accounts of each program's genesis converged with respect to perspectives and incidents relevant to this study, and so allowed investigation of the hypotheses.

responsible for the show. The pair, in collaboration, had successfully produced and set-designed other series in the 1960s. The two became interested in the project when Gotlieb explained that rather than have a regular host, they would create a "special" every week. Actually, JWT executives would accept such a program only if they could get commitments from at least three famous hosts to appear several times a year. Although, the name of Frank Sinatra (a G.A.C. client) was mentioned, the first year's list of "core" hosts involved slightly less-stellar personalities—Bobby Darin, Alan King, and Eddie Arnold.

Gotlieb, his boss Sam Cohn, Smith, and Hemlon also presented their ideas to Kraft executives in the Chicago home office. Both the Kraft people and the agency executives liked the idea and the format. The firm prided itself on the "Music Hall" name and wanted it in front of the public on a regular basis. Smith and Hemlon had a "track record" of polished programming. Moreover, the "Colgate Comedy Hour," an early network TV show, had been successful using a similar format, and ABC's more recent "Hollywood Palace" had succeeded using various hosts. Kraft executives were assured that the hosts and themes of the show would fit the contemporary, though rather conservative, family-oriented image the firm tried to exude. Comedian Alan King's sometimes biting humor made the executives a bit nervous, but they realized that his urban style was needed as a counterbalance to Arnold's rural demeanor. They were also willing to pay a little more than was typical for variety programming to associate with a quality show. To draw attention to the series, early installments of the show would feature the popular Herb Alpert and the Tijuana Brass, Louis Armstrong, and Rock Hudson. The Kraft executives agreed to the series, about five months after Gotlieb had first proposed it.

JWT executives proposed the show to NBC, the network Kraft had associated with since radio days. The network, struggling behind CBS in the ratings, had been trying to interest Kraft in sponsoring a variety or anthology show. Program executives, led by Mort Werner, a former agent, felt those formats were the vehicles whereby they would overtake CBS. Werner and his staff accepted Kraft's alternative to the NBC suggestions, and they also accepted the JWT executive's insistence that the "Music Hall" be aired on Kraft's traditional Wednesday, 9 p.m. slot. (The slot allowed Kraft to advertise its products the night before the traditional American Thursday and Friday shopping days.) Since JWT controlled the show and G.A.C. packaged it, the network had very little to do with the program once it was scheduled. Given this go-ahead, Smith and Hemlon hired writers, a choreographer (the prominent Peter Gennaro), and other staff members. The first program was ready to air within two months.

The "Music Hall" was typical of variety shows of the time in not having to test a "pilot" program. Situation comedies and other episodic series *were* expected to pass network audience tests. "Arnie" was no exception. The idea for the program began with a phone conversation between David Swift, a successful television and film writer/producer/director, and actor Telly Savalas. Savalas indicated he wanted to star in a television show, and Swift responded somewhat later with a lightly funny storyline about a Greek-American blue collar worker who is elevated to a white collar job and finds himself making many adjustments as a result. Not wanting the exhausting burden of guiding a television series, Swift brought the idea to his friend Grant Tinker, who had recently moved from a position as West Coast production head of NBC to a position of production chief at 20th Century Fox Television. Liking the idea, Tinker and his boss, William Self, took it through the normal development channels at CBS—to Frank Barton, a West Coast development executive, and Perry Lafferty, head of the network's West Coast development area. Both knew of Swift's reputation for successful films and TV programs. They liked the idea for "Arnie" and, in summer, 1969, ordered a script—and Swift complied. The CBS West Coast executives liked the pilot script, but Michael Dann, the network's New York programming chief, had to give the final approval to produce a pilot. Dann was concerned about the public's acceptance of a blue collar worker, but Grant Tinker convinced him to approve the pilot.

Around that time, Telly Savalas bowed out of the project. The Fox people together with CBS casting personnel suggested Hershel Bernardi, who had recently done "Zorba the Greek" on Broadway, as a replacement. Perry Lafferty recalls that he and his staff had encouraged Swift, the director, to take advantage of the mechanical, predictable nature of audience testing:

> We had every kind of satisfaction for the audience. A man got promoted to a different level. His job improved. He got things for his wife, was kind to her and the family. So everything was wonderful. . . . We designed it to test well, and it tested great![3]

Pleased with "Arnie" 's audience-response scores, Mike Dann scheduled it for Saturday evening, 9-9:30, between the long-running "My Three Sons" and the new "Mary Tyler Moore Show." The pilot, taped in fall, 1969, was ready to be shown to prospective advertisers.

The six months it took from idea presentation to the completion and acceptance of the "Arnie" pilot closely matched the time taken to develop and complete the first "Kraft Music Hall" installment. In the case of "Facts of Life," the process took only three months. The impetus for the show and its quick development was NBC's very low position in the ratings race during fall, 1978, and spring, 1979. Fred Silverman had recently taken over the

---

[3]Unless otherwise noted, all quotations are taken from the author's interview with the person quoted.

presidency of the network, and he and his staff were looking for program ideas to shore up the network's sagging schedule.

One of the few successful NBC shows debuting in the fall of 1978 was "Different Strokes," a situation comedy about a rich white widower, his daughter (Kimberly), his two adopted black sons, and their white housekeeper (Mrs. Garrett). The comic center of the show was the young Gary Coleman, but Silverman felt Charlotte Rae, who played the housekeeper, had enough personality to carry a show on her own. In spring, 1979, he told a member of his West Coast development staff, Stuart Sheslow, to develop a spinoff from "Different Strokes" in which Raye would have "something" to do with girls.[4]

Shortly thereafter, Sheslow suggested the idea of this spinoff to Al Burton, head of development for T.A.T., the very successful firm which produced the series. Sheslow's view of the new series, which he would call "Garrett's Girls," was to have Rae become a custodian of some rather tough students in a girls school; the show would be a kind of female "Welcome Back, Kotter," the ABC hit of a few season's back. For his part, Burton, believed that a such a show would explore some important issues about growing up—a kind of teenage *Passages*. His notion was that Mrs. Garrett would take a position at Kimberly's private girls school and become an anchor around which the problems of the girls could hinge. He saw the *private* school as better reflecting T.A.T.'s "quality" image. The company's principals, Norman Lear and Alan Horn, were skeptical that the program would be nothing more than a "cheap shot at [sexual] jiggles," Burton recalls. He assured them it would really be a teenage *passages* (recalling the popular book by Gail Sheehy), and they acquiesced. They rejected the title "Garrett's Girls" as sexist, however; the tentative title became "Growing Up." They wanted to air the spinoff quickly.

The "pilot" was to be Episode 22 of "Different Strokes". Two writers completed the script on the Monday before a mandatory Friday taping in May. T.A.T. executives were astonished at the script's crudeness. Rather than the "passages" idea, the writers seemed to have gone for low comedy akin to that of *Animal House*. Two "Different Strokes" writers were brought in to give the script some "coherence" and "polish" (to quote Burton). Still, Horn informed Silverman that T.A.T. was taping the show under protest. That the episode was televised was due in large measure to Silverman's persuasive abilities. NBC, testing it on the night it aired, told T.A.T. that audience response was quite favorable.

Soon after the May airing, NBC executives ordered from Horn and Burton 4 more episodes to run as a "short flight" series. The network people

---

[4]Sheslow suspected that Silverman's reference to girls was to give the show a conceptual separation from "Different Strokes," which dealt with boys.

felt the series had potential and, moreover, they needed to fill the half hour after "Different Strokes" for four Friday nights beginning late August. They felt a short flight series of "Growing Up" (soon to be renamed "Facts of Life") would have a good change in that time slot.

Horn and Burton, concerned about the bad experience with Episode 22 and the short lead time NBC was giving them, said they would consent to produce the episodes only if NBC first ordered 4 scripts that both T.A.T. and the network would approve in advance. All parties agreed, and Glen Padnick, a T.A.T. executive, came up with a storyline he felt would establish the "passages" theme of the program: One of the teens in Mrs. Garrett's dormitory is afraid she (the teen) is a lesbian. Sheslow liked the storyline, and two writers from the successful T.A.T. show "One Day at a Time," Julie and Dianne Kirgo, were brought in to write the script. The lesbian theme got tangled with the NBC censors, however, and in the end the script was diluted to portray a girl who is ridiculed because she is a tomboy. The Kirgo sisters angrily removed their names from the credits, replacing them with "Brad Rider," purposely a man's name, to emphasize their exasperation with "a bunch of old men" writing about girls' problems. Though a bit disheartened, Burton contended that the *Passages* flavor of the episode remained. As he said, "the pace of television production is such that we didn't have the time to be disappointed."

The Unconventional Series

As hypothesized earlier, the unconventional programs such as "Rowan and Martin's Laugh In," "All in the Family" and "United States" all took much longer than six months from initial proposal to airing. Moreover, in each case network executives had grave reservations about televising the show, even after it was scheduled. One crucial reason the series ultimately did air related to the initiative of particular network officials who, for both occupational and organizational reasons, decided to encourage the unorthodox.

In the case of "Rowan and Martin's Laugh In," the primary network official to fit this role was Ed Friendly, NBC's Vice President in Charge of Special Projects during the mid-1960s. In the years prior to "Laugh In" 's September, 1967, debut, Friendly had often voiced his conviction that the network should experiment with "all comedy" formats. Since the mid-1950s, television humor that was not "situation comedy" had essentially meant monologues or skits on song-and-dance "variety shows." Ernie Kovacks' ingenious "blackout" humor, short-lived on CBS during the early 1950s, had pointed in a different direction, but none had followed. Friendly helped supervise NBC's rather ill-fated version of "That Was the Week That Was" ("TW3"), the biting British news satire program. After that experience, he decided that what television really needed was a television version of *Hel-zappoppin*, the more frantically paced (and much less news-conscious) stage smash of the 1940s.

Creative interest in takaing a risk on an unusual comedy idea came to Friendly from two sources—producer George Schlatter and the comedy team of Rowan and Martin. In the mid-1960s, Schlatter was developing a modest reputation for his work on television variety shows. His dream, however, was to bring outrageous, quick-paced humor to the medium on a sustained basis. He recalls going to all the networks for about three years in the early and middle part of the decade "trying to sell the idea . . . of bright and fast comedy" that would use a free-wheeling, multi-media format, no host, and a group of unknown comedians (Barthel, 1968, p. 154). Friendly recruited him to do a variety special with some of the ingredients he favored ("NBC Follies"), but no network seemed interested in giving Schlatter full reign with his all-comedy notions.

Dan Rowan and Dick Martin, a struggling comedy duo for several years, had shown strong potential for regular prime-time television in the eyes of NBC's brass when they replaced Dean Martin during the summer of 1966 and garnered good ratings. Network executives tried to interest them in starring in a regular variety program, but the two insisted upon an unusual, all-comedy, vehicle which Schlatter was ultimately to produce. Friendly became a champion of this show. His initial program deal was for one special with the implicit possibility of it becoming a series. In fact, Friendly, who wanted to leave the network for the potentially more lucrative independent production business, seems to have been convinced of the show's prognosis. After buying the special for NBC, he resigned from the network to become Schlatter's business partner. NBC program chief Mort Werner gave his blessing to that unorthodox move, and Friendly retained much influence at the network. In a sense, the "Laugh In" company had a network executive in its midst and on its side, tilting the program toward a series commitment.

The program which Schlatter, Rowan, Martin, head writer Paul Keyes, and their staff put together was a collage of elements from vaudeville, burlesque, film, and television; and much of it was derivative. What was new for television here were the manic style and pace, quickened considerably over typical TV comedy through sharp electronic editing, which pruned jokes to their punch lines.

While NBC's program executives found the program funny, they questioned its intelligibility and "blue"-ness for the general public. Moreover, when the special was audience-tested, it received poor marks. Nevertheless, NBC had found a sponsor, Timex. Because the watch manufacturer had financed previous NBC specials, the network offered it the "Laugh In" special at a significant discount, in a time slot adjacent to the fall, 1967, Miss America Pageant. The hope was that it would attract young viewers.

The program got mediocre ratings—about 26 percent of the audience. Nevertheless, the "Laugh In" principals tried to persuade the NBC Program Committee to allow the show to air as a series. The special had drawn excitedly favorable comments from TV critics, a fact they were sure would impress the network executives. Yet the program people were not easily convinced. Aside from previously-raised objections, they felt that such a quick-paced program, which relied on many rapid-fire jokes, could not maintain its energy for an hour each week. They suggested the show be shortened to a half hour if it aired. Friendly and Schlatter demurred, contending that an hour-long weekly "Laugh In" was possible. In the end, the show entered the NBC lineup as a mid-season replacement. The NBC brass had begun to worry seriously that traditional variety programs and stars—the Jackie Gleasons, Perry Comos, and "Kraft Music Hall"'s—were losing their hold on the audience. Overall, NBC was running consistently behind CBS in the popularity of its prime time programs. Thus, it was felt that an unconventional specimen like "Laugh In" should be given a chance. Moreover, the show, bereft of stars, was relatively inexpensive. Still, the scheduling of "Laugh In" seems to show some ambivalence about the series. The program replaced the network's fast-fading "Man From U.N.C.L.E." against two CBS Monday night powerhouses—"Gunsmoke" (then the number 2 rated show) and "Lucy" (then number 1). As a *Saturday Evening Post* article (Dietz, 1968, page 35) later noted, "Insertion into 'U.N.C.L.E.'s time slot was not exactly a vote of confidence." "Laugh In" writer Dighby Wolfe suggests that such scheduling reflected the network's exasperation at CBS's control over the Monday night time slot. "Laugh In" was considered expendable, and perhaps something as outrageous and different might indeed compete well with "Gunsmoke" and "Lucy."

The strong ambivalence which accompanied NBC programmers' acceptance and scheduling of "Rowan and Martin's Laugh In" as a series was also seen in CBS programmers' acceptance and scheduling of "All in the Family," the situation comedy which the network began to air in January, 1971. At first glance CBS was, as Richard Adler (1979, p. xvii) has observed, "the network least likely to broadcast a program like 'All in the Family,' " startling as it was in its direct confrontation with bigotry and its use of racial and ethnic slurs never before heard on television. The network had perennially led NBC and ABC in the ratings by striving for audience loyality through proven stars and programs. In 1970, however, CBS departed from its traditional style, for two related reasons. One was the presence of a new network president, Robert Wood, who, despite a very limited experience in programming, was ambitious to show his leadership in the most visible of network areas—the selection and scheduling of prime time series. The second was Wood's belief that while CBS was first in the overall ratings, its was falling behind NBC and ABC in reaching a population segment that was becoming increasingly important to advertisers: young (18-49 old), urban adults.

About that time Norman Lear and Bud Yorkin already *had* something that people in the industry deemed different from anything on American TV—a show they called "All in the Family." Lear and Yorkin had worked successfully (as writer and producer, respectively) in television and film during the 1950s, and had joined forces in 1959. In 1968, Lear learned of a hit British comedy series about a bigot constantly at odds with his family, especially his son-in-law. Intrigued by the idea, Lear acquired the American rights to develop a series based on the show. With his agent from Creative Management Associates (C.M.A.), he proposed the idea to development executives at ABC. The network's president, Marty Starger, liked Lear's "treatment" and approved it for a pilot that was shot in January, 1979. When ABC executives saw the pilot, however, they became concerned over the program's controversiality, and, eventually, rejected a second pilot. Neither version had done well in audience tests, and the executives decided the overall concept was too risky for commercial television.

After the ABC rejection, Lear and Yorkin went back to making movies and seriously considered a film version of "All in the Family." In February 1970, Yorkin mentioned to Sam Cohn (at C.M.A. in New York) that he and Lear would consider working in television again if "All in the Family" were picked up, Cohn called Michael Dann, the program chief at CBS, and persuaded him to see the second of the pilots ABC had rejected. It so happened that before Robert Wood's appointment as network president CBS program executives had rejected a property based loosely on "Till Death Do Us Part" called "Man in the Middle." Still, Dann screened the program, liked it, and recommended it enthusiastically to Wood. After conferring with an uncertain CBS Chairman William Paley and a nervous CBS chief censor William Tankersly, Wood decided to buy the show. Perry Lafferty, then head of CBS programming on the West Coast, was sure that Wood's novice status at the network helm encouraged his risk-taking. Wood, looking back, agrees and adds that his early years as network president "were the freshest." Afterwards, "you learn the rules too well and don't think in new directions."

After Wood bought "All in the Family," however, his executives questioned the advisability of airing the pilot as it stood; they specifically urged less objectionable language. Lear, who remained successful in the film industry, had no desire to return to television if it were not on his terms. Debate within CBS about the show stretched through the early summer. Audience tests paralleled those at ABC and upheld those at CBS who wanted to change the pilot. Finally, Wood decided that, despite its negative test results and its controversial material, the pilot should air without major script changes. "All in the Family" fit his youth-oriented, urban image for the network; he hoped the controversial material would generate viewership. It was mid-summer, 1970, when he gave Lear the go-ahead to produce 13 episodes. Somewhat later, Wood decided to begin airing the show in January. Lear reshot the pilot to recast the daughter and son-in-law, but he would *not* change words or ideas. Quickly, word spread that "All in the Family" was Wood's concern, and crucial problems of phrasing became a matter of discussion between the network president and chief censor Tankersly. Wood stood by Lear in maintaining the language and plot of the pilot. However, CBS' ambivalence emerged in scheduling the show against two very strong forces—the ABC "Movie of the Week" and the NBC "Tuesday Night Movie"— and *after* CBS's own "Hee Haw," a rustic version of "Laugh In" that, as a lead-in, cultivated the very audience that "All in the Family" was presumably purchased to counter. Lear and Yorkin argued against this "death slot," to no avail. But even more troubling to them was a decision by Wood and other CBS executives to begin the series with what was to have been the apparently less-shocking second episode. Lear's refusal of this switch and threats to disband the "All in the Family" company culminated in the first airing of the original sequence.

 Comparing the genesis of "All in the Family" with the genesis of "Arnie" illustrates the claim by CBS personnel that "All in the Family"'s journey through network development was quite different from that of more typical shows. The initial development of corporate chairman Paley in considering "All in the Family"'s acceptance, the involvement of network president Wood in day-to-day production issues regarding that show, and the general circumvension by Norman Lear of typical censorship lines of command were unusual for the time. In the case of another unconventional show, "Rowan and Martin's Laugh In," Ed Friendly's involvement with the program at both the production and network ends, and the airing of a "pilot" special (rarely done then with variety), took it, too, out of the typical development channels of the time.

In comparing the conventional "Facts of Life," with "United States," the bittersweet anomaly of early 1980, we see a similar trend. While "Facts of Life" was conceived through the suggestion and guidance of NBC's program development department (one typical development procedure), "United States" was created with NBC development people playing virtually no role from conception to taping (a rare phenomenon in 1980).

The person with the unorthodox idea that became "United States" was Larry Gelbart, a writer-producer who had penned and (with Gene Reynolds) supervised the enormously successful 1972 television adapation of the film M*A*S*H. Around 1975, Gelbart had left the series to write for the stage and cinema. Still, about a year after leaving television, he began to conceive a television series he felt would make it worthwhile for him to return to the medium. Believing that family situation comedies of the 1970s were simply stale "variations on originals I don't think anybody remembers anymore,"

Gelbart felt he wanted "to go back to basics. Simply to go back to a man and a woman, a husband and wife, and a family. And to treat it . . . like 1980, not 1950." During 1976 he suggested his idea "to some people at CBS" who were interested in creating a series for actress Linda Lavin. The executives expressed interest, but when Gelbart said he was not yet prepared to get more involved in a program than consult and perhaps write a pilot, they dropped the proposal. Some months later, Gelbart became more eager and suggested it as a vehicle for actress Mary Tyler Moore. Moore and her husband, Grant Tinker (by then a successful independent producer), considered it seriously. However, when Gelbart wanted a year for scriptwriting before starting production, they declined.

Gelbart brought his idea to NBC President Fred Silverman in December, 1978. The two had known each other for some while. After a friendly clash with Gelbart about network program quality at a Writers Guild panel discussion, Silverman, acknowledging Gelbart's expertise and flair for originality, had publicly offered to allow him to program a block of time on ABC. However, Gelbart did not present concrete suggestions, and ABC program executives—riding high on the highest rated network—did not seem anxious to push him. It was only after he became seriously interested in creating the series about marriage that Gelbart approached Silverman, now at NBC, and reminded him of his offer. He wanted virtual autonomy to produce a series that would take a "witty," "honest," and unconventionally "adult" look at marriage. Moreover, he wanted NBC to allow him (as executive producer) and Gary Markowitz (his stepson, as producer) to have as much time as needed to refine an entire season's worth of scripts before production would begin.

Not even having received a "treatment" for the proposed new show, Silverman bought a season's worth of episodes. NBC was plummeting into third place in the ratings in late 1978, and Silverman, appointed president of the network just a few months before, was hoping Gelbart's track record would rub off on the network. Also, Silverman may have wanted Gelbart's stage and screen prestige to help improve his image. For his part, Gelbart says he was not interested in ratings. He, Markowitz, and Chuck Kalish (the supervising producer) took great pains to overturn many of the traditional situation comedy conventions. There would be no audience, no laugh track, no uniform floodlights, no proscenium perspective, no "three camera" setup. The actors would not be television regulars.

An NBC censor was present on the show, but Gelbart took complaints about such interference (and there were several) to much higher levels in the network. The program development department took no part in the show's evolution. Some executives thought the central couple too wealthy, the show too "highbrow," and simply insufficiently funny. An audience test of the initial episode confirmed their beliefs though Gelbart neither requested nor received any feedback. Yet, when, after agreeing to a January 1980 start, NBC executives postponed the series until March, the "United States" company began to realize something was drastically wrong.

NBC did air the first episode in March, but in a time slot which seemed to reflect Silverman's exasperation with Gelbart's final product. Not arguing with the show's literacy, distinctiveness, and ability to generate prestige, program executives felt the series did not have elements that would attract a huge audience. They decided not to risk placing the show at the center of prime time, where high ratings and "audience flow" was badly needed. They placed the series at 10:30 Tuesday nights, after "The Big Show," a new variety extravaganza. Opposing "United States" was an adventure series on ABC ("Hart to Hart") that began at 10, and a two hour CBS movie that began at 9. Clearly, viewers of the other networks were unlikely to switch at 10:30. Moreover, Gelbart feared that "The Big Show" was hardly a proper lead-in to his sophisticated property. Silverman assured Gelbart the network would try to program the last half hour of "The Big Show" with sophisticated comedy. Gelbart was not convinced; to him the scheduling meant that NBC programmers' uncertainty about what to do with his show had led them to "electronic euthanasia."

ANALYSIS

The first hypothesis offered earlier was that unconventional program innovations are most likely to be generated and accepted by organizations experiencing unusual changes or competitive pressures. As the previous pages have shown, that prediction was confirmed in our case studies. The networks that chose to accept the unconventional ideas (in two cases after another network refused) were lagging in the ratings (as in the case of NBC when it bought "Rowan and Martin's Laugh In" and "United States") or (as in the case of CBS when it bought "All in the Family") were perceived by top management as seriously deficient in ratings-related areas. The hypothesis was not supported, however, regarding the producers who generated the shows in the first place. In the case of producers Norman Lear ("All in the Family") and Larry Gelbart ("United States"), at least , the motivation for tenaciously pushing an unorthodox program idea was not related to extraordinary changes or competitive pressures. Rather, it was related to the producers' awareness of having a power base *outside* the television industry which allowed them attractive alternatives to television work if a network did not accept their proposals.

This lack of support for the hypothesis at the production end is perhaps understandable when one realizes that while the networks are large organizations, that characterization does not fit the Lear-Yorkin association in the pre-"All in the Family" days, Larry Gelbart's status as an individual writer-producer, or, for that matter, George Schlatter's position at the start of "Laugh In." Independent creative individuals heading their own small firms would seem to have been free to pursue unconventional program ideas whether or not unusual pressures or changes were affecting the firms. Perhaps the prediction that unusual organizational pressures are particularly conducive to the generation of unconventional program ideas would hold in the case of large firms that begin to falter (such as Disney and Universal). In this study the hypothesis most relevant to the production firms is the suggestion that the members of unestablished firms are more likely than the staff of established firms to encourage and generate unconventional innovations, since the latter are much more likely than the former to be preoccupied with the need to protect and expand existing product lines.

That second hypothesis, and the three other numbered predictions offered in this paper, *were* confirmed quite strongly. With regard to the second hypothesis, it was found that, while all three conventional shows were developed by people or production firms enjoying ongoing work and comfortable success in the television industry, the three unconventional programs derived from people who were at moderate to low points in fitfully successful TV careers (as in the case of "Laugh In") or who had been out of television work for some years and wanted to return only on their own terms (as in "All in the Family" and "United States"). The third prediction was supported as a corollary to the first two, since it suggested that the coming together of an unestablished production firm with a network experiencing extraordinary problems or changes most favors the development and airing of unconventional shows. Consonant with the fourth prediction, the acceptances of two of the unconventional shows ("All in the Family" and "United States") at the network level were linked directly to the accession of new network presidents. The other unconventional show ("Laugh In"), while not illustrating the consequence of a new president's arrival, did exemplify the case of an executive risking his current position to move to a more powerful one as a direct result of championing an unconventional program. Confirming the fifth hypothesis, all three unconventional shows moved through different network-related development routes than did their conventional counterparts; and, confirming the sixth hypothesis, the unconventional shows took a much longer time to move from the initial program suggestion to completion for network airing.

At the same time that the findings supported various hypotheses regarding unconventional innovation, they also implied that risk-taking under those conditions would only go so far. One recurrent theme was network reluctance to air unorthodox shows in favorable time slots. Larry Gelbart's comment about the enthanasic scheduling of "United States" echoed comments by the producers of "Rowan and Martin's Laugh In" and "All in the

Family" about the unfortunate scheduling of their programs. Such statements might be dismissed as theatrical posturings by creators remembering anxious times. However, the comments of more dispassionate observers and the circumstances surrounding the airing of those programs do suggest that the unconventional series, much more than the conventional ones, evoked strong ambivalences in network schedulers. The programs were clearly unorthodox, and while key executives had taken the risk of buying them, those same executives and their program committees were hesitant about risking attractive and valuable time slots when airing them.

More important with respect to hesitations in network risk-taking was a feature of network program acceptance that implied severe limits on the range of unfamiliar approaches likely in unconventional shows on commercial television. That feature was the relatively small web of interpersonal relationships which dominated the process. Even in this study of only six programs, certain names—Grant Tinker, Perry Lafferty, Sam Cohn, Norman Lear, and others—recurred across time and across networks. Past activities and past acquaintances were keys to membership in the web—and to present potential. Professional friendships were often crucial to initiating or facilitating network interest or acceptance. It is, for example, important to recall that for both the conventional and unconventional shows, all of the principals involved at the production and network levels had considerable experience in the entertainment industry, and most had known one another prior to that program involvement.

This web of relationships serves an important function. Choosing producers from within it helps protect network executives from the ultimate risk—not having technically acceptable products delivered to them on time. Yet, while this web of relationships does seem to allow network executives to rest easy, it also seems to function (intentionally or not) to limit even unconventional "risk taking" to producers who have developed at least some track record within the entertainment community. Implicitly, these producers have indicated that, despite their unconventionality, they understand and follow many of the commonly accepted values and procedures of popular entertainment. By choosing people whom they consider, in some sense at least, "safe" producers of "entertainment," the networks imply a rather severe limit on the range of experimentation and unorthodoxy they will accept even in their unconventional shows.

This suggestion warrants a good deal more investigation. In fact, the findings and tentative generalizations of this comparative case study open a multitude of questions and research directions on the meaning of unconventionality in various mass media and the conditions that foster it. While the wellspring of unconventionally creative ideas is likely to be an individual (Wainwright and Gerlack, 1968, p. 12), the encouragement of such ideas, their development, and their implementation are likely to relate intimately to the social and organizational contexts in which those individuals exist. Understanding these factors and their interrelationships will move researchers a long way toward understanding the reasons for change and continuity in mass media.

REFERENCES

ADLER, R.B. (1979). "All in the Family: A Critical Appraisal." New York: Praeger.

BALDWIN, T., and LEWIS, C.E. (1972). Violence in television: The industry looks at itself. In G.A. Comstock and E.A. Rubinstein (Eds.), "Television and Social Behavior." Washington: U.S. Government Printing Office.

BARNOUW, E. (1975). "Tube of Plenty." New York: Oxford University Press.

BARTHEL, J. (1968), Hilarious, brash, flat, peppery, repetitious, topical, and in border-line taste. *New York Times* Magazine (Oct. 6, 1968), 32-33 ff.

BROWN, L. (1971). "Television: The Business Behind the Box." New York: Harcourt, Brace Jovanovich.

BURNS, T., and STALKER, G. (1961). "The Management of Innovation." London: Tavistock.

CANTOR, M. (1972). The role of the producer in choosing television content. In G.A. Comstock and E.A. Rubinstein (Eds.), "Television and Social Behavior." Washington: U.S. Government Printing Office.

CANTOR, M. (1980). "Prime Time Television." Beverly Hills, California: Sage.

CRANE, D. (1976). Reward systems in art, science, and religion. *American Behavioral Scientist* 19, 719–734.

DIETZ, L. (1968). Where TV comedy is at. *Saturday Evening Post* (Nov. 30), 32–37.

DiMAGGIO, P., and HIRSCH, M. (1976). Production organizations in the arts. *American Behavioral Scientist 19,* 735–752.

DOWNS, A. (1967). "Inside Bureaucracy." Boston: Little Brown.

HIRSCH, P.M. (1972). Processing fads and fashions: An organization-set analysis of cultural industry systems. *American Journal of Sociology 77,* 735–752.

JOHNSON, C. (1970). Dying is not an option. *Innovation 18,* 40–45.

KHANDWAILLA, P.N. (1977). The design of invention and innovation. *In* P.N. Khandwailla (Ed.), "The Design of organizations." New York: Harcourt, Brace Jovanovich.

MARCH, J.G., and SIMON, H.A. (1958). "Organizations." New York: John Wiley.

MARQUIS, D.G. (1976). The anatomy of successful innovations. *In* R. Rothberg (Ed.), "Corporate Strategy and Product Innovation." New York: Free Press.

MELODY, W.H. (1973). "Children's Television: The Economics of Exploitation." New Haven Connecticut: Yale University Press.

National Industrial Conference Board. (1967). "The Challenge of innovation." New York: National Industrial Conference Board.

Panel on Invention and Innovation. (1967). "Technological Innovation: Its Environment and Management." Washington, D.C.: U.S. Government Printing Office.

PERROW, C. (1980). "Complex Organizations." Glenview, Illinois: Scott, Foresman, and Company.

PETERSON, R.A. (1976). The production of culture: A prolegomenon. *American Behavioral Scientist 19,* 667–669.

PETERSON, R.A., and BERGER, D.G. (1975). Cycles in symbol production: The case of popular music. *American Sociological Review 40,* 158–173.

Rogers, E.M., and ROGERS, R.A. (1967). "Communication in Organizations." New York: Free Press.

ROTHBERG, R. (1976). Production innovation in perspective. *In* R. Rotherberg (Ed.), "Corporate Strategy and Product Innovation." New York: Free Press.

SCHON, D.A. (1966). The fear of innovation. *International Science and Technology 14*, 70–78.

SHANKS, B. (1976). "The Cool Fire: How to Make It in Television." New York: Vintage.

SPENCER, L., and DALE, A. (1979). Integration and regulation in organizations: A contextual approach. *Sociological Review 27*, 679–702.

STEELE, L. (1975). "Innovation in Big Business." New York: Elsevier.

TUCHMAN, G. (1974). Assembling a network talk show. *In* G. Tuchman (Ed.), "The TV Establishment." Englewood Cliffs, New Jersey: Prentice Hall.

TUROW, J. (1980). Television sponsorship forms and program subject matter. *Journal of Broadcasting 24*, 381–397.

TUROW, J. (1978). Casting for television: The anatomy of social typing. *Journal of Communication 28*, (No. 4), 18–24.

WAINRIGHT, C., and GERLACH, J. (1968). "Successful Management of New Products." New York: Communication Arts.

YOUNG, R. (1970). No room for the searcher. *Innovation 10*, 50–56.

9

The Onus of Minority Ownership: FCC Policy and Performance Expectations in Minority-Oriented Broadcasting

Loy A. Singleton
Department of Radio–Television–Motion Pictures
University of North Carolina, Chapel Hill, North Carolina 27514

Government policy regarding minority ownership of broadcast stations is an issue of increasing importance. Although Blacks and Latinos now constitute nearly 20% of the U.S. population, they own disproportionately few of the 8668 commercial broadcasting stations in this country. Consequently, the Federal Communications Commission's minority ownership taskforce has observed that "unless minorities are encouraged to enter the mainstream of the commercial broadcasting business, a substantial portion of our citizenry will remain underserved" (U.S. Federal Communications Commission, 1978a, p. 1).

Accordingly, the FCC has established a policy supporting increased minority ownership and has adopted measures designed to encourage the sale of stations to minority entrepreneurs (U.S. Federal Communications Commission, 1978b). The Commission has also been awarding merit to minority entrepreneurs in comparative license application proceedings, a policy which has been challenged and upheld in federal court.[1]

The result has been a significant but relatively small increase in the number of minority owners. It is now estimated there are 138 minority-owned radio and television stations in the U.S.[2] Thus, minority ownership policy to date has succeeded to the extent that it has increased the number

---

1. See: *TV 9 Inc. v. FCC*, 495 F. 2d 929 (D.C. Cir., 1973); *cert. den.*, 419 U.S. 986 (1974). See also *Garrett v. FCC*. 513 F. 2d 1063 (D.C. Cir., 1975).

2. This estimate is based on N.A.B. research and is the same figure currently cited by the Minority Enterprise Division of the FCC Broadcast Bureau. (*N.A.B. Radio/TV Highlights* 1980.)

of minority-owned stations from nearly none to about 1.5% of the total stations on air. Unfortunately, in the long run, the same policy may have some unintended negative effects in addition to this positive one.

The Commision has based its pursuit of increased minority ownership on the public interest objective of increased program diversity in general and on increased service to minorities in particular. The FCC has said that the policy steps it has taken to increase minority ownership are based on the assumption "that such measures will result in programming reflecting the needs and interests of minority groups" (U.S. Federal Communications Commission, 1979). In the same ruling it has clearly stated that minority broadcasters must bear a significant part of the burden for the success or failure of the policy: "the effectiveness of this policy in achieving the . . . public interest objective of diversity will depend in part on the ability and willingness of minority owners and employees to provide such programming."

This paper argues that by linking the success of minority ownership policy to an increase in minority programming, the FCC has inadvertently handicapped present and prospective minority broadcasters; the handicap referred to in the title of this paper as the "onus" of minority ownership.

BLACK-ORIENTED AND PRIMARY SPANISH-LANGUAGE RADIO: AN OVERVIEW

Programming in more than 60 languages is heard regularly on U.S. radio stations. However, two types of minority-oriented programming clearly predominate in total audience and number of stations. According to Standard Rate and Data Service information, 270 radio stations carry at least some Spanish language programming regularly, making Spanish the most programmed language in the country after English. That Spanish is clearly the second language of American radio is apparent when the number of stations carrying the next three most popular languages is noted: Polish, Italian, and German are programmed regularly on 63, 55, and 43 stations, respectively (U.S. Federal Communications Commission, Inquiry, 1979).

However, even more popular than Spanish-language programming is Black format or Black-oriented programming. More than 400 radio stations broadcast a significant amount of Black-oriented programming, making it the most popular minority-oriented format in U.S. radio broadcasting. Together, Spanish-language and Black-oriented radio, serving the nation's largest linguistic and racial minorities, are the most widespread types of minority radio in the U.S.

Although most of these stations carry Spanish-language or Black-oriented programs as part of a varied format, there are some stations which rely primarily on one of these two minority audiences. The discussion which follows is based on data taken from the FCC renewal files and telephone surveys of these primary minority-oriented stations; stations whose primary business is programming to and selling minority audiences. The stations referred to as primary Spanish-language radio (PSLR) broadcast more than 50% of the time in Spanish; 72% of them broadcast Spanish exclusively. Because of the variety of music which falls under the rubric of "Black" radio, the Black-oriented stations referred to in this study are only those which broadcast a 100% Black-oriented format, regardless of the type of music aired.

PSLR Station Distribution and Ownership

In the United States the existence of commercial radio stations which broadcast primarily in Spanish can be traced back to the 1940s. According to the FCC renewal file data available at the time of this study, there are 64 PSLR stations operating in the continental U.S. The majority (78%) of these stations are found in the Southwestern states, but an increasing number can be found in Midwestern and Northeastern metropolitan areas. For instance, there are PSLR stations in Chicago, New York, Hartford and the District of Columbia. Regardless of the region of the country in which they may be located, PSLR stations tend to be situated in medium-size and larger markets. Chicago, Los Angeles, Miami, New York, San Francisco-Oakland, and San Antonio all have multiple PSLR stations. Only 9% of PSLR stations are in small towns or rural areas. This follows the pattern of distribution of persons of Spanish origin in the U.S., 85% of whom live in metropolitan areas (U.S. Bureau of the Census, 1978).

The ownership of PSLR stations is predominantly non-Latino. According to data compiled from FCC renewal files, non-Latinos own 75% (48) of the stations identified in this study. They also tend to own the stations in the larger markets. Of the PSLR stations in the top-ten Latino markets, 90% are owned by non-Latinos. A study of Southwestern PSLR stations suggests that the stations owned by non-Latinos are more often those which are the most successful—the wealthiest stations in terms of financial assets (Gutierrez and Schement, 1979).

Black-Oriented Radio Distribution and Ownership

Like PSLR broadcasting, Black-oriented radio has a distinct geographic distribution. Using Standard Rate and Data Service format information and a confirmatory telephone survey, 134 Black-oriented stations were identified which claim to be 100% Black-oriented in format (Radio Stations Regularly Scheduling Black Programs, 1980). Of these stations, 70% (42) are located in southern states, where 53% of the U.S. Black population resides (Black Radio Market Study, 1980). However, like PSLR, Black-oriented radio stations can also be found in major metropolitan areas outside this primary population region. There are three exclusively Black-oriented radio stations in Los Angeles and in Chicago, Philadelphia, and New York as well. There are six in Washington, D.C. and two in Detroit. Again this follows the distribution of the target audience: 75% of Black Americans live in urban areas (Black Radio Market Study, 1980, p. A-9). Only 31% of the Black-oriented stations in this study are located outside major metropolitan areas.

Like its Spanish-language counterpart, Black-oriented radio is owned primarily by persons who are not members of that industry's primary audience. Only one third of the 134 completely Black-oriented stations are owned by Blacks, making Black broadcasters only slightly more successful than their Latino counterparts, who own 25% of PSLR stations. National Data comparing Black and non-Black control of station assets are not available at this time.

In summary, minority-format radio in the U.S. is dominated in terms of total audience and in numbers of stations by Spanish-language and Black-format radio. There are 64 PSLR stations which concentrate on Spanish-language programming and 134 which are exclusively Black-oriented. In both cases the stations are owned primarily by non-minority entrepreneurs, the condition which the FCC's minority ownership policy is designed to alter. The effect of this policy on programming is examined next.

NON-ENTERTAINMENT PROGRAMMING PERFORMANCE IN PSLR AND BLACK-ORIENTED BROADCASTING

The relationship between the owner of a radio station and the characteristics of that station's programming is a complex one, particularly when the effects of owner race are being examined. A logical first step in investigating this relationship is to examine the quantitative data collected by the FCC as part of its evaluation of a station's performance at license renewal time. All broadcast stations have until recently been required to provide the FCC percentages of news, public affairs, and other nonentertainment programming aired during a designated composite week. These percentages do not measure the quality of such programming or the owner's personal commitment to public service. However, they *are* the primary quantitative data available to the FCC in assessing a licensee's public service programming performance. They are particularly relevant to this discussion because minority radio industry performance in these areas has been subject to criticism over the years for failing to serve adequately the needs of minority audiences (see Surlin, 1973).

Using FCC license renewal forms, the composite week data were obtained for the 64 PSLR stations and for 124 (93%) of the Black-oriented stations.[3] The news, public affairs, and other nonentertainment programming percentages were compared for minority and nonminority owned stations. Regardless of owner race, the levels of public service programming vary widely in PSLR and Black-oriented radio. For instance, the percentage of news programming in Black-oriented stations ranged from 6.7% to as much as 14.9%. In PSLR stations the news percentage ranged from as little as 2.4% to over 20%. Percentages reported in the public affairs and other nonentertainment categories varied similarly, resulting in positively skewed distributions which distorted the mean in each case.

In order to examine the statistical relationship between owner-race and programming percentages while minimizing the effect of extreme values, median percentages were calculated in each programming category for the PSLR and Black-oriented stations in the study. Then the PSLR and Black-oriented stations were divided separately into two groups for each programming category: those performing above the median and those falling below it. Each "above" and "below" group was then subdivided according to owner race. The overall proportions of minority and nonminority owners in the PSLR and Black-oriented stations were used to calculate expected values in a chi-square analysis of the proportion of minority and nonminority owned stations above and below the median in each programming category.

The results are summarized in Table 9.1 for PSLR and in Table 9.2 for Black-oriented stations. Generally the proportion of minority and nonminority owned stations above and below the median in all categories closely

TABLE 9.1   PSLR Nonentertainment Programming Performance By Owner Race

Programming Category (Median)	Stations Programming Below PSLR Median		Stations Programming Above PSLR Median	
	Latino Owned	Non-Latino Owned	Latino Owned	Non-Latino Owned
News (7.9%)	10	23*	7	22***
Public Affairs (3.2%)	10	22*	5	26**
Other (4.0%)	10	23*	5	24**

*p>.50

**p>.25

***p>.90

(p values associated with one sample chi-square statistics)

---

3. For administrative reasons about 10% of station renewal data is unavailable at any given time. See "Release of Additional Materials in Deregulation Proceedings," FCC *Public Notice*, Jan. 11, 1980.

TABLE 9.2   Black-Oriented Radio Nonentertainment Programming Performance By Owner Race

Programming Category (Median)	Stations Programming Above Median		Stations Programming Below Median	
	Black Owned	Non-Black Owned	Black Owned	Non-Black Owned
News (6.6%)	20	41**	19	42*
Public Affairs (2.3%)	23	38*	17	45***
Other (8.3%)	20	46*	21	45†

*p>.50
**p>.90
***p>.25
†p>.75

(p values associated with one sample chi-square statistics)

resembled the distribution of these owners in the samples as a whole. In terms of the chi-square analysis, none of the categories yielded a chi-square statistic significant below the .25 level; most were above the .50 level. Thus no statistically significant relationship between owner race and amount of station composite week programming was indicated for PSLR or for Black-oriented stations. T-tests and regression analyses using normalized data from the Black-oriented stations have further confirmed these findings (Singleton, 1981; Schement and Singleton, 1981). In short, owner ethnicity does not appear to be a useful predictor of the quantity of public service programming aired on primary Spanish-language or Black-oriented radio stations.

THE ONUS OF MINORITY OWNERSHIP: POLICY DISCUSSION

The data imply that, at least in terms of *amount* of public service programming, changing the owner-race of a minority-oriented station will not necessarily improve the station's performance. This gives rise to the question: Why would anyone think it would? That is, assuming that minority broadcasters face the same, if not more formidable, economic constraints as their nonminority counterparts in the radio marketplace, why should they be expected to outperform them in public service programming? Yet the implication of FCC policy seems to be that, while nonminority owners are expected to meet only minimal standards in public service programming performance, minority owners must go beyond that for the policy to appear successful: the onus of minority ownership.

It is possible that further research on the qualitative aspects of such programming—such as its relevance, positioning, or production expense—

may indicate superior performance by minority owners. It is likewise possible that, as data collected in the PSLR study indicate, minority owners tend to own "poorer" stations than their nonminority counterparts and cannot afford to produce the quantity or quality of programming they desire. However, until such evidence is available, the FCC cannot demonstrate that its policy has significantly increased the overall amount of nonentertainment programming serving the needs and interests of minority groups by changing the owner race of minority-oriented stations.

This leads to an even more fundamental question: If prospective minority owners cannot and should not fairly be relied upon to improve radio industry performance in public service programming for minorities, why should they be expected to program to the minority audience at all? Assuming that minority entrepreneurs are no different from others, their primary motive for entering broadcasting is profit. As Stan Raymond, a Black broadcasting consultant, has stated, Black ownership does not always imply Black format: "These new owners will program to the audience that's profitable for them" (Black Radio Market Study, 1980, p.A-24).

Present owners of minority-oriented stations may already have satisfied much of the demand for this type of programming in the prime minority markets. If so, is it appropriate for the success of minority ownership policy to depend, as the FCC has said, "on the ability and willingness of minority owners . . . to provide such programming"? (U.S. Federal Communications Commission, 1979). The implication seems to be that if minority entrepreneurs are not willing to provide such programming in the less profitable markets which remain open to them, they are responsible in part for the failure of the very policy designed to help them.

In light of these considerations and the results of this research, perhaps the FCC should reconsider whether increased minority program service is a useful or fair basis upon which to advocate increases in minority ownership. Increased minority program service implies a racially based double standard in performance expectations on the Commission's part. Prospective minority owners may be unfairly caught in the middle between such FCC expectations and the hard economic realities of station programming in a competitive industry.

FCC policies aimed at increasing the amount of minority ownership of broadcasting stations have been sorely needed and long in coming. However, the FCC's professed rationale for its existing policies in this area may have inadvertently created an unfair burden for minority owners; the success of the policy hinges on their dedication to minority programming. If increased programming for minority groups is a legitimate policy goal, then perhaps all licensees, regardless of race, should participate. Moreover, increased minority ownership should simply be advocated on the same basis as equal employment opportunity: as a necessary part of a broad effort to bring minorities into this country's economic mainstream. The FCC should rely for support, as the FCC minority ownership taskforce has suggested, upon the "more intuitive concepts of equity . . . especially in light of this country's history of racial injustice" (U.S. Federal Communications Commission, 1978a, p.3).

REFERENCES

Black radio market study. (1980). *Television/Radio Age* (Feb. 25).

Federal Communications Commission: Inquiry and proposed rulemaking; deregulation of radio. (1979). *Federal Register* (Oct. 5) Part III, 57683, Table 8.

GUTIERREZ, F.F., and SCHEMENT, J.R. (1979). "Spanish-Language Radio in the Southwestern United States." Austin, TX: Mexican-American Studies Center, Institute for Latin-American Studies, University of Texas at Austin. (Monograph No. 5.)

N.A.B. Radio/TV Highlights. (1980). *6* (Mar. 24), 12.

Radio stations regularly scheduling Black programs. (1980). *Spot Radio Rates and Data* (April 1), 21.

SCHEMENT, J.R., and SINGLETON, L.A. (1981). The onus of minority ownership: FCC policy and Spanish-language radio. *Journal of Communication 31* (No. 2), 78–83.

SINGLETON, L.A. (1981). FCC minority ownership policy and non-entertainment programming in Black-oriented radio stations. *Journal of Broadcasting 25*, 195–201.

SURLIN, S.H. (1973). Black-oriented radio's service to the community. *Journalism Quarterly 50*, 556–560.

U.S. Bureau of the Census. (1978). "Current Population Reports." (Series P-20, No. 328, "Persons of Spanish Origin in the United States.") Washington, DC: Government Printing Office.

U.S. Federal Communications Commission. (1978a). "Minority Ownership in Broadcasting: Minority Ownership Taskforce Report." Washington, DC: Government Printing Office.

U.S. Federal Communications Commission. (1978b). "Statement of Policy on Minority Ownership of Broadcasting Facilities." 68 FCC 2d 979.

U.S. Federal Communications Commission. (1979). "Deregulation of Radio." 73 FCC 2d 457.

10

Home Sweet Factory: Perspectives on Mass Society

VINCENT MOSCO
Department of Radio–Television–Film
Temple University
Philadelphia, Pennsylvania 19122

INTRODUCTION: EROSION OF THE PUBLIC SPHERE

The public sphere is a region of social life in which people come together freely to offer information, analyses, perspectives, criticism, and advice to advance their ability to meet changes in society. The goal of the public sphere is to provide people the fullest possible collective participation in the decisions that affect their lives. The public sphere is the terrain of democracy, but it may also be the endangered species of a mass-mediated society.

Critical theorists have repeatedly mourned, the demise of the public sphere. Habermas, sees in its decline the central evidence of crisis in contemporary capitalism:

> At one time the process of making proceedings public (publizität) was intended to subject persons or affairs to public reason, and to make political decisions subject to appeal before the court of public opinion. But often enough today the process of making public simply serves the arcane policies of special interests; in the form of "publicity" it wins public prestige for people of affairs, thus making them worthy of acclamation in a climate of non-public opinion. (Habermas, 1979, p. 200).

This emphasis on individual famous *people*, as opposed to a public, and on what Young calls *mass* rather than public opinion forms the thematic core for two descendants of Habermas (Young, 1979). Sennett (1974, p. 287) unmasks the contemporary public personality, the product of the Star System, as a thin vestige of a vibrant community life:

> The impact of television on politics is usually discussed in terms of the politician having to behave as though he were an actor. This cliche is true in one way but profoundly misleading in another.

What is believable about the politician as a personality are his motives, his sentiments, his "integrity". All these are at the expense of concern about what he does with his power. The content of politics is thus narrowed by the perception of personality in it.

For Bordieu (1979, pp.129-130) the task is to demystify the product of the pollster:

> In brief, in saying that public opinion does not exist, I mean it does not exist in the form which some people, whose existence depends on this illusion, would have us believe. At present, there is, on the one hand, mobilized opinion, formulated interests; and on the other, certain inclinations, opinions in an implicit state which, by definition are not really opinions, if by opinion we mean a formulated discourse with a pretension to coherence.

Of course this concern for the public sphere attracts the interest of more than the social theorist. The pages of popular magazines, of *Self, Me, People*, and *Mademoiselle*, contain an almost obsessive concern with this issue. Considerable attention has been devoted to their slavish devotion to the personal (*Mademoiselle's* February 1981 headlines: How to LOVE the Skin You're In; 97 Snazzy Spring Looks!; BREASTS: Making Yours Look (and Feel) Beautiful; BIG O? BIG DEAL! The Facts Behind the Fiction). But in the attention to narcissism that such bodily adoration inspires, there is the need to ask what this tells us about the public realm. Here we find more than a mechanistic withering of the public terrain that corresponds to the growth in narcissism. For a profound uneasiness envelops the recognition that individuals must relate to the public—to work, to neighborhood—but no one knows precisely how to do it *right*. The chief response is to privatize the public sphere. The appropriate response to the need to deal with the public world is to "dress" for it though without appearing to privatize completely the public realm. For the uncertainty about how to act publicly extends to the realization that it cannot be made completely into a private space. This tension is reflected in *Self* magazine's instructions on how to "make it" in the office:

> COMPANY PARTIES AND OUTINGS—YOU'RE NOT THERE FOR FUN
> While most people recognize that their performance at company meetings will affect their careers, they underestimate the significance of company parties and company outings. These are also "dog and pony shows." You're being observed. The first rule of attending business/social affairs is the same as the first rule for attending a meeting. Dress well. Wear your best clothes to the company party and quality sportswear to the company outing. Company parties and outings are not places to let your hair down.

Between Habermas and *Self* lie a range of empirical analysts and political activists who speak to the importance of public life in advanced capitalism.

Interestingly, both conservatives and radicals in the U.S. have begun to focus on similar structural solutions to differently perceived distortions in the relationship of public to private. Conservatives such as Peter Berger fear that unless an alternative is found, the prospect is for a totalitarian absorption of private life into the distorted public sphere of a coercive state. Berger (1976) therefore proposes strengthening not state, nor id, but those mediating structures, "family, church, voluntary association, neighborhood, and sub-culture" which "still give a measure of stability to private life."

The left, of course, advises that the danger is other than the state overwhelming private life. Rather, capitalism narrows the private sphere into the channel of commodity consumption. Those elements of the public sphere which resist absorption are at best tolerated, at worst trivialized and attacked. Traditionally, the left has sought to make the state the site of resistance to capitalist expansion into the private sphere. The U.S. Commerce Department, Federal Radio Commission, and, until recently, the FCC have in succession provided the arena for opposition to the invasion of the home by broadcast advertising, (see Barnouw, 1978, and Mosco, 1979). Without rejecting this strategy, though clearly shaken by the right wing victories in the recent British and U.S. elections, the left has begun to pay more attention to some of the same mediating structures that Berger describes. Though the recent defense of family and neighborhood grows more out of a need to reverse their absorption into commodities than to make them bulwarks against the state. One hears more frequently today that it is both tactically and politically essential for the left, particulary in the U.S., to erase the perception that its program would leave little more for the individual than a state apparatus, however democratized. Thus there is the call for strengthening family ties, for using electronic media, particularly new means of communication such as cable television. (See Boyte,1980, and Moberg, 1980.)

The relationship of public to private sphere is an issue for communicators of all sorts—for theoreticians, purveyors of mass culture, as well as for the political activist. This paper advances our understanding of this issue by examining the dominant theoretical perspective in which this issue is embedded—mass society theory. Against this view is a mushrooming of radical critiques of this perspective, critiques enriched by the application of economic imagery to our understanding of the private sphere. It is not essential for Chrysler to build K-cars in your living room for the private sphere in America to reflect the theme Home Sweet Factory. This paper deepens these radical critiques by examining the private sphere as an arena of struggle to counter hegemony and create a thriving public sphere. It concludes with some thoughts on a revision of our thinking about the private/public sphere dichotomy.

MASS SOCIETY: THE MAINSTREAM

The concept of a democratic public sphere is at best a secondary current in social science. Mass society occupies the mainstream. Indeed, the concept *mass society* entered the lexicon with *sociology*, each introduced by Auguste Comte, whose statue at the Sorbonne proclaims him "Père de la Sociologie." Comte's vision of industrial society was a divided one: Will this be an industrial age of plenty guided by the priest *cum* surgeon Sociologist, or the age of division, of isolated individuals wandering in aimlessness? (Comte, 1972).

This split view would structure the debate about mass society for two centuries. The latter, the pessimistic view of man in mass society, of the lonely crowd, would lead the debate and indeed shape the course of theorizing in sociology and "mass" communications. Nowhere is this view expressed with more care and passion than in the work of Comte's intellectual heir Emile Durkheim. Durkheim's work contains a unity of focus that is not fully appreciated because it threads through a number of diverse substantive areas. He wrote of religion, the family, crime, education, suicide. But all of these topics are little more than expressions of, or vehicles for, conveying the message that industrial society is mass society; that mass society is a loose collection of anomic individuals, "liquid molecules" as he calls them, tied to one another by little more than the bond of mutual economic dependence. The most explicit presentation of this bleak vision of mass society is in *Suicide*, ironically Durkheim's most empirical work. Perhaps out of confidence in the statistical basis of his view that suicide has risen dramatically throughout Europe, Durkheim (1951, p. 388) uses the final chapter to ruminate on the implications of this trend:

> Historical development . . . has swept cleanly away all the older social forms of organization.

All that is left is individuals in competition for material goods—a competition that the means of communication make more profitable and thereby more morally impoverished. Durkheim sees in suicide the symptom of a wider social malaise, the rise of mass society. The decline of organized religion, the reduction of the family to "nonentity," the rise of the modern state, whose growth to Durkheim only masks its moral impotence, leaves the individual without social resources. A pessimistic Durkheim (1951, p. 391) concludes with an appeal to recreate community around occupation, though he gives this option little chance before the onslaught of modernity.

Durkheim's view remains central to the understanding that scholars bring to the study of social relations in a mass media age (De Fleur and Ball-Rokeach (1975, pp. 133-161). It has been sharpened more by events than by intellectual accomplishment. The horrors of World War, economic depression, and the rise of fascism make, what was once an unusual challenge to the Enlightenment–born vision of secular progress, a popular view of the human condition. In a critique, Daniel Bell (1962, pp. 21-22) captures the spirit of mass society and its link to media:

> The conception of the "mass society" can be summarized as follows: The revolutions in transport and communications have brought men into closer contact with each other and bound them in new ways; the division of labor has made them more interdependent; tremors in one part of society affect all others. Despite this greater interdependence, however, individuals have grown more estranged from one another. The old primary group ties of family and local community have been shattered; ancient parochial faiths are questioned; few unifying values have taken their place. Most important, the critical standards of an educated elite no longer shape opinion or taste. As a result, mores and morals are in constant flux, relations between individuals are tangential or compartmentalized, rather than organic. At the same time, greater mobility, spatial and social, intensifies concern over status. Instead of a fixed or known status, symbolized by dress or title, each person assumes a multiplicity of roles and constantly has to prove himself in a succession of new situations. Because of all this, the individual loses a coherent sense of self. His anxieties increase. There ensues a search for new faiths. The stage is thus set for the charismatic leader, the secular messiah, who, by bestowing upon each person the semblance of necessary grace and of fullness of personality, supplies a substitute for the older unifying belief that the mass society has destroyed.

The works of specific 20th century descendants of Durkheim make Bell's summary perhaps too tame. Karl Mannheim (1940) writes of the crushing burden of bureaucracy and the meaningless functional rationality that it inspires. Ortega Y Gassett (1957) laments the decline of standards, social and aesthetic, that the "revolt of the masses" has engendered. The result of the diffusion of culture, particularly through the "sinister" mass media, is to dilute the quality of cultural production. A bland mediocrity replaces human aspiration and achievement.

Bell's critique of this view wanders over contradictions in usage and ambiguities of terminology before arriving at the essence of his concern:

> It is at heart a defense of an aristocratic cultural tradition—a tradition that does carry with it an important but neglected conception of liberty—and a doubt that the large mass of mankind can ever become truly educated or acquire an appreciation of culture (Bell, 1962, p. 28).

For Bell, this overlooks the facts of life in the United States. In this respect his optimistic variant of the mass society theme places him in the tradition of de Tocqueville. The latter's *Democracy in America* celebrates the mass experience of America. The United States, at least the U.S. in the mid-nineteenth century, is a thriving *pluralist* nation of joiners:

Americans of all ages, all stations in life, and all types of disposition are forever forming associations. There are not only commercial and industrial associations in which all take part, but others of a thousand different types—religious, moral, serious, futile, very general and very limited, immensely large and very minute. Americans combine to give fêtes, found seminaries, build churches, distribute books, and send missionaries to the antipodes. Hospitals, prisons, and schools take shape in that way. Finally, if they want to proclaim a truth or propagate some feeling by the encouragement of a great example, they form an association. In every case, at the head of any new undertaking, where in France you would find the government or in England some territorial magnate, in the United States you are sure to find an association (De Tocqueville, 1964, p. 515).

A century later, Bell sees little in this assessment that needs revision:

It is asserted that the United States is an "atomized" society composed of lonely, isolated individuals. One forgets the truism, expressed sometimes as a jeer, that Americans are a nation of joiners. There are in the United States today at least 200,000 voluntary organizations, associations, clubs, societies, lodges, and fraternities, with an aggregate (but obviously overlapping) membership of close to 80 million men and women. In no other country in the world, probably, is there such a high degree of voluntary communal activity, expressed sometimes in absurd rituals, yet often providing real satisfaction for real needs (Bell, 1962, p. 32).

In Bell's view, then, the connection between industrialization and an atomized mass society is broken. America has, in fact, realized the hope of Durkheim for a genuine occupational community. Referring to America's "ingenuity in shaping new social forms" Bell (1962, p. 28) cites "trade unions whose leaders rise from the ranks—there are 50,000 trade-union locals in this country that form little worlds of their own." Far from a society of mindless masses, America has realized a genuine *pluralist* mass culture. It is left for Foster Rhea Dulles, whose family produced heads of the State Department and CIA, to make the obvious link between this view and a pluralist conception of politics. In his history of popular recreation in America, Dulles (1963, p. 349) celebrates the growth of sport in depression America:

3,700 recreational buildings, 881 new parks, 1,500 athletic fields, 440 swimming-pools, 3,500 tennis-courts, 123 golf-courses, and 28 miles of ski trails. Twelve hundred cities had in all seventeen thousand acres of parks reserved for sports activities, and they were annually spending $60,000,000 on their upkeep. Bathing beaches and swimming-pools, with an estimated annual attendance of some 200,000,000, were the most popular of their facilities, but there were also 8,800 softball diamonds and 3,600 baseball diamonds at which the player attendance was estimated at 31,000,000; 11,000 tennis-courts with an attendance of 11,000,000; and public golf-courses used by a total of 8,000,000.

Here was the truly democratic approach to this phase of recreation. These millions of urban workers—men, women, and children—were finally enjoying the organized sports that had been introduced by the fashionable world half a century and more earlier. Democracy was making good its right to play the games formerly limited to the small class that had the wealth and leisure to escape the city.

Like the pluralist view of politics which sees power widely distributed among many interests, mass society is a pluralist marketplace of diverse participants. But also like the pluralist view of politics, the optimistic variant of the mass society perspective is now under question by its once staunchest supporters.

The pluralist political analyst, once enthusiastic supporter of mass participation, now laments the inability to act, the stalemate that comes from too many pressures, too much pluralism.[1] How, they ask, can a nation like the United States establish, not to mention *execute,* an energy policy, when a dozen or more interest groups wield veto power?[2] In the same way that Samuel Huntington shifts from founding father of pluralist political science to prophet of the doom inherent in the "excesses of democracy," Bell (1976, p. 54) shifts from singing the praises of mass culture to worrying as America descends "from the protestant ethic to the psychedelic bazaar." The *End of Ideology* gives way to *The Cultural Contradictions of Capitalism,* to "pop hedonism," to the "death of the bourgeois world-view," to the modern hubris:

> the refusal to accept limits, the insistence on continually reaching out; and the modern world proposes a destiny that is always *beyond:* beyond morality, beyond tragedy, beyond culture (Bell, 1976, p. 50).

For Bell, the ramifications of this cultural shift are profound. A promiscuous culture clashes with the rational economic machine that is the essence of a capitalist social structure. According to Bell (1976, p. 37) we experience

> the radical disjunction between the social structure (the techno-economic order) and the culture. The former is ruled by an economic principle defined in terms of efficiency and functional rationality, the organization of production through the ordering of things, including men as things. The latter is prodigal, promiscuous, dominated by an anti-rational, anti-intellectual temper in which the self is taken as the touchstone of cultural judgments, and the effect on the self is the measure of the aesthetic worth of experience. The character structure inherited from the nineteenth century, with its emphasis on self-discipline, delayed gratification, and restraint, is still relevant to the demands of the techno-economic structure; but it clashes sharply with the culture, where such bourgious values have been completely rejected—in part, paradoxically, because of the workings of the capitalist economic system itself.

---

[1] For a detailed examination of this shift see Mosco (1980).

[2] The latest expression of this concern for "the limits of democracy" is offered by former counsel to President Carter, Lloyd Cutler, in "To Form a Government" (1980).

Unfortunately, the latter point, the contradiction (as opposed to disjunction) in capitalism that fosters its own demise, is not explored. The culture is culprit. To a polity overwhelmed with the press of single issue politics, we add a culture whose limitless manifestations ("even madness . . . is now conceived to be a superior form of truth"—Bell, 1976, p. 34) make a mockery of traditional means to legitimate the system. This is indeed the central problem:

> One problem . . . is whether the system itself can manage the huge overload of issues. This depends, in part, on "technical" economic answers and equally on the stability of the world system. But the deeper and more difficult questions are the legitimations of the society as expressed in the motivations of individuals and the moral purposes of the nation. And it is here that the cultural contradictions—the discordances of character structure and the disjunction of realms—become central (Bell, 1976, p. 83).

The solution is clear: to preserve capitalism, curb the excesses of democracy, curtail the madness of the cultural sphere.

RADICAL CRITIQUE: HOME AS FACTORY

Where Bell sees contradiction, radical critics of the mass society view see the intimate connection between a capitalist economy and its cultural sphere, between the mechanized workplace and the home. The critique begins at the level of functional interdependence; the private sphere supports the workplace by offering space for recuperation and the channeling of workplace anger, typically onto women. The critique deepens in recent work that questions the division between workplace and home. The home is more than a vent for repressed rage; it too is the site of production, though not of steel ingots or cardboard boxes, but of the *audience commodity*. We examine the profound implications of this reorientation in thinking about the relationship between economics and culture. This prepares for a third and final movement—the view of the cultural sphere as an arena of struggle.

Culture as Recuperation

Within traditional Marxism, culture is a reflection of economic relations. Culture is functionally interdependent with, and not merely a reflection of, economics. The cultural or private sphere provides an arena of support to fundamental economic activity. Samir Amin (1974, p. 8) puts this sense of interdependence well in his analysis of the relationship between work and non-work time:

Social time is split into non-working time and working time. But here too the former exists only to serve the latter. It is not leisure time, as it is called in the false consciousness of alienated man, but recuperation time. It is functional recuperation that is socially organized and not left up to the individual despite certain appearances.

It is in this sense that Stanley Aronowitz (1973) refers to leisure as "colonized." Also, as Heidi Hartmann and others have shown, the private sphere is the major site of women's oppression, the clearest expression of patriarchy. The personal degradation that men increasingly experience as a result of trivialized work is given some measure of compensation in the pattern of male control in the home. According to Hartmann (1979, p. 19) the growing participation of women in the labor force does nothing to substantially alter this relationship:

The "ideal" of the family wage—that a man can earn enough to support an entire family—may be giving way to a new ideal that both men and women contribute through wage earning to the cash income of the family. The wage differential, then, will become increasingly necessary in perpetuating patriarchy, the male control of women's labor power. The wage differential will aid in defining women's work as secondary to men's at the same time as it necessitates women's actual continued economic dependence on men.

The private sphere in capitalism is then the arena of recuperation and re-production. Workers recoup the physical and psychic strength to return to work, in part through the reproduction of sexual hegemony, the dominance of men over women, changed in form, though largely undiminished in strength by the recent growth in women's participation in the labor force.

The Audience Commodity

The recuperation thesis has been considerably deepened in the work of Dallas Smythe. To appreciate the significance of Smythe's contribution we need to see it as a fundamental change in our way of seeing the relationship between work and leisure. Where once there was division, two spheres—work and leisure/economy and culture—now there is one: the sphere of commodity production. The private sphere is the site for the production of audiences that broadcasting stations and other media entrepreneurs sell to advertisers. The primary commodity of the private sphere, particularly of the invasive commercial communications industry, is the audience: "a non-durable producers good which is bought and used in the marketing of the advertisers product" (Smythe, 1977, p. 6).

According to Smythe (1977, p. 3), once one uncovers the blindspot that has masked the audience commodity, one uncovers the underlying symmetry of capitalism:

The material reality under monopoly capitalism is that all non-sleeping time of most of the population is work time. This work time is devoted to the production of commodities-in-general (both where people get paid for their work and as members of audiences) and in the production and reproduction of labor power (the pay for which is subsumed in their income). Of the off-the-job work time, the largest single block is time of the audiences which is sold to advertisers. It is not sold by workers but by the mass media of communications. . . . But although the mass media play the leading role on the production side of the consciousness industry the people in the audiences pay directly much more for the priveledge of being in those audiences than do the mass media.

Smythe's analysis raises a number of issues and considerable controversy (Murdock, 1978; Smythe, 1978). What then of media messages? According to Smythe, the messages of advertisers are the instruments that speed the circulation of audience commodities (the message is the medium?). Furthermore, the programs (news, entertainment, stories) are, following Liebling, a free lunch. They are tossed in at the Tavern of the Audience Commodity as an added enticement to serious drinkers. But for those of us who believe with Milton Friedman that capitalism offers no free lunch, might we not conceptualize the news and entertainment as the wage for working to produce the audience commodity? Furthermore, if the private sphere is not playtime in mass society, nor simply recuperation time, but rather *work*, the process of building the audience commodity, then what do we make of the eight hour day? To what extent can we continue to refer to a reduced work week as one of the benefits of 20th-century industrial society or one of labor's great victories, when workers spend so much of their time, outside of factory or office, even outside of the general definition of houseworker, *laboring* under the pressures imposed by the demand management system of monopoly capitalism?

CULTURE: ALTERNATIVE AND OPPOSITIONAL

In its effort to counter the dominant mass society view, the radical critique has generally emphasized the idea of *hegemony*. Culture is not the expression of timeless values debased by mass diffusion, as the pessimistic mass-society view holds, nor is it enriched by a plurality of contributors, as the optimists see it. Rather, it is the embodiment of domination, the subtle insinuation of class rule into daily existence. This results in the widespread view that audience production and cultural reproduction are *common sense*. As Raymond Williams (1980, p.38) points out, hegemony, when used as Gramsci intended, transcends the bounds of base and superstructure. It is more than mere opinion or mental manipulation:

It is a whole body of practices and expectations; our assignments of energy, our ordinary understanding of the nature of man and of his world. It is a set of meanings and values which as they are experienced as practices appear as reciprocally confirming. It thus constitutes a sense of reality for most people in the society, a sense of absolute because experienced reality beyond which it is difficult for most members of the society to move, in most areas of their lives.

Hegemony is the unquestioned social value, nationalism in the return of hostage Americans from Iran. It is the unquestioned practice, the commercial break twelve minutes into a television program. In fact, once discovered, hegemony is so powerful a notion that we tend to lose sight that it is merely one part of a process that requires *incorporation*. Schools, the family, the media, all are engaged in a process of incorporating people into a dominant or hegemonic culture. They teach, not merely an ideology that sits atop the heads of people, easily imposed but as easily sloughed off. They teach us how to live, a code that selects from all possible ways of living those ways which conform to the needs and pressures of producing and reproducing capitalist social relations. But this requires incorporating from existing patterns of social life; it requires bending, shaping, and often crushing ways of living that differ from the needs of an audience commodity system. According to Aronowitz (1973, pp. 118–119) this introduces an inherent tension into the workings of hegemony:

> What this means is that while a ruling class can appropriate existing cultural forms and symbols and to a certain extent convert them into means of legitimizing its hegemony, it cannot *create* culture any more than it can create means of production. It thus depends in the last analysis on the exercise of creativity by others as they attempt to adapt their everyday lives under the impact of socioeconomic changes.

What Aronowitz describes is the dialectical tension between a hegemonic system of social relations that reproduces itself by incorporating new generations, new groups of people. In the process of incorporation, there is tension and struggle.[3]

The concepts *hegemony, tension,* and *struggle* are useful because they correspond to major social groups that interact in the cultural sphere. Borrowing concepts from Williams, the *dominant* group in society seeks hegemony, seeks to impose a pattern of social relations onto the general society. In the process of imposition, the dominant group confronts both *alternative* and *oppositional* groups. Alternative groups grow out of the tension between dominant and non-dominant forms of cultural expression. They resist restrictions imposed by the dominant pattern of social relations, but do so

---

[3]For a study of how this process operates, see Goodman (1979). This is an analysis of how a dominant culture used settlement houses, schools, and the police to cleanse and absorb the street and play life of immigrant communities at the turn of the century.

within the framework of dispute settlement sanctioned in the dominant culture. A good example of an alternative group growing out of tension with the dominant culture is the public-interest media-reform movement in America. The National Citizens Committee for Broadcasting represents people who feel that the dominant system of commercial mass media is overly restrictive. It limits media access to the wealthy. The NCCB protests and seeks fuller access by using the court system and the U.S. regulatory machinery. It thus represents an "alternative" view *within* the established framework. On the other hand, some "opposition" groups seek to alter fundamentally the formation itself, e.g., *The Guardian* or community radio stations such as those linked to the Pacifica network.

The introduction of the notions alternative and oppositional culture adds important dimensions to existing research on cultural relations. For one, it broadens the onesided emphasis on *hegemony* that quite necessarily has occupied major research efforts to date. For all of their differences, the early Frankfurt School, Althusser on the all-encompassing Ideological State Apparatus, Schiller on mind management, Ewen on the growth of the advertising industry, and Smythe on the audience commodity, the view has been similar. The capitalist consciousness industry exerts near omnipotent hegemony over people. But viewed dialectically, contemporary culture is more than a powerful instrument of ruling class hegemony. It *is* that, but more.

How have people used their collective cultural energy to resist the consciousness industry and build an alternative class culture? In what ways have people gone out on strike against the dominant culture? Or how have people simply hoarded their cultural power as a form of resistance? How might people usefully resist today? Examples include powerful resistance to the incursions of commercialism first into newspapers and magazines (Benson, 1979) and then the electronic media (Barnouw, 1978) to efforts to root out the sexism, racism, and class bias of the media (Berk, 1979; Glasgow University Media Group, 1976-1980; U.S. Commission on Civil Rights (1979). On the other hand, how have working class people formed their own oppositional culture? Just before World War I, openly socialist publications like the Kansas-based *Appeal to Reason* boasted a subscription list of 750,000, while the *International Socialist Review* sold 50,000 copies of each issue. How might we enhance, through careful analysis of the dialectics of alienated culture, popular cultural control? Recent efforts, ranging from strategies to create alternative programming to the politics of gaining public control over, or at least access to, established media, offer interesting suggestions (Downing, 1980; Kellner, 1979).

Hans Enzensberger (1976) offers further insight into this view by breaking with the traditional condescending scorn that the Frankfurt School has heaped upon the mass media. He points out how inherently emancipatory media technologies are utilized in a contradictory, that is, repressive way.

Specifically, mass media which allow for decentralized programming, two-way communication, which open the way for collective production, are used quite to the contrary. Programs are centrally controlled; operation is according to the one transmitter/many receiver model; the goal is to create isolated passive consumers with production in the hands of specialists and the entire system controlled by property owners or elite bureaucrats. But the latter is historically produced and not an *inevitable* consequence of information technologies. Recent technological developments from cable television and video discs to small earth station satellite systems make the social relations of capitalist media production, distribution, and consumption more contradictory (National Citizens Committee for Broadcasting, 1979).

Aronowitz extends this view beyond the sphere of potentially oppositional technology to what he sees as the irreduceably liberating quality of mass culture itself. According to Aronowitz (1979, p.50):

> The power of mass culture resides not only in the degradation and commodification of human needs, but in its capacity to express and produce those needs. The images of mass culture may be the only sphere within daily existence that points beyond the mundane towards the erotic. Mass culture cannot be understood simply as a degraded form of cultural life. For it is its utopian element that gives it power.

We need to explore further the free spaces of mass culture, those territories that defy reduction to political economy, not out of curiosity over their persistence, but to expand their boundaries.

CODA: THE PUBLIC SPHERE, PRIVATE SPHERE, AUDIENCE SPHERE

This paper has taken us through three movements. The first, the dominant mass-society perspective on the leisure sphere, views that sphere as the payoff for whatever subjugation the individual must endure in the workplace. For some analysts, the payoff is very costly. It results in individual isolation, the lonely crowd, and in a culture made mediocre by its mass diffusion. For others, the vast informal networks of a mass society make the lonely crowd more appearance than reality, enrich rather than debase cultural values. The second movement sharply criticizes the mass society view for its failure to stress the intimate connection between the workplace and home. In its most radical form, this view asserts that for the purposes of producing and reproducing, the social relations of capitalism, work and leisure are the same. The leisure sphere is site for the production of the audience commodity, collections of individuals delivered by media to advertisers who bid for their particular audience characteristics. Laborers gather in factories to produce shoes size 6-12, people gather in living rooms to produce audiences of teenagers or "ladies ages 19-49." The third movement deepens the radical critique by complementing the latter's stress on *hegemony* with a view of cultural *struggle*. The private sphere is not only a channel through which capital creates the audience commodity and reproduces social relations and cultural values conducive to the commodity form. It is also a site of resistance for alternative and oppositional groups driven by economic, political, and cultural alienation. The tensions and contradictions that hegemony seeks to suppress are not easily contained. The result is cultural struggle.

Where does this leave the malaise about public and private spheres that Habermas, *Self* magazine, and political activists right and left find so disturbing? Those like Sennett, who express concern about the decline of the public sphere, link that decline to the emphasis on the private, the self, that raises narcissism to a dominant position in the social psychology of industrial society. But when people like Lasch or *Self* magazine turn to the private sphere we find a terrain as deeply unsatisfying. The private sphere is isolated in form only. Its substance has been invaded by the corporate and political institutions that comprise the public sphere in industrial society.

A substantial problem with these analyses is that we do not know whether we are dealing with existing or idealized versions of public and private sphere. Furthermore, is it axiomatic that growth in one sphere threatens the other? Is it possible, as most imply, that a process of mutual contamination can make for a shrinkage in both? If so, what is left?

I have what amounts to a simple thought about these questions that I hope further debate can clarify and assess. Drawing on the work of Smythe, consider the usefulness of introducing the concept *audience sphere* as that area of human activity that capital has shaped into a marketable commodity. This would reserve for the *public sphere* the social activity in which people come together to offer information, opinion, and criticism on issues that concern neighborhood, community, region, or the entire society. The private sphere is that region of human activity concerned with personal intimacy, with friendship and family, with personal love and hate. Historically, capitalism results in the penetration of public and private spheres by the process of building the audience commodity. The central *public* debates in capitalism are media events in which candidates for public office and elected officials are judged on their ability to deliver, not on a policy promise, but an audience to advertisers. The most intimate of human activities, sexuality, friendship, animosity, are equally devised for making of *private* life the audience commodity. The magazine in the living room contains a Winston ad featuring a macho image proclaiming that he doesn't judge his cigarette only by its length; the TV in the bedroom says its okay for men to go off together— provided they bring along Michelob.

To suggest that the audience sphere invades both public and private domains preserves the meaning of the terms and avoids confusing implications about the relationship between public and private spheres. The "fall of public man" results not from the intrusion of personality into politics, but from the intrusion of the audience commodity. It is not intimacy that overwhelms the public sphere, but a false intimacy that builds the audience commodity. Likewise, it is not the intrusion of the public sphere that destroys intimacy, but a false sense of community that creates neither public spirit nor private life, but the audience commodity. Consequently, to struggle against the erosion of intimacy is not necessarily to oppose public life, but rather to oppose turning the personal, the intimate, into commodities. And likewise, to struggle for the fullest possible public participation in decisions that affect our lives is not to oppose intimacy, the family, the private sphere, but the intrusion of a profitably packaged version of that sphere.

The distinction among private, public, and audience spheres is of more than analytic significance. Those seeking to advance democracy, collective action, the building of a democratic public sphere have either been stridently critical or very defensive about the private sphere of self, personal relations, family, and intimacy. The ability of the Right to capture widespread support in America can be traced in part to the failure of progressives to distinguish their critique of what capital has done to the relations and institutions of the private sphere, from support for a vital sphere of intimacy. Why support a political movement that opposes the family? The left needs to make clear that it opposes not the family, nor neighborhood, nor the symbols of freedom and commitment that enrich peoples lives, but a system that makes these institutions marketable commodities.

In conclusion, discovering the audience sphere is one step toward removing both public and private life from the endangered species list of our mass-mediated society.

REFERENCES

AMIN, S. (1974). In praise of socialism. *Monthly Review 26* (No. 4), 1–16.
ARONOWITZ, S. (1973.) "False Promises." New York: McGraw-Hill.
ARONOWITZ, S. (1979). The end of political economy. *Social Text* (No. 2), 3-52.
BARNOUW, E. (1978). "The Sponsor: Notes on a Modern Potentate." New York: Oxford.
BELL, D. (1962). "The End of Ideology," Revised ed., New York: Free Press
BELL, D. (1976). "The Cultural Contradictions of Capitalism." New York: Basic.
BENSON, S.P. (1979.) Advertising America. *Socialist Review 9* (No. 1), 143–155.
BERGER, P. (1976.) In praise of particularity: The concept of mediating structures. *Review of Politics 38*, 399–410.
BERK, L.M. (1979.) The great middle American dream machine. *In* Alan Wells (Ed.), "Mass Media and Society." Palo Alto, CA: Mayfield.
BORDIEU, P. (1979.) Public opinion does not exist. *In* A. Mattelart and S. Siegelaub (Eds.), "Communication and Class Struggle," Vol. 1. New York: International General.

BOYTE, H.C. (1980.) "The Backyard Revolution: Understanding the New Citizen Movement."
Philadelphia: Temple University.

BRAVERMAN, H. (1974.) "Labor and Monopoly Capital." New York: Monthly Review Press.

COMTE, A. (1972.) "La Science Sociale." Paris: Gallimard.

CUTLER, L.N. (1980.) To form a government. *Foreign Affairs 59*, 125–143.

DE FLEUR, M., and BALL-ROKEACH, S. (1975.) "Theories of Mass Communication," 3rd. ed.
New York: David McKay.

DOWNING, J. (1980.) "The Media Machine." London: Pluto.

DULLES, F.R. (1963). "America Learns to Play: A History of Popular Recreation 1607-1940."
Gloucester, MA: Peter Smith

DURKHEIM, E. (1951.) "Suicide: A Study in Sociology." Trans. by J.A. Spaulding and G. Simpson.
New York: Free Press

ENZENSBERGER, H.M. (1976.) Constituents of a theory of the media. *In* H. Newcomb (Ed.),
"Television: The Critical View." New York: Oxford.

EWEN, S. (1976.) "Captains of Consciousness." New York: McGraw-Hill.

GARNHAM, N. (n.d.). "Towards a Political Economy of Mass Communication." Unpublished
manuscript, Polytechnic of Central London.

Glasgow University Media Group. (1976-1980). "Bad News," Vol. 1-2. London:Routledge and
Kegan Paul.

GOODMAN, C. (1979.) "Choosing Sides: Playground and Street Life on the Lower East Side."
New York: Schocken Books.

HABERMAS, J. (1979.) The public sphere. *In* A. Mattelart and S. Siegelaub (Eds.), "Communication and Class Struggle: Vol. 1, Capitalism, Imperialism." New York: International
General.

HARTMANN, H.I. (1979.) The unhappy marriage of Marxism and feminism: Towards a more
progressive union. *Capital and Class* (Summer).

KELLNER, D. (1979). TV, ideology, and emancipatory popular culture. *Socialist Review 9* (No.
3), 13-53.

LIVANT, B. (1979). The audience commodity: On the "blindspot" debate. *Canadian Journal of
Social and Political Theory 3* (No. 1), 91–106.

MANNHEIM, K. (1940.) "Man and Society in an Age of Reconstruction." London: K. Paul, Trench
and Trubner.

MOBERG, D. (1980). Retooling the industrial debate. *Working Papers for a New Society* (Nov./
Dec.), 32–39.

MOLLOY, J.T. (1981). Office parties: The new "dog and pony" shows for women. *Self* (Feb.),
122–123.

MOSCO, V. (1979). "Broadcasting in the United States." Norwood, NJ: Ablex.

MOSCO, V. (1980). "The State and Information Resources: Theoretical Perspectives and Political
Practice." (Paper presented at the Association for Education in Journalism, Boston, MA.)

MURDOCK, G. (1978). Blindspots about western Marxism: A reply to Dallas Smythe. *Canadian
Journal of Political and Social Theory 2* (No. 2), 109–119.

National Citizens Committee for Broadcasting. (1979). "New Technologies and Their Application
to Individual and Community Uses." Washington, DC: National Citizens Committee for
Broadcasting.

ORTEGA Y GASSETT, J. (1957). "The Revolt of the Masses." New York: Norton.

SENNETT, R. (1974). "The Fall of Public Man: On the Social Psychology of Capitalism." New
York: Vintage.

SMYTHE, D. (1977). Communications: Blindspot of western Maxism. *Canadian Journal of
Political and Social Theory 1* (No. 3), 1–27.

SMYTHE, D. (1978). Rejoinder to Graham Murdock. *Canadian Journal of Political and Social
Theory 2* (No. 2), 120–127.

TOCQUEVILLE, A. DE, (1964). "Democracy in America," Vol. 2, Part 2. New York: Anchor Books.

U.S. Commission on Civil Rights. (1979). "Window Dressing on the Set: An Update." Washington, DC: U.S. Government Printing Office.

WILLIAMS, R. (1980). Base and superstructure in Marxist cultural theory. *In* R. Williams, "Problems in Materialism and Culture." London: Verso.

YOUNG, T.R. (1979). "The Public Sphere and the States in Capitalist Society." Livermore, CO: Red Feather Institute for Advanced Studies in Sociology. (Transforming Sociology Series No. 50.)

PART III

Mass Media Content

11

Fairy Tales in the Age of Television:
A Comparative Content Analysis

CATHERINE E. KIRKLAND
Annenberg School of Communications
University of Pennsylvania
Philadelphia, Pennsylvania 19104

While critics of modern popular culture are concerned with the violence and stereotypical portrayals they find in the mass media, supporters of and apologists for the media stress their continuities with folk culture and classical literature and drama. This paper discusses the findings of a study (Kirkland, 1981) based on the premise that fairy tales and television drama, representing either end of the historical continuum of popular culture, are indeed similar in certain characteristics that some critical researchers have attributed to mass media.

The task posed for this investigation was to subject a representative sample of historically popular fairy tales to the same kind of content analysis that has been applied to samples of dramatic television content, to determine whether more similarities or more differences would be found between these two symbolic "worlds" of storytelling. A comparative analysis was made of selected Grimm's fairy tales and samples of both prime-time and weekend-daytime (children's) programming. The methodology and data of the ongoing Cultural Indicators research on the content of network television drama was used (see Gerbner et al., 1980). The comparison was concerned with the presentation of particular fictional themes, patterns of character casting and fate, and violent story action. Examination of these characteristics provided a broad and relevant base from which to test the assumption of continuity between these two different storytelling modes.

Gerbner (1978) has noted that we make the invisible network of culture visible through various forms of storytelling. We structure our behavior according to this implicit network; storytelling of all kinds, as a basic aspect of humanization, tends to make us behave in socially acceptable ways and tells us what those ways are. Fairy tales have fulfilled an important role in this process of acculturation. Originally handed down orally from generation to generation, and later collected and printed for mass consumption, they continued to provide the basis for much of the socialization of children in literate families. Not only could they be read to children by parents, but children were then able to read the stories themselves. At least before the advent of television fairy tales often provided a child's first glimpse into the world of fiction.

Yet it seems that fairy tales, as the surviving remnants of an oral tradition, have been largely replaced in their role as primary instruments for the socialization of the young. The basic assertion of the Cultural Indicators research is that "television drama is in the mainstream — or is *the* mainstream — of the symbolic environment cultivating common conceptions of life, society, and the world" (Gerbner and Gross, 1973, p. 2).

The goal of this study was to ascertain whether a continuity exists between fairy tales and TV drama in what they tend to present as socially valued — and valid — roles and behaviors; in other words, what expectations about the nature of social reality they are likely to cultivate in their respective audiences.

The fairy tale sample consisted of 92 stories selected from the 1972 Random House edition of *The Complete Grimm's Fairy Tales*. These stories are virtually identical to those found in the 1901 version of *Grimm's Household Tales*, containing the original English translations.

Data for the sample of television drama were obtained by computer access of available Cultural Indicators files, from 1969 to 1979, cumulative. The source of these files is one week of TV programming transmitted in the fall of each year across all three major networks. The data for prime time (8-11 p.m. EST each day) and weekend-daytime drama (children's programming, 8 a.m.-2 p.m. Saturday and Sunday) were included in order to broaden the scope of the study. The addition of children's television programming facilitated a parallel between two different types of storytelling which today are aimed at the same specific audience. Results of the Cultural Indicators message system analysis of TV drama were taken from a 10-year period to provide the most comprehensive and accurate picture possible of the symbolic world of television fiction. A total of 750 prime-time programs and 544 weekend-daytime programs made up the sample.

The recording instrument used in the content analysis of the selected fairy tales was adapted from the revised (as of 1978) Cultural Indicators instrument. There were three units of analysis: general story themes, leading characters, and violent story action. Fictional themes, providing an overall context for the more particular examination of characters and action, were measured in terms of both average attention (their appearance in the stories) and emphasis (the relative significance of a given theme).

The analysis of leading characters was concerned with patterns of casting and fate in the world of fairy tales. A demographic and descriptive profile of the fairy tale population was constructed with particular attention to sex, social age, social class, and character type. Character fate was assessed by items relating to overall success and to involvement in violence.

Defined as "the overt expression of physical force (with or without weapon) against self or other compelling action against one's will on pain of being hurt or killed, or actually hurting or killing" (Gerbner, 1980, p. 67), fictional violence portrays the structure of social relations in a symbolic world. The roles adopted by different groups of characters in violent actions reveal underlying patterns of social dominance and vulnerability. By looking at who commits violence, who suffers it, what types of characters use violence successfully, what types are punished for wielding it, and to what extent, a fictional hierarchy can be constructed of those who control through violent means and those who tend to be controlled — or eliminated.

The features of violent actions per se were also examined in order to contrast the nature of the incidents which most baldly reaveal the structures of social power presented in fairy tales and television drama.

The comparison of fairy tales to TV fiction uncovered some basic similarities as well as highlighting certain differences. Both exhibit social and gender bias, and the theme of violence appears frequently and is emphasized in both worlds, but these tendencies are differently manifested. One might not expect fairy tales to exhibit an emphasis on violence similar to that of TV. In fact, examples from the Grimm collection are even more explicitly gory, and evil characters quite frequently earn bizarre comeuppances —e.g., Snow White's stepmother is forced to dance herself to death wearing red-hot iron shoes; a traitorous serving maid is put into a nail-studded barrel and rolled down an incline; and a malevolent wizard who keeps the dismembered bodies of his former wives in a blood-filled basin is burned alive by the ladies' irate relatives. The first of two key findings was concerned with character casting and fate.

In both fairy tales and television drama, male and female roles are sharply demarcated. Male characters outnumber females in both these worlds. Females are more often younger or older than males, who appear most often as settled (middle-aged) adults. Women are also consistently more likely than men to be romantically attached, married, and involved with the traditional female concerns of home and family life. Yet fairytale women are proportionately more likely than their male counterparts — and more likely than females on TV drama — to be portrayed as both bad and unsuccessful in the pursuit of their goals. In addition, females in fairy tales are more frequently involved in both violence and killing than those in television fiction — and are more often the victims of fatal violence. Thus, while fairy tales feature a traditional split in the portrayal of women — virtue versus wickedness — television drama's stereotypical presentation of female characters is one-dimensional. Women in TV drama play more marginal and harmless roles than their fairy tale counterparts; and models of evil femininity so prevalent in fairy tales are missing in television.

In terms of social age, fairy tales present a more generally representative population than that apparent in TV fiction, where settled or middle-aged adults dominate, both numerically and otherwise. Of most significance is the disparate portrayal of elderly characters in these storytelling worlds. The elderly are of greater importance in fairy tales, not only in terms of the proportionately larger size of this group as compared to TV drama, but in its enhanced role. While elderly characters in both worlds are more likely than those in other age groups to be pictured as bad and unsuccessful, eccentric, and physically handicapped, these traits are presented humorously in TV drama. In fairy tales, however, elderly adults characterized in this manner are endowed with the power attendant on their initially successful wielding of magic and violence, a power which demands that these characters be taken seriously. This difference is mirrored in the comparative involvement of elderly characters in violence. The elderly in fairy tales tend to be agents rather than victims of non-fatal violence, but they are eventually as likely to be killed as to be successful in fatal confrontations. Elderly characters in TV drama, on the other hand, are portrayed as both vulnerable *and* expendable; they are victimized across the board.

Thus elderly figures are negatively portrayed in both fictional worlds, but in fairy tales this is largely because they employ unscrupulous methods to (unsuccessfully) safeguard consolidated power and established status. The elderly in fairy tales play a significant, if not altogether fortunate, role since it is through their hands that power is passed on to the next generation. The elderly are indispensable to the maintenance and perpetuation of this social hierarchy.

In television drama, however, elderly characters fulfill no such vital function because they have very little power to begin with; their roles are marginal and their presentation, as with female characters, is essentially one-dimensional. The cyclical process of the passing down of power from one generation to the next which is so obvious in fairy tales has no counterpart in television drama, where settled adults remain the permanent possessors of social dominance.

These findings for sex and social age are not isolated trends. When considered in conjuction, they indicate the first key difference between the worlds of fairy tales and television drama. The fairy tale population includes a unique group of characters, largely female, largely elderly figures outside the conventional social-class hierarchy, in whom evil and power are inextricably linked. Frequently appearing as wicked witches or greedy, unscrupulous stepmothers, these characters are likely to be guilty of crime or wrongdoing, to wield magic for evil ends, and to hurt or kill other characters — but they are ultimately appropriately punished and rendered powerless. These antagonists are essential to the fairy tale messages of travail and triumph, and to the cyclical transference of dominance in this fictional realm.

One may hypothesize that these characters are remnants of a pre-industrial age when women's inferior status was unquestioned; when the mentally and physically handicapped were objects of superstition and fear, and their strange behavior frequently interpreted as manifestations of supernatural powers; and when the cumulative knowledge of a society was embodied not in books and libraries but in its elderly. As the dispensers of cultural wisdom, the transmitters of folk customs, traditions, and values, a community's elders possessed considerable authority. Elderly females, as knowledgeable as their male counterparts, were still of inferior status; their power, therefore, was a negative one and was often likely to be construed as evil. They were, nevertheless, strong figures and the objects of awe if not reverence.

Television drama, however, has no such identifiably different group of antagonists, because no such group exists today. The reservoirs of social knowledge are no longer deposited in individuals. Today, age serves no comparable productive purpose; a child's role models are less and less often parents and grandparents and, instead, are more commonly those provided by the mass media, where both heroes and villains are most likely to be mature males successfully established in middle-class careers. Regarded as economically and socially dysfunctional, the elderly, the mentally handicapped, and the physically disabled alike are now safely institutionalized and solicitously shielded from the public gaze.

The second key difference between fairy tales and television drama has to do with the nature and presentation of violence in these symbolic worlds. Although the role of violent actions in each is the same — the demonstration of power through successful involvement in hurting or killing — and although its end product is invariably the establishment or reinforcement of adult male dominance, the manner is which this is accomplished varies.

Fairy tale violence occurs within a world where participants are more likely than not to be acquainted, where violent actions are caused by human or humanized agents, and where violent intent springs either from malice or revenge. The threat of violence is simple and direct, and posed most often by close ties between characters.

Violence in prime-time drama, on the other hand, while equally serious in tone, is less likely to have definite repercussions. Few incidents actually result in injury or death. Whereas fairy tale violence serves to reinforce moral edicts, its function in television drama is not quite so clear-cut. Because participants in violence (particularly criminal violence) in this symbolic world tend to be strangers — different from the TV audience and the leading characters with whom this audience identifies — the infliction of violence on individual characters from outside — from hostile, unknown forces — would seem to create a more generalized insecurity.

Fairy tale violence is a clearly moralistic showdown between good and evil in which good inevitably wins out. Its consequences — and its message — are simple, direct, and obvious. Violence in television drama, however, is not only more frequent but more amorphous in character. TV violence occurs in a more social context, in that encounters more often involve unacquainted participants; perpetrators of fatal violence, both good and bad types, are more often successful than not; violence frequently erupts in the absence of any evil provocation; and violent actions are less likely to result in injury or death for the characters involved. The fact that violence is more often inflicted by strangers — characters who are different or unfamiliar — indicates the existence of a television hierarchy of fear, consisting of those characters most likely to fulfill these roles. TV violence thus tells us what kind of people should be feared and quite effectively reflects and reinforces widespread social prejudices.

All these factors suggest the greater ability of television violence to cultivate insecurity, a diffuse anxiety concerning a wide range of social types, in its audience. Fairy tale violence, in contrast, relays a distinct lesson. Evil violence perpetrated by a specific group of characters is always punished, and good violence always serves the particular purpose of retaliation. The black-and-white nature of violence in fairy tales, and its nearly always satisfying resolution, would seem, ultimately, to alleviate the insecurity that is both aroused and sustained by violence in TV fiction.

One might then speculate that the very simplicity of fairy tale violence reflects and once reinforced the didactic, authoritarian social structures which first gave rise to these stories, and that violence in TV drama similarly echoes the confusion and disintegration of a mass society in the midst of unsettling transition.

Such speculation about the timebound social relevance of these fictional forms poses the question: why have fairy tales survived — and will television drama prove to be as timeless? (The content of popular fairy tales has also undergone various transformations. What are the nature and functions of the changes that can be witnessed in the "watered-down" versions preferred by Disney and current children's readers?) Having ascertained what these two symbolic worlds are *like* along a few significant dimensions, we must then ask what it is that they *do*. Understanding how human behavior is shaped by cultural environment requires a greater perception of the manner in which the symbolic message systems we call entertainment cultivate our needs and expectations as well as our satisfactions. In addressing the problem of the comparative meanings and functions of fairy tales and television drama for their respective audiences, the results of this study may indicate the direction that further examination can most profitably take.

REFERENCES

GERBNER, G. (1978). (Lecture at The Annenberg School of Communications, University of Pennsylvania.)

GERBNER, G. (1980). Death in prime time. *Annals of the American Academy of Political and Social Science 447*, 64–70.

GERBNER, G., and GROSS, L. (1973). "The Social Reality of Television Drama." (A proposal for renewal of a grant, abstracted from *Cultural Indicators*.) Philadelphia, PA: Annenberg School of Communications, University of Pennsylvania.

GERBNER, G., GROSS, L., SIGNORIELLI, L., and MORGAN, M. (1980). The mainstreaming of America: Violence profile No. 11. *Journal of Communication 30* (No.3), 10–29.

KIRKLAND, C.E. (1981). "The World of Fairy Tales in the Age of Television: A Comparative Analysis." Master's thesis, University of Pennsylvania.

12

A Media Definition of Alcoholism*

TRICIA S. JONES
Department of Communication
Ohio State University
Columbus, Ohio 43210

Alcohol abuse has been of major social concern throughout U.S. history. It is currently estimated that there are over ten million alcoholics in the United States, and the rate of alcoholism, particularly among women, is increasing rapidly.

Concern over the prevalence of alcohol abuse is reflected in the mass media and, more recently, specialized media such as medical journals and government reports.

Over the past two centuries the depiction of habitual drinkers or alcoholics has been shaped by social conceptions of deviance and mental illness (Levine, 1977). The image of the alcoholic as well as the suggested treatment of alcoholism has fluctuated substantially. Generally, the assessment of alcoholism as a progressive disease has been maintained for the past 175-200 years. However, the conception of alcoholism as a disease did not always ensure compassion for the alcoholic. Rather, the perpetuation of the skid-row stereotype formed a crucial component of the effort to deal with the social problem of alcoholism (Lender and Karnchanapee, 1977).

Perhaps the best known social movement concerning alcoholism in the United States was the temperance movement, which spanned the 19th and 20th centuries. The temperance movement vacillated between depicting the alcoholic as a victim and bombasting the alcoholic as a pest and a menace (Levine, 1977). The portrayal of the alcoholic as a victim coincided with the movement's reformist notions of the early 19th century. Yet, the latter part of the 19th and the early 20th centuries witnessed a shift in focus from the reformist notion to an overriding concern for prohibition.

---

*Presented to the Conference on Communication and Culture, Temple University, April 1981.

The temperance movment successfully used literature and the graphic arts to popularize the problem of alcoholism (Lender and Karnchanapee, 1977). From the 1870s through the early 1900s these "temperance tales," distributed in novels, short stories, plays, and illustrations, portrayed the alcoholic as a skid row bum. This sterotype paints the "drunkard" as socially undesirable, irreligious, immoral, lazy, and/or criminal.

The impact of the temperance tales on public opinion was reportedly massive. The perseverance of the temperance movement up to the 1940s effectively prevented the emergence of a strong alcoholism treatment program (Rubington, 1973). Baron (as reported in Rubin, 1979) contributed an excellent critique of the temperance movement's overwhelming negative effect on attitudes, action, and research concerning alcoholism.

Since the 1940s, the disease concept of alcoholism has been increasingly accepted by the public, although the perception of alcoholism as a moral problem is often held in conjunction with the concept of alcoholism as a disease (Haberman and Sheinberg, 1969). The disease concept of alcoholism has spawned extensive treatment efforts, which are more sympathetic to and less condemning of the individual alcoholic. The resulting effect was a focus on therapy rather than punishment.

In light of the focus on therapy, researchers have examined the attitudes of health workers toward alcoholics. Generally, and surprisingly, this research suggests that professionals who work with alcoholics have negative attitudes toward the people they are supposed to help (Stafford and Petway, 1977). Hanna (1977) reported that health workers surveyed in 1963 maintained the "alcoholic as derelict" stereotype. Her follow-up survey in 1971 indicated that views of health workers had not changed. Furthermore, the negative perceptions of alcoholics directly affected the type of treatment the alcoholics received.

Little research has been done concerning the general public's attitude toward alcoholics or the effect of media information on these attitudes. Orcutt et al. (1980) surveyed law enforcement officers, detoxification workers, students, and residents of a Southern community to ascertain their attitudes toward alcoholics. The student and public samples described alcoholism as both a moral problem and a disease, and to a lesser extent, as only a disease. The law enforcement sample viewed alcoholics as threatening, immoral, and, to a lesser extent, as diseased, while the overwhelming majority of detoxification workers viewed alcoholism as a disease. The results of this survey were supported by results of similar surveys done in Iowa and Florida which suggest that public and professional conceptions of deviant drinking have become increasingly medically oriented in recent years (Orcutt et al., 1980).

Very little has been done concerning the effects of media information on public attitudes toward alcoholism. Dickman and Keil (1977) assessed the effects of public television programs on public awareness of the problem of alcoholism. A survey of 1200 Pennsylvania residents revealed that the few who had seen the public television broadcasts considered the media one of the most important information sources available and suggested that the media information had some effect on creating or increasing awareness of personal alcoholism problems.

Apparently the attitudes toward alcoholics and alcoholism have changed over the past two centuries—in part, due to the portrayal of alcoholics in the media. This cautiously advanced supposition indicates the value of examining media information in order to understand current descriptions of alcoholics and alcoholism. Analysis of information about alcoholism presented in popular magazines was used to answer the following questions:

(1). How have alcoholics been described in the media?
    (a). Does the source of the message affect the description of alcoholics?
    (b). Have the descriptions changed over the past two decades?
(2). How has the media portrayed the social impact of alcoholism?
    (a). Does the source of the message affect the portrayal of social impact?
    (b). Has the portrayal of social impact changed over the past two decades?

METHODS AND PROCEDURES

Sources of information analyzed in this study were popular news magazines (NM) and popular domestic women's magazines (DWM). Popular magazines were selected because of their availability to the general public. Approximately 250 articles concerning alcoholism appeared in popular magazines from 1960-1979. Focusing on news magazines and domestic women's magazines reduced the article pool to 100 articles. From these articles, 50 articles—25 from news magazines and 25 from domestic women's magazines—were selected on the basis of the following criteria: (a) Length of the article, minimum of 350 words, and (b) Absence of overlap between articles (several articles were reprinted in complete or edited form in other reviewed magazines). An attempt was made to secure adequate samples from both decades (1960-1969, 1970-1979); however, fewer articles concerning alcoholism appeared in popular magazines during the former decade.

A content analysis was performed to investigate:

(1) a "societal impact" measurement involving four subareas:
    (a). locale,
    (b). tone of the articles,
    (c). social effects of alcoholism,
    (d). major themes about alcoholism.

Table 12.1   Source Magazines

News Magazines:	Newsweek
	Time
	US News and World Report
	Denver Post
Women's Magazines:	Good Housekeeping
	Better Homes and Gardens
	Redbook
	McCall's
	Ladies Home Journal
	Seventeen
	Harper's Bazaar

(2) a personal description measurement involving two subareas:
(a). demographic information about the alcoholic (sex, marital status, family role, age, race, socio-economic status, and employment)
(b). adjectives used to describe alcoholics.

RESULTS

Results of this analysis are presented for each major research question. Data is reported in terms of percentages of articles using a specific description. The major focal areas of each research question are discussed in terms of differences between sources and decades.

1. How Have Alcoholics Been Described in the Media?

Sex.   Overall, the sex of the alcoholic was specified more often in the women's magazines (DWM) articles than in news magazine (NM) articles. 42% of the NM articles did not specify the sex of the alcoholic; 36% described alcoholics as male, and 14% described alcoholics as female. 54% of the DWM articles described alcoholics as female, 12% described them as male, 12% described both male and female alcoholics, and 22% of the DWM articles did not specify the sex of the alcoholic.

The trend over time was omission of sex specification in news and women's magazines. Concurrently, news magazines began to describe alcoholics of both sexes in the 1970-1979 decade. Women's magazine articles in the 1970s described alcoholics as females twice as often as in the 1960s, and began to describe alcoholics as males in the 1970s.

Marital Status.   76% of the NM articles and 44% of the DWM articles did not specify the marital status of the alcoholic. NM articles described the alcoholics' marital status as single, married, and divorced. As expected, the majority of DWM articles (52%) described alcoholics as married. No descriptions of divorced alcoholics were reported in the DWM articles. Both news and women's magazines exhibited a tendency over the two decades to disregard marital status as a relevant characteristic of alcoholics.

Family Role.   The family role of the alcoholic was not provided in 68% of the NM articles. When specified, 12% of the NM articles dealt with the father/husband role, 12% with the mother/wife role, and 8% with a child's role. As expected, a large number of DWM articles, 44%, described the alcoholic's family role as mother/wife. Of these articles 36% did not specify the family role.

The trend over the two decades for both the NM and DWM sources was to forego description of the family role. Similarly, both types of magazines increasingly described alcoholics in the mother/wife role. During the 1960s, news magazines did not describe the alcoholic in a child's role, although two of the 1970s articles did use this descriptor. DWM articles did not describe the alcoholic in a father/husband role during the 1960s, although the DWM articles of the 1970s included these roles.

Age.   In both types of magazines, alcoholics were usually described as adults. NM described alcoholics as adults 60% of the time, as adolescents 12%, as preadolescents 3%, as elderly 3%, and did not specify age in 22% of the articles. DWM articles referred to adults 78% of the time, to adolescents in 8%, and did not specify age 14% of the time. The only significant change from the 1960s to the 1970s was the descriptions of preadolescent, adolescent, and elderly alcoholics in the NM articles of the 1970s.

Race.   References to the race of an alcoholic were rare in both NM and DWM articles. Of the NM articles 70% did not specify race; when specified, race of the alcoholic was either White or Black. Of the DWM articles 80% did not specify race. When the race of the alcoholic was designated, alcoholics were described most often as White. Over the two decades, both types of magazines increasingly omitted descriptions of race. However, none of the news articles of the 1960s discussed race, while 40% of the NM articles of the 1970s did.

Socio-economic Status.   There was not a predominant pattern in the description of the socio-economic status of alcoholics in either NM or DWM articles. Approximately 45% of the NM articles did not specify SES, while 32% of the DWM articles did not specify this variable. Both sources described alcoholics as upper class in 20% of the articles. Middle class descriptors were used in 24% of the NM articles and 40% of the DWM articles; while lower class descriptors were used in 12% and 8% of the articles, respectively. The only apparent change over time was the occurrence of upper and lower class descriptors in the DWM articles of the 1970s.

Employment.   NM and DWM articles did not describe the alcoholics employment in the majority of articles. When employment was described, NM's detailed employment as production 12%, managerial 8%, professional 4%, religious 4%, and domestic 4%. DWM's, on the other hand, tended to describe employment as domestic 16%, although clerical 4% and religious 8% types of employment were also described. From the 1960s to the 1970s, both types of magazines broadened the descriptions of alcoholics' employment. In the 1970s, NM articles discussed production, managerial, and professional employment, while DWM articles expanded to include descriptions of clerical and religious types of employment.

Adjectives.   Due to the complexity of analyzing this category, the results will be discussed in the following order: core adjectives used in NM articles, core adjectives used in DWM articles, and trends of usage from 1960-1969 to 1970-1979.

NM articles most often described alcoholics as out-of-control (20%), shameful (14%), lonely (12%), or drunken (10%). To a lesser degree they described alcoholics as adolescent (6%), dependent (6%), and fearful (6%).

DWM articles most often referred to alcoholics as shameful (14%), out-of-control (12%), physically repulsive (8%), self-disgusting (8%), and lonely, (8%). The adjectives helpless (6%), fearful (6%), and suicidal (6%) were also used in the DWM articles.

Over the two decades, different trends were apparent for the two sources. In the NM articles from the 1960s to the 1970s there was an increasing trend to describe alcoholics as shameful and out-of-control, and a decreasing tendency to describe alcoholics as lonely and suffering. In the women's magazines from the 1960s to the 1970s there was an increasing tendency to describe alcoholics as lonely, shameful, suicidal, out-of-control, inadequate, and guilty; and a decreasing tendency to describe alcoholics as self-disgusting.

A brief analysis of the personal description of alcoholics in news magazines and women's magazines illuminates differences attributable to source and decade. From the 1960s to the 1970s in both types of magazines there was an increasing tendency to omit references to an alcoholic's sex, marital status, family role, race, and socio-economic status. When these characteristics were specified, there was very little stereotyping; rather, a broader definition emerged which suggests that alcoholism transcends sexual, racial, or class distinctions. Core adjectives, regardless of the time of the article, described an alcoholic as a lonely, frightened, shameful, suffering adult. There was a noticeable lack of perjorative adjectives such as sinful, immoral, or evil.

2. How has the Media Portrayed the Social Impact of Alcoholism?

Locale.   The majority of articles in both types of magazines did not refer to the locale of the alcoholic. NM articles discussed alcoholics in work settings (20%), home settings (8%), and government settings (8%); while DWM articles usually discussed alcoholics in a home setting (42%).

From the 1960s to the 1970s, NM articles increasingly referred to work and government locales. Likewise, DWM articles discussed work locales in the 1970s, although not in the 1960s.

Tone.   There was a significant disparity in the tone of the NM and DWM articles. In half of the NM articles, the tone was objective, while 28% of the articles were sympathetic to the problems of alcoholics, and 22% were disapproving of alcoholics. Most of the DWM articles were disapproving (68%), 28% were objective, and only 8% were sympathetic. Both sources exhibited a tendency over time to discuss the problem of alcoholism objectively, although the women's magazines of the 1970s had more disapproving articles than in the 1960s.

Effects.   Most of the articles in both news and women's magazines discussed the effects of alcoholism. News magazines concentrated on work effects (17%), personal, family, and work effects (14%), legal effects (9%), medical effects (9%), and legal and medical effects (9%). Women's magazines discussed personal and family effects (22%), personal, family, and work effects (22%), personal effects (12%), and legal and medical effects (12%).

Over the decades there was a trend for NM and DWM articles not to discuss the effects of alcoholism. There was an increasing tendency in the news magazines to discuss work and medical effects and a decreasing tendency to discuss legal effects. Women's magazines increasingly discussed legal and medical effects.

Themes.   This analysis was complicated in that the average number of themes per article was five for NM articles and nine for DWM articles.

NM articles predominantly employed the following themes: Alcoholics Anonymous as therapy (11%), other therapies (9.5%), therapies effective (8.5%), alcoholism as a disease (7.5%), alcoholism increasing (7.5%), psychological causes of alcoholism (7.5%), and reports of studies (7.5%). DWM articles relied on the following themes: Alcoholics Anonymous as therapy

(11.5%), therapies effective (10%), alcoholism as a disease (10%), personal histories of alcoholics (9%), psychological causes of alcoholism (7%), other causes of alcoholism (7%), psychological therapies (7%), alcoholism increasing (7%), and alcoholism as addicition (6.5%). In both sources, the alcoholism as a disease and the alcoholism as addiction themes cooccurred. Discussion of causes of alcoholism was accompanied by discussion of alcoholism therapies, although this trend was more common in women's magazines than news magazines.

Several trends in theme usage are apparent over the two decades. In both sources there was increasing usage of the increasing alcoholism theme, the discussion of causes of alcoholism, therapies for alcoholism, and effective therapies theme. NM articles of the 1970s discussed the reasons for alcoholism increasing, criticisms of therapies, and reports of studies more than in the 1960s, however, the 1960s NM articles discussed the legal role in the definition of alcoholism. The use of personal histories increased in the DWM articles over the decades, specifically personal histories of noncelebrities.

DISCUSSION

The results of this analysis present a general definition of alcoholism found in popular magazines of the past two decades. The definition varies depending upon the source and decade of its publication.

News magazines usually did not discuss the demographic characteristics of alcoholics. When such characteristics were described, alcoholics were portrayed as white adult males, usually middle-class workers in production or managerial capacities. Alcoholics were described as out-of-control, shameful, lonely, or referred to as drunkards.

Women's magazines specified demographic characteristics more often than news magazines, referring to alcoholics as white adult middle-class married females in a mother/wife role and/or engaged in domestic employment. Alcoholics in the women's magazine articles were described as shameful, out-of-control, physically repulsive, self-disgusting, and lonely.

The target audiences of the two sources may explain the differences in portrayal of alcoholics. News magazines are targeted toward the general population, and are generally concerned with widespread social phenomena. The depiction of alcoholics in NM articles corresponds to the image of the working American. The women's magazines are targeted toward homemakers predominantly. The emphasis upon shamefulness and social undersirability may stem from perceptions of female alcoholics as less socially acceptable than male alcoholics. Women alcoholics are viewed more negatively because they deviate more from accepted behavior (Stafford and Petway, 1977). Beckman (1978) reports that women alcoholics have lower self-esteem than male alcoholics or female nonalcoholics. The increasing number of women alcoholics, partially reflected in this portrayal of alcoholics in DWM articles, corresponds to changing social norms and pressures (Keil, 1978).

The emphasis on shamefulness and lack of control found in both sources' definitions reflects moralistic attitudes toward alcoholism, yet stresses the victimized role of the alcoholic. Overall, the results of the personal depiction of alcoholics in this study seem to coincide with reports of public attitudes toward alcoholics (Orcutt, et al., 1980).

The societal impact of alcoholism as revealed in the results fits conceptually the personal depictions of alcoholics. News magazines placed the alcoholic in work or governmental settings, objectively discussed the effects of alcoholism on the work, personal life, and family of the alcoholic, and detailed the legal and medical effects of alcoholism. Women's magazines described alcoholics disapprovingly and placed them in home settings focusing on alcoholism's impact on personal, family, and work situations.

Both sources conceptualized alcoholism as disease and addiction, and discussed causes and therapies of alcoholism. News magazine articles generally portrayed alcoholism as a societal rather than individual phenomenon, whereas women's magazine articles placed more emphasis on the individual alcoholic. The disapproving tone used in most of the DWM articles supports the assumption of highly negative attitudes toward women's alcoholics. The predominant and increasing use of the alcoholism as disease and addiction themes supports assumptions that the skid row stereotype is being slowly replaced with more medical views of alcoholism (Levine, 1977).

The effects of these media definitions of alcoholism on public attitudes and treatment of alcoholics is at this point mere conjecture. However, assuming some media impact on public attitudes, the different definitions found in news and women's magazines may reflect interesting differences in attitudes toward alcoholism held by the readers of these magazines.

REFERENCES

BECKMAN, L.J. (1978). Self-esteem of women alcoholics. *Journal of Studies on Alcohol 39*, 491–498.

DICKMAN, F. and KEIL, T. (1977). Public television and public health. *Journal of Studies on Alcohol 38*, 584–592.

HABERMAN, P.W., and SHEINBERG, J. (1969). Public attitudes toward alcoholism as an illness. *American Journal of Public Health 59*, 1209–1216.

HANNA, E. (1977). Attitudes toward problem drinkers. *Journal of Studies on Alcohol 38*, 95–105.

KEIL, T. (1978). Sex role variations and women's drinking: Results from a household survey in Pennsylvania. *Journal of Studies on Alcohol 39*, 859–868.

LENDER, M. and KARNCHANAPEE, (1977). Temperance Tales: Antiliquor fiction and American attitudes toward alcoholics in the late 19th and 20th centuries. *Journal of Studies on Alcohol 38*. 1347–1370.

LEVINE, H. (1977). The discovery of addiction: Changing conceptions of habitual drunkenness in America. *Journal of Studies on Alcohol 38*, 143–169.

ORCUTT, J., CAIRL, R., and MILLER, E. (1980). Professional and public conceptions of alcoholism. *Journal of Studies on Alcohol 41*, 652–661.

RUBIN, J. (1979). Shifting perspectives on the alcoholism treatment movement: 1940–1955. *Journal of Studies on Alcohol 40*, 376–395.

RUBINGTON, E. "Alcohol Problems and Social Control." Columbus, OH: Merill.

STAFFORD, R. A. and PETWAY, J. M. (1977). Stigmatization of men and women problem drinkers and their spouses. *Journal of Studies on Alcohol 38*, 2109–2121.

13

Who Shall I Be: A Study of the Novel as Ideology

NELDA K. DALEY
Department of Sociology and Anthropology
Radford University
Radford, Virginia 24142

OVERVIEW

From a population reflecting the reading tastes of college-educated American women, fifty novels written by women between 1950-75 were randomly selected for analysis. (See Daley, 1975, for a full methodological description.) It was found that female characters, even in novels written by women, accepted traditionally "masculine" patterns as the yard stick to measure all adult behavior. This was also the finding of Broverman et al. (1970) with regard to clinical estimations of adult mental health. Data from the fifty novels show that the female characters in the novels, much like their counterparts in society, have come to devalue traditional feminine status-roles and opt to perform "masculine" status-roles. Thus, the novels appear to promote "masculine" behavior (self-interest, assertiveness, career- and self-achievement-orientations) as "good" behavior, and to devalue selfless, nurturing, communal behaviors. The novels do not question whether or not values relevant to the "male-value dominated culture" are inherently worthwhile (Bernard, 1976; Bem, 1976). Nor do the novels show what data from society show—for example, that success for a woman in a male-value-dominated culture is nearly impossible, since women rarely receive the kind of domestic support necessary for a total career and self-achievement orientation (Bird, 1979; Burke and Weir, 1976; Curtis, 1976; Freeman, 1975; Grappa, 1980; Gross, 1980; Hoschild, 1975; Rubin, 1976).

CHANGES IN WOMEN'S CHARACTER IN THE NOVELS FROM 1950-1975

Women throughout history have worked on farms or as wage earners outside the home. In almost all cases, however, this role was seen as secondary to their roles as "managers" of households. The wife/mother was usually the last to go into the labor force, not because of her low status, but because it was recognized that her work in the home was *essential* and that, due to her knowledge and expertise, she was not easily replaced by other family members. However, women did not assume that they would never have to work (Tilly and Scott, 1978). Thus, women have always worked at some time or another during their lifetime, but their supportive, communal activities were valued more highly than the income they could bring to the family.

Thus, it comes as no surprise that nearly as many wives have worked in the 1950s novels (72.3%) as in the 1970s novels (83.0%). What is of concern to us is other data from the novels which illustrate the increased value placed upon work outside the home, despite the fact that a higher percentage of women are married in the 1970s novels. Only 74.5% of the women are married in the 1950s novels, as compared to 90.6% in the 1970s novels. The data from the novels show that women in the later novels, despite their higher marriage rate, seek out and value individual success over domestic, supportive activity.

Comparing 1950s to 1970s data, one sees that several home-centered concerns have decreased. The percentage of wives who see either their husband or their children as the locus of their concern has decreased dramatically. The proportion of wives whose lives center around their husbands drops from 37% to less than 18.5% while the percentage of wives whose lives are centered around their children drops from 40.7% to 29.6%.

Housework remains an important concern, although not a focal one, in the lives of the 1970s characters. Housework as an important concern for the wives declines from 88.9% in the 1950s novels to 47.6% in the 1970s novels. Further, a large percent of women continue to spend more of their time on housework than anything else. Nearly half (45.5%) of all wives in the 1950s novels spend most of their time on housework, while 24.1% of the wives in the 1970s novels do so.

Finally, the wives in the 1970s novels are much more independent of their husbands. Those wives looking to be "taken care of" decline from 46% in the 1950s novels to 16.2% in the 1970s novels.

Thus, in the later novels, although there is a healthy minority of wives who see their home, children, or husbands as the center of their lives, the majority of women are more and more concerned with their lives outside their homes. The largest decline in concern is with housework, with over 40 percentage points difference between the two periods. This reflects real-life data which show that working wives tend to lower their housekeeping standards to a more "causal" and often more comfortable standard ("Do Working Wives Have Better Marriages?" 1976). Their husbands as a focal concern declines nearly 20 percentage points, while their children as a focal concern drops only a little more than 10 percentage points. Thus, even those women who are home-centered are more likely to be concerned with their children than with their homemaking or their husbands. This too reflects real-life data (Curtis, 1976). Up to this point, then, the women in the novels seem to be very much like the modern married woman, working for wages, taking care of children, doing household chores, but "standing on their own two feet."

However, we see that the types of behavior that increase are also those that reflect the masculine values of success. The career as the wife's central concern increases from 11.1% to 33.3%. Further, an even larger increase occurs among the percentage of women who spend the bulk of their time in work outside the home (from 18.9% to 44.8%). Thus, the novels show that more and more wives are putting the bulk of their concern and time into wage-earning work rather than communal, supportive work.

In addition, if we look at the sexual behavior of the wives in the novels, we find that, more and more, their behavior appears to be like that traditionally attributed to men. Using extramaterial sex as an indicator of self interest over communal interests, we find that the percentage of wives who have affairs in the novel drastically increases. Only 17.1% of the wives in the 1950s novels engaged in extramarital sex. This figure comes close to the 25% figure Kinsey (1953) found for women in general. However, the percentage of wives engaging in extramarital sex in the 1970s novels jumped to 43.3%. This figure more nearly approximates the rate of 50% found for husbands by Hunt (1974) than data for wives which has been variously reported as 17% (Hunt, 1974), 26% (Bell and Peltz, 1974), and 30% (Levin, 1975). Thus, the women in the novels seem to be espousing what might be understood as a masculine "recreational" definition of sex (Gagnon and Simon, 1972) rather than the female single standard of fidelity for both husband and wife (Christensen, 1973). Using extramarital sex as an indicator of self-interest in the novels is particularly telling because real-life data indicate that women, rather than accepting the masculine definition of sexuality, have actually decreased their approval of extramarital sex (Christensen, 1973). Also, since extramarital sex is seen as a real threat to the family (Christensen and Gregg, 1970), this increase in extramarital sex indicates a real break in commitment to their families on the part of women in the novels. Thus, the dramatic increase in the wives who engage in extramarital sex combined with increased concern for their careers seem to point to a real decline in concern for domestic, supportive attitudes, and a real increase in self-interest.

Although the data "accurately" reflect the predicament of the modern woman (i.e., dual career problems), the novels present women who have accepted the masculine definition of success and value self-interest over communal, supportive interests. It appears that the authors of these novels by and about women have closed out other possible realities and have relied instead on the masculine game plan, as it were. Since literature is one of the few areas in which alternate possible realities can be explored, this acceptence of the "masculine" rules for success by women authors is particularly ironic and telling.

REFERENCES

BELL, R.R., and PELTZ, D. (1974). Extramarital sexual experience among women. *Medical Aspects of Human Sexuality 8* (No. 3), 10–32.

BEM, S.L. (1976). Probing the promise of androgyny. *In* A.G. Kaplan and J.P. Bean (Eds.), "Beyond Sex-Role Stereotypes." New York: Little, Brown.

BERNARD, J. (1976). Sex differences: An overview. *In* A.G. Kaplan and J.P. Bean (Eds.), "Beyond Sex-Role Stereotypes." New York: Little, Brown.

BIRD, C. (1979). "The Two-Paycheck Marriage." New York: Rawson Wade.

BROVERMAN, I.K., CLARKSON, F.E., ROSENKRAUS, P.S., and VOGEL, S.R. (1970). Sex role stereotypes and clinical judgments of mental health. *Journal of Clinical and Counselling Psychology 34,* 1–7.

BURKE, R., and WEIR, T. (1976). Relationships of wives employment to husband, wife, and pair satisfaction. *Journal of Marriage and the Family 38,* 279–287.

CHRISTENSEN, H.T. (1973). Attitudes toward marital infidelity: A nine culture sample. *Journal of Comparative Family Studies 4,* 197–214.

CHRISTENSEN, H.T., and GREGG, C.F. (1970). Changing sex norms in America and Scandinavia. *Journal of Marriage and the Family 32,* 616–627.

CURTIS, J. (1976). "Working Mothers." New York: Doubleday.

DALEY, N.K. (1975). "The Image of the Woman in the Contemporary American Novel: 1950-1954 and 1968-1972." Unpublished dissertation, Wayne State University.

Do working wives have better marriages? (1976). *Family Circle* (Nov.), 58–64.

FREEMAN, J. (1975). How to discriminate against women without really trying. *In* J. Freeman (Ed.), "Women: A Feminist Perspective." Palo Alto, CA: Mayfield.

GAGNON, J.H., and SIMON, W. (1972). "Sexual Conduct." Chicago, IL: Aldine.

GRAPPA, J.M., O'BARR, J.F., and ST. JOHN-PARSONS, D. (1980). The dual career couple and academe: Can both prosper? *Anthropology Newsletter 21* (No. 4), 16.

GROSS, H.E. (1980). Dual-career couples who live apart. *Journal of Marriage and the Family 42,* 567–577.

HOSCHILD, A.R. (1975). Inside the clockworks of the male careers. *In* F. Howe (Ed.), "Women and the Power to Change." New York: McGraw-Hill.

HUNT, M. (1974). "Sexual Behavior in the 1970s." Chicago, IL: Playboy Press.

KINSEY, A.C. (1953). "Sexuality in the Human Female." Philadelphia, PA: Saunders.

LEVIN, R.J. (1975). The Redbook report on premarital and extramarital sex: The end of the double standard? *Redbook Magazine 145* (No. 6), 38–44, 190–192.

RUBIN, L.B. (1976). "Worlds of Pain." New York: Basic Books.

TILLY, L.A., and SCOTT, J.W. (1978). "Women, Work, and the Family." New York: Holt, Rinehart and Winston.

14

The Problem of Regularities in Television Program Content

ROBERT R. SMITH
Department of Radio–Television–Television–Film
Temple University
Philadelphia, Pennsylvania 19122

Those of us concerned with the way television programs relate to social reality have two problems which precede our work as social scientists. The first is that the programs themselves are difficult to examine individually in detail as one might a poem or a Dürer engraving. The discrete programs are of less importance than their commonalities. Consequently, we have to find methods of dealing with programs en masse without becoming involved in the examination of specific programs. Thus, it is important to look for patterned regularities occuring across episodes, series, genres, media, and so forth. This concern with regularities in program content is a welcome and constructive development. It has allowed theorists in the mass media to move ahead of humanists who are preoccupied with the unique.

There is another problem which has had less welcome consequences. Our interest in television has been motivated partly by a desire to understand, but partly also by a desire to reform. There may be moments when the urge to understand may conflict with the desire to reform. The result in such cases may be a willingness to make risky leaps from very sound descriptions of content to thinly supported hypotheses about the social consequences of that content.

It may be time to acknowledge the complexity of the problem of effects, and to back away from an attempt to relate media content to consequences in ways which are too specific to be of general significance (e.g., advertising research) or too general to be empirically investigated (e.g., Marshall McLuhan). I would like to lead a retreat from the concern with consequences to a reevaluation of our knowledge of program regularities. How much do we know? What don't we know about the ways in which program content is organized?

Let me review our progress on this pilgrimage from a humanistic concern with the individual program, to a social scientific concern with content and cultural effects. The first step is the systematic description of program content relevant to a specific concern. The danger in this kind of analysis is what might be called preemptive shaping of results. It does not go beyond that which can be supported by the data, but it shapes the data so that it can be used by someone who, for other reasons, wishes to make the leap to effects which cannot be empirically established. The first part is respectable social science; the second—the leap—is what law schools describe as legal reasoning.

Some workers in the field have focused on the methodological problems and have made a different sort of contribution: the refinement of technique apart from social consequences. Klaus Krippendorff's work may provide the best example of this sort of focus.

But restraint is a difficult and not always admirable virtue. And the pragmatism for which American intellectuals have become renowned and ridiculed has led us to attempt systematic linkages between programs and audience attitudes or behavior. Let me cite two examples which typify the best of the genre: Leckenby and Surlin's "Incidental Social Learning and Viewer Race: 'All in the Family' on Children" (1976) and Meyer's "The Impact of 'All in the Family' on Children" (1976). Leckenby and Surlin, in a conclusion characteristic of this variety of research, found that "there is clearly a relationship between frequency of watching family programming . . . and the acceptance of the view of major characters in the programming." Meyer concluded:

> As an instrument for "learning," the kinds of behaviors depicted on "All in the Family" which are apparently having the greatest impact on most children are not the moral/ethical lessons . . . physical appearance of the characters, role stereotypes, comedy behavior etc., are the ingredients which seem to dominate children's perceptions of the content.

In each case, the "effect" could be explained by pre-selection; those who prefer certain content watch heavily those programs bearing that content. In short, this line of inquiry leads to results which ultimately become problems of data analysis—an attempt to find the most socially arresting conclusion which can be supported by the data.

This leads to the dispute involving George Gerbner, Paul Hirsch, (1980, 1981) and Michael Hughes (1980). What is disputed is not the data upon which the interpretations are made, but how far one can go before a conclusion becomes conjecture. What we have been reading is not an indictment of scholars, but rather the exploration of the limits of a technique. Descriptive research may not lead to the kinds of conclusions we are seeking. Frequently, the result is a leap to conclusions that cannot be easily supported.

Another line of inquiry is to look into television's hidden structures. Those involved with this line of inquiry have been concerned that television's content is impersonal (i.e., it does not bear the mark of an individual maker) and repetitive. Although critics from a theatrical or literary tradition may have difficulty with mass-media content, it offers some interesting possibilities for examination. Gilbert Seldes led the way, but continued throughout his long career to seek the unique, the personal, and the excellent. Others following him have been more willing to acknowledge that the genius of television—one is reluctant to identify individual geniuses, only the brilliance of the total achievement—lies in its endless minor variations upon repetitive themes.

Raymond Williams (1975) noted this about news programs in which he identified the "flow" rather than the content of individual news stories as the essential content. Others have been concerned with structures of news items as miniature dramas.

This concern with the structure of programs or sub-sets of programs has its origins in one of the first Americans to reverse the traditional cognitive flow from the old world to the new: Charles Sanders Peirce.

Although Peirce's contributions have been adopted by other fields, his focus, as Thomas Sebiok has quoted him, was the lifelong study of the nature of signs. That is, in Peirce's words "the doctrine of the essential nature and fundamental varieties of possible semiosis" (Sebeok, 1976, p. 6). Peirce's contemporary, the French linguist Ferdinand de Saussure, began the most influential linguistic development of semiotic analysis. But Peirce did not limit his analysis to language; he took the entire range of signs as his domain. For our purposes, this means television, radio, videotext, and video.

Despite the lack of development of Peirce's outlook by those interested in television, film analysts have developed this approach. Unfortunately, most of their work is concerned with the understanding of the idiosyncratic, the individual film, and does not contribute to those problems which are characteristic of mass—large volume, large audience—communication.

In recent years, however, some scholars have turned their attention to the repetitions of the mass media. Adler's "All in the Family: a Critical Appraisal" (1979) provides a clue to this native American line of inquiry. Of 36 essays in the collection, only three (Arlen, Rosenblatt, and Rabinowitz) reflect an awareness that the importance of the show may lie in its structure (e.g., hero, theme) rather than in its manifest content (that is, racism, changing sexual mores).

If one seeks examples of such criticism, a useful collection is Arens and Montague's "The American Dimension: Cultural Myths and Social Realities" (1976). In the collection, particularly the analysis of *Star Trek* by Peter Claus and the essays on football by Arens and Montague indicate the direction of such studies. They are free from much of our concern about effects and more concerned with the ways in which television functions in our culture. Unfortunately, they are also free of a systematic analysis, and the occasional insights stem more from humanistic intuition than from the application of a method. It adds to our knowledge, but does not give us tools with which to pursue the search.

Another book, is Fiske and Hartley's *Reading Television* (1978). Here we find an attempt to test a research tool combined with perceptive analyses. Unfortunately, the tool is not up to the task. Yet, this may be the most instructive model available to us. The worth of their analyses is greater than the worth of their method, and thus provides us with a good book, but a frustrating model. It is, in some ways, similar to the work of Roland Barthes, who has constructed elaborate models of semiosis, but whose analyses have a strange tendency to become political criticism. (In his case, I suspect that the method contains shortcomings that predetermine the outcome of the the the analysis.)

The path we should be following is not one prepared by Barthe, Arlen, Levi-Strauss, Fiske and Hartley, or Arens. Rather, we should backtrack to their sources and begin again. This may be a radical suggestion, but, in a new field, it does not call for an extensive act of historical reconstruction.

The source, as I have indicated, is Peirce. His broad-based definitions of signs and his freedom from ideological commitment provide us with concepts both simpler and more useful than those of his followers. For instance, Barthes' triad (signifier/signified/signification), though based on Peirce, is essentially Hegelian and imposes a limit on the study of signs which imprisons their meanings. Thus, Barthe may see an advertisement containing a French soldier and flag as having imperialistic content (France means military strength and the combination means patriotism). It also contains subsets of signification—the social class of the soldier, his military rank, race, the setting, etc.—all of which may set in motion numerous interacting signs.

Who does this? Where can we look for examples? There are moments when Arlen, Sebeok, Fiske and Hartley, and others achieve it. But we do not have a model which allows them to sustain this level of analysis.

Peirce proposed not only the triad signifier/signified/signification, but also suggested the study of the triadic relation of comparisons (qualsigns, or indications of quality embedded in signs); the study of the triadic relations of performance (icons, indices, and symbols); and the triadic relations of thought (the rheme, the dicent, and the law) (Hawkes, 1977). In this simple repetition of Peirce's work you will note that I have described a triple pyramid, a nine-sided analysis. This is the unexplored complexity and the promise of the work of this American master.

Given this more complex and subtler tool for analysis, one can hope for a better understanding of what it is that holds us as we watch television, where similar things happen predictably again and again and again.

REFERENCES

ADLER, R. (1979). "All in the Family: A Critical Appraisal." New York: Praeger.

ARENS, W., and MONTAGUE, S. (1976). "The American Dimension." Port Washington, NY: Alfred.

FISKE, J., and HARTLEY J. (1977). "Reading Television." London: Methuen.

HAWKES, T. (1977). "Structuralism and Semiotics." Berkeley, CA: University of California Press.

HIRSCH, P.M. (1980). The "Scary World" of the Nonviewer and Other Anomalies. *Communication Research 7*, 403–456.

HIRSCH, P.M. (1981). On Not Learning From One's Own Mistakes. *Communication Research 8*, 3–37.

HUGHES, M. (1980). The Fruits of Cultivation Analysis: A reexamination of some effects of television watching. *Public Opinion Quarterly 44*, 287–302.

LECKENBY, J.D., and SURLIN, S.H. (1976). Incidental Social Learning and Viewer Race. *Journal of Broadcasting 20*, 481–494.

MEYER, T. (1976). The Impact of "All in the Family" on Children. *Journal of Broadcasting 20*, 23–33.

SEBEOK, T. (1976). "Contributions to the Doctrine of Signs," Bloomington, IN: Indiana University. (Studies in Semiotics, vol. 5.)

WILLIAMS. R. (1975). "Technology and Cultural Form." New York: Schocken Books.

Part IV

BEHAVIOR AND ACCULTURATION

15

Television and the Obliteration of "Childhood": The Restructuring of Adult/Child Information Systems*

JOSHUA MEYROWITZ
University of New Hampshire
Durham, New Hampshire 03824

In the last half century, psychologists have enriched our knowledge of the cognitive, linguistic, and physiological stages through which children pass as they grow to adulthood. Bruner, Piaget, Gesell, Kagan, and Kohlberg are only a few of those who have worked at plotting the course of human growth and development. Their research has indicated that children are qualitatively different from adults and that children of different ages are different from each other.

What these studies of children have generally ignored, however, is the current evolution in the social manifestations of "childhood." It is not unusual for social actions to change along with the publication and popularization of research findings. What is peculiar in this case, however, is that the change is in direct opposition to the thrust of the research. The psychological studies would suggest that children be treated very differently from adults, and yet the present trend is to treat children more like "little adults" and to have people of different ages share much more similar roles, rights, and responsibilities than in the past. Ironically, then, social scientists have intensified efforts to discover the *facts* of childhood, just as the social *experience* of

*This essay is based on a portion of *No Sense of Place: Electronic Media and Social Behavior,* Oxford University Press, forthcoming. These ideas were first developed in the author's doctoral dissertation, New York University, 1979.

The author wishes to thank Candice Leonard, Paul Levinson, Robert Mennel, Paul Goodwin, Joe Dominick, David Leary, Ian Jarvie, and Patricia Fleming for commenting on an earlier draft of this essay.

childhood is disappearing. This study explores the possibility that the changes in childhood are related to our shift from a "book culture" to a "television culture."

This paper has a three-fold purpose: to describe the evolution in childhood, to identify a common denominator linking media with the socialization process, and to compare print and television in terms of their impact on child socialization. I argue that media interact with socialization by affecting the pattern and sequence of access to social information, and that television radically restructures adult/child information systems and forces a shift in social development and behavior.

THE END OF "CHILDHOOD"

In the first half of the 20th century, childhood was considered a time of innocence and weakness. The child was sheltered from the realities of life. The child was dressed differently from adults. There were separate "languages" for children and adults; there were words and topics that were considered unfit for children's ears. There was a strict age-grading system, supported by the school, which designated what a child of any given age should know and do.

In the last thirty years, however, there has been a remarkable change in that image. Many traditional adult/child distinctions have virtually disappeared from our culture. A walk on any city street or in any park suggests that the era of distinct clothing for different age-groups has passed. Just as children sometimes dress in three-piece suits or designer dresses, so adults often dress like "big children": in Mickey-Mouse or Superman T-Shirts, dungarees, and sneakers. And people of all ages wear "designer jeans." If we accept that there is a powerful relationship between distinct modes of dress and distinct social statuses (Treece, 1959), then there is significant evidence that many age-determined roles are fading.

Children and adults also have begun to behave more alike. Even casual observations indicate that posture, sitting positions, and gestures have become more homogenized. It is no longer unusual to see adults in public, sitting cross-legged on the ground or engaging in "children's play." Indeed, the latest generation of playthings—video and computer games—are not only labelled "for all ages," but are designed for, and avidly played by, adults as well as children.

Even adult psychological temperament appears to be changing. The much-discussed attitudes of the "me-generation" can be viewed as adult manifestations of the ego-centrism traditionally associated with childhood. A recent movement in developmental psychology is to avoid classification of behavior according to chronological age. The concept of "age-irrelevancy" is growing (Hall, 1980; Neugarten, 1981). The homogenization of roles is evidenced in the increasing school drop-out rate among the young, coupled with the increasing enrollment in adult education. Extended retirement ages, career shifts, and the establishment of summer camps for adults all suggest that there is a trend toward a single, all-age behavior and role conception. Socially speaking, then, we are not only losing traditional conceptions of childhood, we are also losing traditional conceptions of "adulthood."

Distinct languages and vocabularies for different ages are also disappearing. Many slang words, phrases, obscenities, and grammatical constructions are shared across a broad spectrum of age-groups. Children speak more like adults and adults speak more like children. Perhaps even more dramatically, they are speaking this way in each other's presence. The linguistic evidence of adult authority in relation to children is also fading. Children often call adults, in some cases their parents, by first names.

There are fewer and fewer topics which society can agree are unfit for discussion with children. In any case, children seem to know about the taboo topics *before* they are included in children's formal education. Sex and drug education programs, for example, have had to chase the runaway increase in teenage pregnancy and drug abuse.

While many continue to embrace the old clichés of adulthood and childhood, the homogenization of status has, in a sense, been culturally and legally documented. If we look at our entertainment and legal systems, the changes are explicit. The television and film roles played by children and adults have changed markedly. While the Shirley Temple character of the past was merely a cute and outspoken *child*, current children stars, such as Brooke Shields and Gary Coleman, are seemingly *adults* imprisoned in children's bodies. They portray characters aware of corruption and sin, and in some cases are deeply involved in such behaviors themselves. Conversely, many so-called "adult" characters, such as those portrayed by Burt Reynolds and Elliot Gould, have the needs and emotions of overgrown children. A similar trend in roles can be seen in the differences between the early domestic comedies on television and current programs. The parent/child distinctions in "One Day at a Time," for example, are marginal compared to those in "Father Knows Best." Even the program titles suggest a different view of authority and social order.

The legal status of children has also shifted. In 1967, for example, the Supreme Court gave children the right to counsel. Later decisions have provided children with virtually every adult legal right. In the last few years, there have been a number of cases where children have contacted lawyers on their own to fight parent or school authorities (Footlick, et al., 1977). On the other side of the coin, special lenient treatment of juveniles is being abolished in many states because children are increasingly committing "adult crimes" such as murder and armed robbery (Berlin, 1976).

For many, the homogenization of legal status for all ages has not yet reached a satisfactory level. Children have come to be seen as another disenfranchised "minority" in need of liberation. Sociologist Elise Boulding (1977, p. 39) argues that the Children's Rights Movement "should be included in the general process of consciousness raising about the human condition." Marian Wright Edelman (1978, p. 16), Director of the Children's Defense Fund (CDF), writes that "After seven White House conferences for children and countless reports and speeches on children's problems, they remain the poorest and most under-represented and under-served group in American society." Educator John Holt (1974, p. 18) has outlined a "bill of rights" for children, to insure that the "rights, privileges, duties, responsibilities of adult citizens be made *available* to any young person, of whatever age, who wants to make use of them." The rights enumerated by Holt include the right to vote, to work, to have privacy, to own property, to sign contracts, to choose sexual partners, to travel, to have one's own home, and to choose one's own guardian.

If these proposed changes seem far-reaching and even frightening, we must nevertheless recognize that they are an indication of the trend in current attitudes toward children. We must also recognize that the relationships between parents and children have *already* changed dramatically. Kenneth Keniston (1977, p. 33), who directed the Carnegie Council study on children, notes that

> a greater sense of parity between parents and children has certainly evolved. There is more democracy in families today, and parents are more likely to admit their flaws and inadequacies to their children. There is no longer the automatic "parents always know best" attitude.

For better or worse, then, "childhood," as it was once defined, no longer exists.

MEDIA AND SOCIALIZATION: A COMMON DENOMINATOR

Most of the research on children and media cannot explain these changes in adult/child roles. Indeed, the issue of a change in childhood in general has not even been approached. Research has focused on the effects of specific media content on specific behavior of children (aggression, for example). (For recent reviews on children and television, see Comstock, 1975; Murray, 1980; and Williams, 1981.) But beyond the issue of particular behavioral effects lies the larger question of why we no longer have child-like children. To study the possible role that media play in these changes, we need to look past the effects of media content on children at given stages of socialization; we need to examine how media may affect the socialization process itself.

One way to do this is to identify a common denominator linking media and socialization.

Human growth involves at least three developmental components: biological, social, and psychological. Biologically, children pass through various stages of physical growth and maturation. Socially, there is a corresponding process where children interact with adults and are taught appropriate social roles. The psychological component seems to depend upon the other two; maturational factors may set outside limits on psychological maturity, but social factors can retard or enhance the rate of development.

While the biological sequence of human development may be "natural," or innate, the social stages are largely arbitrary and conventionalized. Indeed they vary greatly from culture to culture (Muuss, 1975, pp. 3-10). As anthropologist Arnold Van Gennep (1960) has noted, even rites of passage seemingly dependent on physiological development often occur at arbitrary points. He suggests that "puberty rites" are misnamed in that they do not necessarily coincide with the individual's biological puberty.

What then is the key factor that distinguishes one social status from another? As I have argued in detail elsewhere, distinct social roles and statuses are dependent in large measure on distinctions in access to social information (Meyrowitz, 1979, pp. 146-180). The movement from one social status to another generally involves learning the "secrets" of the new status or role. Every stage of socialization involves both exposure to and restriction from social information. Traditionally, for example, we tell sixth graders things we keep hidden from fifth graders. Socialization, therefore, is a form of "graded access" to information; children are exposed to "adult" information slowly and in set stages.

Viewing socialization as a process related to patterns of access to information reveals a relationship with media, for media also involve the dispersal of information. Indeed, when a society moves from the primary use of one communication medium to the primary use of another, there may be a shift in the patterns of access to social information, including those that relate to the social development of children.

While much lip service has been given to the fact that we are in an "electronic age," and while virtually every writer on electronic media comments on their ability to bypass former barriers to communication, there have been few systematic studies of the impact of these new patterns of information flow on the social structures and roles associated with a print culture.

It is surprising that most of the studies on the impact of the television medium have ignored the study of the *medium* itself. Television tends to be studied as if it were a passive "conveyor belt" that brings potentially significant goods/messages to the consumer/viewer. The medium is viewed as important only in so far as people receive its messages. Television content is a very popular area of study simply because 98% of American households own television sets. The medium itself is viewed as a neutral delivery system.

Implicit in many studies of television is the assumption that parental authority, coupled with regulation of broadcasters, will solve the problem of children being prematurely exposed to "adult" information. Apparently it is believed that such dual control can maintain the "innocence of childhood."

What this popular perspective misses, however, is that television is not a passive conveyor of information, equivalent to or interchangeable with earlier channels of communication such as books. Television and print, regardless of specific content and parental control, create different patterns of access to social information and therefore affect the socialization process in different ways. As detailed below, television and print differ in their "code," their physical characteristics and conditions of attendance, and in their general structuring of adult/child information systems. These differences may account for the recent changes in childhood and adulthood.

RESTRUCTURING ADULT/CHILD INFORMATION SYSTEMS

Television's Simplistic "Code"

In a print society, a person has to read and write well in order to gain full access to the society's stock of knowledge and communication networks. Even a dime novel requires a minimal reading proficiency; a short note to one's mother requires some writing ability. Because we are taught to read and write when we are very young, we often forget that reading and writing are incredibly complex skills that require years of learning and rote practice. Even among adults in the most industrialized societies, the literacy rate has never reached 100%. Reading and writing involve an abstract code of semantically meaningless symbols that must be memorized, internalized, and forgotten—forgotten in the sense that when people read and write letters of the alphabet they *hear words* rather than focus on the shape and form of writing. (See Havelock, 1976, p. 46.)

One of the implications of this complex code is that the young child is automatically excluded from social communication that takes place through writing and books. Further, a child learns to read in stages. There is a logical sequence to the stages based upon increasing steps of linguistic and grammatical complexity. One has to read simple children's books before reading complex adult books. Through books, therefore, literate adults can communicate with each other without being "overheard" by children, and printed information can be directed at different ages of children simply by varying the complexity of the coded message.

Communication through print allows for a great deal of control over the information to which children have access. It is possible to have books for parents on what books they should or should not allow children to read. This is purely an adult-to-adult interaction of which children are unaware. In a print society, children can be shielded from certain information and, even more significantly, they can be shielded from the fact that they are being shielded.

The same is not true of television. For example, the *content* of parental-guidance warnings on television may be similar to advice given to parents in books, but the structure of the information system is radically different. Television warnings are as accessible to children as they are to adults. These warnings not only cue children to "questionable" programs, but probably increase their interest in them. And even if such warnings actually prompt parental censorship, the control becomes overt, and therefore often unpalatable to both children and adults.

In contrast to reading and writing, television viewing involves a visual code that is barely a code at all. (See Langer, 1957, for a relevant discussion of "discursive" and "presentational" forms.) Even two-year-old children find television accessible and absorbing. One of the primary uses of the medium is as a "baby-sitter." In 1980, children aged two to five watched an average of 29 hours, 14 minutes of television per week (A.C. Nielsen Company, 1981, p. 9). To these active television watchers, words in a book are little more than odd shapes and lines.

Unlike print, the presentational form of television does not allow it to be used to distinguish sharply between the information available to the third grader, the seventh grader, and the adult. Many of the same programs are watched by all age groups. In 1980, "Love Boat," "The Dukes of Hazzard," and "Dallas" were among the most popular shows in *every* age group in America, including ages two to eleven (A.C. Nielsen Company, 1981, p. 15). Even the 11-year-olds, the oldest members of this child group, are only in the sixth grade. Books aimed at the sixth grader generally present a much more idealized view of adult life.

While adults often mention the need for developing more programs that are appropriate for children, studies have shown that children themselves generally prefer "adult programming" and that children often stay up late to watch more adult programs (Webster and Coscarelli, 1979; Mohr, 1979). Adult shows may present children with content they do not fully understand, but the basics of presentation are the same for every television show: picture and sound.

Physical Characteristics and Conditions of Attendance

In addition to being a medium of communication, the book is a physical object. It must be actively sought out and interacted with. It must be carried through the door of the house and stored somewhere. A child is restricted in many ways, therefore, from getting access to certain books because of their size or cost, where the child must go to find them, where in the library or store they are kept, and whom the child must ask to get them. Even the height of a shelf can limit a child's access to print.

In television the individual program has no unique physical dimensions or existence. A person buys a television set (or a cable service), not the specific show. Television content is evanescent; it is consumed and leaves no residue. Once the television is in the home, the programs flow constantly. The child does not have to go anywhere to find a television program, nor ask anyone to see it. While a child has limited access to a book being read by a parent in the family room, a television in the same room is accessible to everyone in it.

As individual objects, books are selectively chosen and given to children. With television, a parent must often choose between giving *all* of television's offerings or *none* of them. A child's book is, in a sense, a "guest" in the house. It makes a "social entrance," that is, it comes through the door and it remains under parental authority. The child's television set, in contrast, is like a new doorway to the home. Through it come many welcome and unwelcome visitors: schoolteachers, salesmen, prostitutes, friends, and strangers.

Further, because the child has not brought the specific television program into the house, there is little guilt of association. For a child to bring a cheap novel or a "dirty" book into the house is to associate with its content; to watch a cheap or dirty television show is to view innocently what has been piped into the home (and is implicitly sanctioned by the parents who provide the television set, and by the larger society which presents itself through this medium).

Such differences in the "code," physical characteristics, and conditions of attendance, suggest that control over what children see and experience through television is not a simple issue of parental authority. Print has many built-in censors that television does not share. Unable to read, young children were once restricted to knowledge of events that took place within or around the home. Television now takes children across the globe, even before they have permission to cross the street.

But surely regulation of what broadcasters are allowed to show will have a tremendous impact on what children know and learn through television! If, for example, only shows such as "Father Knows Best" and "Little House on the Prairie" are permitted, and shows such as "Three's Company" and "One Day at a Time" are banned, will not children be provided only with the information traditionally given to them in a print society? While content variables naturally have some effect, I argue that the effect is not as great as is generally assumed. I also suggest that while such shows as "Father

Knows Best" are, in manifest content, more traditional than shows such as "One Day at a Time," the two programs may be very similar in terms of what they reveal to children about adults. Indeed, many of the early, seemingly traditional television programs may actually have been "subversive," in the sense that they gave away important adult secrets to children and weakened adults' ability to play out traditional parental roles. For even traditional television content cannot override the fact that television, as a shared information system, radically affects adult and child roles.

Traditional Content/Subversive Structure

Distinctions between child and adult behavior depend in part on the restriction of what children know about adult roles. Using a theatrical metaphor, children of the past were given an "onstage" view of adulthood. (For a dramaturgical analysis of everyday social behavior, see Goffman, 1959.) Parents are presented as all-knowing, calm, cool, and collected. The "backstage" view of adulthood—doubts, anxieties, fears, sexual behavior, arguments, and illnesses—were all shielded from children, as well as any knowledge that such a "backstage" area existed. They saw the "onstage" role of adults as *the* reality.

In a print culture, this system could be supported and maintained. Traditional children's books presented stylized, idealized, and stereotyped versions of adult behavior: "See Mommy cook dinner," "See Daddy come home from the office," "See George Washington never telling a lie." Children were presented with the way parents, and adults, in general, attempted to behave in front of them. In going through the grades of school and the corresponding levels of printed material, children were slowly given more and more access to the behind-the-scenes life of adults. This *staggered* access supported role distinctions between children of different ages and it supported distinctions between adults and children. By the time people were let in on most of the adult secrets, they were adults themselves, and they, in turn, protected their younger siblings and children from this information.

Even traditional television programs, however, create a very different information environment. Television programs reveal to children of all ages how parents *prepare* for adult roles, and how parents behave when they are *not* with children. In "Father Knows Best," for example, parents are shown behaving one way in front of their children and another way when they are alone. They are shown as cool and rational with their kids, but when they are by themselves they display doubts and anxieties. Other seemingly traditional programs reveal similar backstage behaviors of teachers, policemen, politicans, and all adult authorities. In contrast to print-educated children, television children learn about depressed parents and crooked cops before they learn (the often contradictory) ideal role models at home or school.

This analysis suggests the primacy of information system structure over manifest content. The child *portrayed* on traditional television shows may be innocent and sheltered, but the child *watching* the programs sees both the hidden behavior and the process of sheltering it from children. "Father Knows Best," for example, reveals to the child viewer the ways in which a father manipulates his behavior to make it appear to his children that he "knows best." From a social dynamics perspective, the particular *content* of the backstage behavior portrayed is less significant than the revelation of the *existence* of the backstage itself. If nothing else, then, children learn through television that adults "play roles" for children. Children learn that the behavior adults exhibit before them is not necessarily their "real" or only behavior. Children, therefore, may become more suspicious of adults, and adults may feel it no longer makes as much sense to try to keep certain things hidden from children.

In a pre-television age, similar disclosure of backstage adult behavior would occur only under unusual circumstances. Such a situation is recorded in Anne Frank's World War II diary. While hiding from the Nazis, Anne was thrust into a confined and not very private space with her parents and another family. The adults could no longer hide their backstage behavior. One of Anne's greatest shocks was the poor behavior of the adults. She wrote: "Why do grownups quarrel so easily, so much, and over the most idiotic things? Up till now, I thought that only children squabbled and that that wore off as you grew up." (Frank, 1953, p. 29). Anne's image and awe of adults was shattered.

Traditional adult/child roles rested on a special ecosystem of information environments. To have greatly different social roles for children and adults requires that adults have control over their backstage behavior. All actors, social and theatrical, need a private rehearsal/relaxation space in order to build to a powerful and consistent performance. When actors lose their rehearsal space, their performance naturally moves toward the extemporaneous. Parents may lose the ability to play traditional roles because television reveals to children the backstage area of adults. From this perspective, many types of programs generally excluded from discussion in the tv-and-children controversy have a tremendous impact on adult/child relationships. Traditional dramatic and comedy programs, news shows, and documentaries, for example, all reveal adult secrets to children. And, perhaps even more significantly, they disclose the "secret of secrecy."

This analysis offers a new interpretation of the seemingly "radical" content of many recent television programs. One major difference is that parents portrayed in these shows often have no private backstage area. The mother in "One Day at a Time," for example, is confused and anxious, even lustful, *in front* of her children. This new portrayal of adults, however, is in keeping with the information that the child-viewer already has. In terms of adult secrets, therefore, there is little difference between these programs and the earlier traditional ones. The new portrayals of adult/child interaction on television, though often condemned, may actually represent an adjustment in the manifest content to match patterns of access to social information established by earlier television programs.

People, of course, have the ability to encode whatever information they wish in television and print media. Yet the different characteristics of the two media tend to establish certain patterns of use. It was never *necessary* for television to reveal any adult secrets. It would be possible to present television programs that parallel the content of books aimed at young children and therefore present only idealized versions of adult roles. Such shows, however, would be bland and unpalatable to adults. Television does not allow for distinctions between programs that are accessible to children and those that are accessible to adults; television has no complex code to filter out young viewers. It is impossible, therefore, to recreate in television the stages of access to information that exist in print. Adults must either abandon television to their youngest children or they must share much of their adult news and entertainment.

Similarly, I am not claiming that there is anything inherent in the medium of print that *demands* that children's books contain no adult secrets. It is possible, for example, to substitute "See Mrs. Smith walk," with "See Mrs. Smith have an abortion." But there is something inherent in print that *allows* adults to control what children know. And general observations of social behavior support the notion that when people *can* control access to private behavior, they do so. (If we know that company is coming, we clean the house; if we have a family argument, we don't share it with the neighbors unless they overhear it; if a political or family scandal can be covered up easily, it usually is covered up.) Television and print characteristics, therefore, interact with general rules of social behavior but nevertheless tend to establish different types of social information systems.

The sharing of information through television has another subtle but significant effect. Traditional distinctions between adult and child information systems actually led to three distinct social arenas: adult/adult interaction, child/child interaction, and child/adult interaction. Lack of explicit knowledge of exactly what the members of the other group knew helped to maintain distinctions in adult and child behavior.

In a print culture, for example, bright children might have gotten access to books on sex and other taboo topics, but they did this privately. This access to information did not drastically alter those children's interaction with their parents. Their parents did not know what their children knew, and the children did not know what their parents knew, or what their parents knew the children knew. Children and adults may have always cursed and spoken about taboo topics, but they usually did not speak of such things in front of each other.

Television undermines behavioral distinctions because it encompasses both children and adults in a single informational sphere or environment. It provides the same information to everyone and, even more significantly, it provides it simultaneously and publicly. Television removes any doubt as to what subjects one's children or parents know about. Any topic on any popular situation comedy, talk show, or news program—be it death, abortion, crime, sex-change operations, political scandals, or rape—can be spoken about the next day in school or over dinner, not only because everyone knows about such topics, but more significantly, because everyone knows that everyone knows. The public and all-inclusive nature of television has a tendency to collapse the former three spheres of interaction into one.

DISCUSSION

It is impossible to say whether the differences in media I have analyzed are the sole causes of the recent changes in childhood and adulthood. In all likelihood, the changes in media interact with other social factors. Yet, certainly, the change from a "book culture" to a "television culture" supports the direction of the evolution toward more homogenized adult/child roles.

The form in which information is now transmitted in our society conspires against controlling what children know about adulthood. Children may still pass through a sequence of cognitive and physiological stages, but the social stages have been blurred. Children still need to learn many things through books, but reading skill alone no longer determines the sequence in which "adult" information is revealed to them. Television undermines the hierarchy of information supported by stages of reading literacy and the age-specific grades of the school system. Television gives children the opportunity to ask the meaning of actions and words they would not yet be exposed to in print, and it thrusts them into a complex adult world which they work to understand. Just as we cannot sharply distinguish among the social statuses of students of different ages if we teach them all in the same classroom, neither can we make very clear status distinctions if we expose everyone to the same information through television.

Many formal reciprocal roles rely on lack of intimate knowledge of the other. If the mystery and mystification disappear, so does the formal behavior. Stylized courtship behavior, for example, must quickly fade in the day-to-day intimacy of marriage. Similarly, television's involvement of children in adult affairs undermines many traditional adult/child roles.[1] Given this analysis, it is not surprising that the first widespread rejection of both traditional child and traditional adult roles should have occurred in the late 1960s among the first generation of Americans to have grown up with television. In the common environment of television, children and adults share too much for them to play out the traditional complementary roles of innocence vs. omnipotence.

If television can alter the social meaning of childhood, then it stands to reason that childhood, as it was defined in the past, is not a natural, or necessary state of being. Indeed, it is implicit in my analysis that our old view of childhood was dependent upon print, and could not have existed in a primarily oral society. The history of childhood supports this argument. In *Centuries of Childhood*, historian Philippe Ariès (1962) describes the "invention" of childhood in the 16th century. Before that time, Ariès claims there was no "childhood" as we have traditionally thought of it. Once past infancy, children began to participate in adult activities and they learned about life directly. Children worked beside adults, drank in taverns with adults, went to war with adults, and slept in the same beds with adults. Children and adults played the same games. There was no special dress for adults or children; there were no topics or words or activities from which children were to be shielded. What few formal schools existed (primarily to train clerics) were not divided into separate age groups. The art of the middle ages often pictured children as "little adults," with identical clothes and facial expressions but smaller in size. Thus, while children have always existed in the physiological sense, the pre-print oral society of Western Europe accorded them few special roles.

Beginning in the 16th century, however, a new concept of the child began to take hold: that of a weak being in need of special care, love, and protection. Ariès does not know why "childhood" suddenly came into being.

---

[1] If television does have an effect on child-adult interaction, then the process must have begun with earlier media, such as film and radio. Neither film nor radio, however, has all of television's relevant characteristics. Movies have an audio/visual code, but a child has to leave the home and travel through the adult world to see a movie. This precludes viewing by very young children, who spend many hours a week watching television. Even for older children, the choice to see *a* movie cannot be compared to the random, flip-of-the-dial television viewing that provides children with information they have not directly sought. Radio, on the other hand, is present in the home, but its "code" is wholly aural and verbal; the listener must fill in the pictures based on *past experience*. This obviously puts the inexperienced child at a disadvantage. Further, radio tends to present a more formal "onstage" view of the adult world. Because of its reliance on words, radio tends to deal in high-level abstractions such as "the hand of God" and "the spirit of democracy." Such things cannot be pictured easily, and television, therefore, turns to the more tangible (and less impressive and mystifying) aspects of everyday speech and behavior.

He offers a demographic analysis, but then admits that the potential causes he outlines did not in fact take place until *after* the new concept developed. The analysis presented here, however, supports the argument that the spread of printing and literacy may have been prime factors in the development of "childhood." Suddenly, to share fully in the adult world a child had to learn to read. Printing may have given a boost to the Renaissance, but it also created a new dark ages for the young and the illiterate. The medium of print removed the child from the adult world in a manner inconceivable in an oral culture. It is no surprise, then, that the image of the weak and naïve child should have developed alongside the growing impact of printing.

Many other features of the growth of childhood as described by Ariès support this analysis. Childhood as a separate time of life developed first among the middle and upper classes, as did literacy. Boys were considered children long before girls were. Boys, after all, were sent off to school to learn to read, while their sisters stayed home and immediately took on the dress and tasks of adult women.

The age-graded school system developed only after the spread of printing. Along with this system came the growing demand on the part of clerics for expurgated versions of the classics. Children, who in an earlier oral culture were exposed to the same violent and vulgar folk tales as their parents, were now deemed too innocent to share fully in "adult" information. Etiquette books for children, along with special guides for their parents, were also printed. With the spread of literacy, child precocity—once as valued as it was common—began to be frowned upon. The *age* of children was used more and more as a guide to what they should know and do. Print separated the world of the adult from the child, created adult/adult interactions that excluded children, and led to an age-grading of information and status based on relative mastery of reading.

This perspective offers a new view of the role of television in the general decline of the American school system. It has already been suggested by others that television hurts the school because television fosters passivity and leads to a generation of youth who demand instant gratification and a degree of control over experience equivalent to the flick of a dial. (See, e.g., Waters, 1977; Morgan and Gross, 1980.) There may be some truth in such attacks, but these arguments overlook the relationship between the *structure* of the school system and the stages and steps of reading. The age-graded system of dispensing information grew out of, and was supported by, a print culture. Since the school controlled access to social information as well as the skill required to achieve that access, it was assumed that those who read poorly knew little. Information was packaged in linear, sequential stages of complexity to match the complexity of the reading code.

The control over access to information fostered by such a system permits adults to shield children from information as well as teach children idealized versions of reality. Young children are first taught the greatness of Presidents, the virtues of our political system, the good intentions of adults, and so forth. As children move through the school system, more information is revealed— but slowly and in set stages—George Washington was, after all, not a very good general; our government does not always work.

In a television society, however, it is not uncommon for young students to "correct" their teachers by jumping out of sequence. A third-grader may interrupt a lesson on the "honor of the Presidency" with some examples from the latest Presidential scandal aired on television. Students may find the school limiting and constraining because it does not teach them enough, or, put differently, because it does not recognize their relatively sophisticated knowledge of society. Television has provided children with a broad mosaic image of their culture. The school needs to clarify the details and correct misperceptions. Instead, the school tries to walk children slowly up the printed steps of social knowledge from complete ignorance to total enlightenment. Television, therefore, may undermine the *structure* of the school more than the potential content of its lessons. The school stubbornly clings to an image of childhood that no longer exists.

The school system is not alone in resisting the end of traditional childhood. The family, the church, the courts, and the medical profession are all faced with new and confounding questions. (Should "children" be given birth control devices and/or abortions without the permission of their parents?) There is more activity aimed at trying to achieve a new social balance by reaching a consensus in answer to such questions than there is a conscious understanding of what is actually happening to childhood.

The attempts to re-establish social equilibrium have taken two distinct forms. On one side, there are those who either refuse to recognize the change in childhood, or, in recognizing it, suggest that children be returned to their earlier social status. On the other side, there are those who are trying to change legal, medical, and other institutions to match the new children.[2] Yet neither group seems to be fully conscious of the nature and degree of the evolution in childhood.

There is a peculiar, yet historically familiar paradox in the current political, social, and scientific activities surrounding children. As Hegel noted, social institutions often become the center of attention just as they are disappearing from a culture. Today's sharpening focus on children's issues is in this sense analogous to the increasingly formalized jousting tournaments of the later middle ages. The growing intensity of these mock battles par-

---

[2]Such differences in view have all the markings of a paradigm-shift in the Kuhnian sense. If the new paradigm of childhood prevails, it will not do so by convincing those who embrace the old paradigm to let go. As Kuhn (1970) suggests, a new paradigm tends to gain support only among the new generation which grows up with it and sees it as natural and familiar.

alleled the *decline* of the role of the knight in battle, and of chivalry in the culture as a whole (Tuchman, 1978, p. 65). Similarly, the current fanfare over "children" has masked the disappearance of childhood as a markedly distinct and special stage of life.

REFERENCES

A.C. Nielsen Company. (1981). "Nielsen Report on Television, 1981." Northbrook, Illinois: A.C. Nielsen.

ARIES, P. (1962). "Centuries of Childhood." R. Baldick (Trans.) New York: Vintage.

BERLIN, M.J. (1976). Tough bills ready, spurred on by the "Laugh" murder. *New York Post* (July 7), 1,7.

BOULDING, E. (1977). Children's rights. *Society 15* (No. 1), 39–43.

COMSTOCK, G. (1975). The evidence so far. *Journal of Communication 25* (No. 14), 25–34.

EDELMAN, M.W. (1978). In defense of children's rights. *Current* (April), 16–20.

FOOTLICK, J.K., AGREST, S., and HUCK, J. (1977). Kids in mental hospitals. *Newsweek* (Nov. 12), 116,119.

FRANK, A, (1953). "Anne: The Diary of a Young Girl." New York: Pocket Books.

GOFFMAN, E. (1959). "The Presentation of Self in Everyday Life." Garden City, New York: Anchor.

HALL, E. (1980). Acting One's Age: New Rules for Old, Bernice Neugarten Interviewed. *Psychology Today* (April), 66–80.

HAVELOCK, E. (1976). "Origins of Western Literacy." Toronto, Ontario: Ontario Institute for Studies in Education.

HOLT, J. (1974). "Escape from Childhood." New York: E.P. Dutton.

KENISTON, K. (1977). More rights for children: What an expert says. *U.S. News and World Report 83* (Oct. 31), 33.

KIHSS, P. (1978). A manual warns social workers of extension of children's rights. *New York Times* (July 2), 24.

KUHN, T.S. (1970). "The Structure of Scientific Revolutions." 2nd ed. Chicago, Illinois: University of Chicago Press.

LANGER, S.K. (1957). "Philosophy in a New Key." 3rd ed. Cambridge, Massachusetts: Harvard University Press.

MEYROWITZ, J. (1979). "No Sense of Place: A Theory on the Impact of Electronic Media on Social Structure and Behavior." Unpublished dissertation, New York University.

MOHR, P.J. (1979). Efficacy of the family viewing concept: A test of assumptions. *Central States Speech Journal 30*, 342–351.

MORGAN, M., and GROSS, L. (1980). Television viewing, IQ, and academic achievement. *Journal of Broadcasting 24*, 117–133.

MURRAY, J.P. (1980). "Television and Youth: 25 Years of Research and Controversy." Stanford, California: Boys Town Center for the Study of Youth Development.

MUUSS, R.E. (1975). "Theories of Adolescence." 3rd ed. New York: Random House.

NEUGARTEN, B. (1981). Age Distinctions and their Social Functions. *Chicago Kent Law Review 57*, 809–825.

TREECE, A.J. (1959). "An Interpretation of Clothing Behavior Based on a Social-Psychological Theory." Unpublished dissertation, Ohio State University.

TUCHMAN, B.W. (1978). "A Distant Mirror." New York: Ballantine Books.

VAN GENNEP, A. (1960). "The Rites of Passage." M.B. Vizedom and G.L. Caffee (Trans.) Chicago, Illinois: University of Chicago Press. (Originally published in 1908.)

WATERS, H.F. (1977). What TV does to kids. *Newsweek* (Feb. 21), 62–70.

WEBSTER, J.G., and COSCARELLI, W.C. (1979). The relative appeal to children of adult versus children's television programming. *Journal of Broadcasting 23*, 437–451.

WILLIAMS, T.M. (1981). How and what do children learn from television? *Human Communication Research 7*, 180–192.

16

The Impact of Television on Space Conception

EDWARD WACHTEL
Queens College
Flushing, New York 11367

The perceptual world we are born into is, in William James' famous phrase, "a blooming, buzzing confusion." The primary cognitive task of childhood is to order this confusion and stabilize the world. Children must learn to see objects as having a permanent shape and form. They must learn to separate parts of the environment. They must learn to separate the environment from their individual selves.

This is no easy task. It will take the average child almost 13 years to see and conceptualize the world as adults. They will be adolescents by the time they have built a mature concept of space and time.

We build our concepts of time and space by making predictions about the world and then testing them in the environments in which we live. But what happens when our environments are changed by the introduction of new technologies? More specifically, what happens when television becomes a substantial part of a child's environment during the years when his or her concept of space is developing?

In this paper, I suggest that television can influence the way that our children build their space conceptions, their visions of reality and their place in it. To describe this possibly enormous influence, four points must be covered: First, how do our conceptions of space and time underly our perceptions of the physical world? Second, how do we develop these concepts? Third, how can television influence this development, and the particular changes in space conception that may result from "heavy" television viewing? Finally, how do these changes in space conception yield a new generation that is more egocentric, more present-oriented, and, in a certain sense, more childlike than were prior generations.[1]

---

[1]The hypothesis presented here has been more fully developed from an historical perspective in *Visions of Order: The Influence of Selected Technologies on Space Conception* (1980).

THE NATURE OF SPACE AND TIME

Albert Einstein once said that "The normal adult never bothers his head about space-time problems" (Seelig, 1954, p. 71). Nonetheless, it is necessary for the development of this paper to so inconvenience ourselves. As adults raised in Western cultures, we generally think and speak as if we could "see" space and "feel" time. We think of space as a kind of empty container in which we can put things. We may speak of a room containing a certain number of cubic feet of space, and in turn we think of ourselves as "occupying" the space in that room.

We think of time as some kind of flow that we can feel, like a river that carries things from the past, through the present, and to the future. For example, if you are bored, you may look at your watch and wonder why time *feels* like it's going so slowly.

In any case, we tend to assume that space and time are real things that exist apart from ourselves. This is not true. They are not objects, things, or quantities. We cannot see or touch them. Modern physics supports what Immanuel Kant (1965) said two centuries ago—that space and time are inventions of the human mind—they are concepts not things. However, they are crucial, core concepts that underlie everything we think and everything we see. Without a space conception, we could not even have a simple perception.

To clarify these points, imagine that we are confronted by an object: a table perhaps. If we ignore color and texture, we might say that we perceive a certain magnitude. There are lines and angles, or, more simply, shape. The table may appear to be near or far, tilted or straight in relation to some other object. If I walked around the table, you would "see" that I was in motion and the table remained still. So, magnitude, shape, nearness, farness, tilt, and motion are some of the formal characteristics of a basic perception. And they are also *spatial and temporal characteristics*. We cannot perceive (or even conceive of) an object without at least some of these characteristics (e.g., what would a table without shape look like?). As Kant (1965, p. 71) put it, "Space is nothing but the form of all appearances of outer sense. It is the subjective condition of sensibility, under which alone outer intuition is possible for us.[2]

Our eyes are not in touch with the outside world. All we have are swirling, shifting, two-dimensional patterns of reflected light. In order to see a table with a fixed shape and distance, or to see anything at all, involves

---

[2]Kant presents separate but parallel arguments for the a priori necessity of time. There are certain differences, (e.g., that time is the formal condition of *all* appearances, while space is the formal condition of outer appearances), but these differences are not particularly relevant to this discussion. See Kant (1965, pp. 74–80) for his special treatment of time.

a complex series of predictions about what is actually "out" there. These predictions are based on our concepts of space and time. So time and space may be characterized as a mental framework of dimensions that we impose on the "blooming, buzzing confusion" that meets our senses. We impose concepts that are in our heads onto the light patterns that meet our eyes, to predict what is out there.

Not only is a space conception necessary for perception of the world, but also for thinking about it. As Julian Jaynes (1976) explained, the first step in becoming conscious is the creation of a mental arena in which we can "arrange" our ideas or "order" our thoughts.[3] For example, if you were asked where you do your thinking, you would probably point to your head. (Other cultures have done their thinking in other places—the Romans, for example, used to think in their breasts.) Regardless of where you think, on examination, you will find that you have invented a fictional place, a "space" in which you can arrange your thoughts as if they too had a physical, spatiotemporal reality. In summary, we might say that space and time are the core concepts we use to order our sense data and even our minds.

DEVELOPING A SPACE CONCEPTION

But where do these concepts come from? They could not be completely innate; otherwise, infants could see at birth, and furthermore, we would have no need of a Newton or an Einstein to explain them to us. In fact, as Jean Piaget (1960; Piaget and Inhelder, 1967) has demonstrated, our concepts of space and time develop slowly from birth. They develop through our sensorimotor interactions with our environment. That is, we learn space and time by touching and looking and by moving and looking. We view objects from many perspectives as we touch them, rotate them, and move around them. Through these interactions of touch, movement and vision, we eventually build a mature space conception. In fact, the child must accomplish this task on two levels: First, during the sensorimotor stage, the child will develop perceptual knowledge of space. This knowledge will permit *behavior* in the physical world. The child, at this point, could (perhaps) chase and catch a rabbit in the woods, or avoid being hit by a car on a city street. Second, during the operational stages, the child must learn to conceptualize and represent spatiotemporal relations. That is, the child must learn to draw

---

[3]Jaynes has presented a brilliant and sweeping hypothesis of the origin of consciousness in his *Origin of Consciousness in the Breakdown of the Bicameral Mind* (1976). I doubt that all of Jaynes' speculations are correct. Nevertheless, his description of the process of building consciousness, and especially his notion of spatialization, echo Kant's view of time and space as prerequisites for conscious awareness, and seem compelling.

or internally visualize the spatial order and motion of objects using Euclidean and perspective relations. The development of these abilities is not completed until (typically) from 9 to 12 years of age.

TELEVISION AND SPACE CONCEPTION

But if a child spends the first 12 years of life building a space conception, what happens when a substantial part of these years is spent in the unique spatial environment that is television? What happens when a child begins to watch television before he or she can speak? What is the effect on a child's spatial development when he or she spends more time engaged in television viewing than in any activity except sleeping? To answer these questions, we must take a look at the child's interaction with television.

First, television presents the child with a world that is already organized. For example, at a televised baseball game, the camera will focus only the relevant spaces—we will see the pitch, the hit, the catch, and the tag at second base. The camera presents us with small pieces of unconnected space—each one containing a relevant action. The child does not get the opportunity to organize the variety of events into one continuous space.

Second, television short-circuits the sensorimotor work that is necessary to coordinate perspectives. T.V. demands that the child sit quite still, watching the screen from a fixed position. There is no opportunity for the child to move around objects, or rotate them. As Piaget emphasized, we can only learn space and time by using our eyes *and* our motor functions—our eyes alone are not enough.

Finally, television presents us with a world of disconnected spaces and times. On television, New York is only a jump-cut or split-screen away from Paris. Similarly, actions that normally take a year may be presented in an instant. Space and time are expanded, contracted, and fragmented at the whim of the producers.

In summary, the picture presented by television not only denies the traditional Western view of a continuous and separate time and space but also denies the child the sensorimotor experience to build this concept. Therefore, I suggest that heavy television viewing may retard the development of a mature space conception.

My prediction can be tested, at least in part. One of the spatial skills that the child must learn is the ability to organize the world with perspective relations. This skill can be tested by using one of Piaget's tasks called the "Three Mountain" experiment. This experiment begins with three objects that can be differentiated easily. (Piaget used paper maché mountains, but later researchers have used cardboard cones of different colors and sizes.) The three objects are arranged on a table with each object as an apex of a triangle. The child is asked to sit at the table and observe the arrangement of the objects. Next, the child is asked, "How would the objects look (or be arranged) if you were sitting on the left side (or the right side, etc.) of the table?" The child then chooses from a variety of photographs of the objects taken from different perspectives. (See Piaget and Inhelder (1967) for a more complete description of the "Three Mountain" experiment and other tasks designed to test for spatial development.)

When children reach the appropriate stage of development they can, of course, choose the picture that represents the viewpoint that was specified. Until that time, they will choose the picture that represents their own viewpoint. They cannot concepualize the world from another place or from another person's position. In Piaget's phrase, they are perceptually egocentric.

It is interesting to note that when Piaget first performed the "Three Mountain" experiment in the late 1940s, he reported that the average age at which children mastered the skill of perspective coordination was about 9 years. Later replications of this experiment have shown a progressive *increase* in age. For example Laurendeau and Pinard (1970) reported that only 25% of 12-year-olds, 22% of 11 year-olds, and 12% of 9-year-olds had mastered this skill.

Can these impressive age differences be attributed to television? The timing is certainly correct—1948 to 1970. But television viewing was not a controlled variable in these tests. Furthermore, the extent to which the experimenter must interact with subjects in these tests makes it imprudent to generalize about age differences when the tests were administered by different experimenters. It is clear, however, that the "Three Mountain" problem and other Piagetian tasks can be adapted to test for differences in spatial development among light and heavy television viewers.

There is one further question to consider. What specific effects can a space conception have on human mind and behavior? If Piaget and other developmental psychologists are correct, then the type of skills discussed here are intimately linked to other attitudes about the world.

For example, in our society we place a premium on the ability to detach ourselves from our own feelings, from our point of view. In fact, the ability to transcend our own egocentrism is a defining characteristic of adulthood. However, the social egocentrism of childhood cannot be overcome until the child transcends perceptual egocentrism. That is, we must learn the spatial skill of perspective coordination; we must learn to conceptualize, *quite literally*, what another person sees before we can conceptualize what another person *knows*. In short, when we use the phrase "point of view" to mean an intellectual or emotional position on an issue, we are not using an idle metaphor. Until the child has built a mature conception of space and time, his or her social behavior may remain egocentric and immature. His or her ability to take a social role, and to understand the roles that others assume, may remain limited.[4]

Finally, a mature space conception—at least in Western culture—entails the ability to split a four-dimensional spatiotemporal reality into three dimensions of space and one dimension of time. Many other Western notions seem to be based on this clean separation of space and time—for example, our assumptions of causality and our notion of history.

If television can interfere with the development of spatial skills, then current and future generations may order the world differently. Their "world view" may begin to resemble the mystical constructions of reality of many "primitive" cultures. They may live immersed in the present. Their vision of the past and future may be limited by minds that are unable to order different times and different places in a logical linear sequence. Our sense of history may be undermined by a growing need for myth, in which the times and places, names and events, of the past are altered to reflect the emotional needs of the present.

These are not simply theoretical predictions. In the past ten years, a number of social critics have noted a trend towards egocentric, present-oriented and mystical attitudes in American society. Could these shifts in psychological orientation be the result of a new vision of order, a new concpetion of space and time? And finally, can television viewing be linked, through empirical research, with this new conception?

This paper offers only a hypothesis that connects television to space conception, and space conception to social attitudes. More research—both theoretical and empirical—is certainly required. However, I hope that the framework suggested here will provide a new approach to the study of television that may reveal not only its influence on our social knowledge and behavior, but also its effects on our most basic intuitions about the nature of reality.

REFERENCES

BORKE, H. (1975). Piaget's mountains revisited: Changes in the egocentric landscape. *Developmental Psychology 11*, 240–243.

JAYNES, J. (1976). "The Origin of Consciousness in the Breakdown of the Bicameral Mind." Boston, MA: Houghton Mifflin.

---

[4]Many of Piaget's critics have tested for (and in some cases, found) role-taking and empathetic abilities at earlier ages than those predicted by Piaget. And yet, they still accept Piaget's assertion of a fundamental relationship between the ability to take another's perspective and the ability to understand (or take) another role. See, for examaple, Borke (1975).

KANT, I. (1965). "Critique of Pure Reason." (Trans. by N. Smith.) New York: St. Martin's Press. (Originally published, 1781.)

LAURENDEAU, M., and PINARD, A. (1970). "The Development of the Concept of Space in the Child." New York: International Universities Press.

PIAGET, J. (1960). "The Child's Conception of the World." (Trans. by J. Tomlinson and A. Tomlinson.) Totowa, NJ: Littlefield, Adams. (Originally published, 1929.)

PIAGET, J., and INHELDER, B. (1967). "The Child's Conception of Space." (Trans. by F. Langdon and J. Lunzer.) New York: W.W. Norton. (Originally published, 1948).

SEELIG, K. (1954). "Albert Einstein." Zurich, Switzerland: Europa Verlag.

WACHTEL, E. (1980). "Visions of Order: The Influence of Selected Technologies on Space Conception." Unpublished dissertation, New York University.

17

Family Processes and the Social Functions of Television

PAUL MESSARIS
Annenberg School of Communications
University of Pennsylvania
Philadelphia, Pennsylvania 19104

What role does parental influence play in children's responses to television? The most frequent answer to this question seems to be that parents who make a special effort *can* modify the effects of television on their children and that, by implication, all concerned parents *should* make such special efforts. Variants of this kind of thinking appear to account for the considerable number of studies of parental—or other adult—"mediation" of the medium's effects on children (e.g., Corder-Bolz, 1980; Corder-Bolz and O'Bryant, 1978; Prasad et al., 1978). The corollary of this position is that, in the absence of explicit parental attempts at "mediation," the influence of television on children is more direct, less conditional.

This paper considers the merits of a somewhat different position. According to this alternative position, parental influence should be thought of, not as a *potential* modifier of television's effects on children, but, rather, as an almost inevitable *precondition* for the existence of such effects. The basic argument behind this position involves two observations: (a) Many—if not most—of the kinds of responses that existing research has linked to television represent behavior or belief which is bound to have received previous, independent reinforcement in the child's social environment, and, in particular, in the child's relationship with its parents. (b) To the extent that one can tell from existing research, it is precisely when such previous reinforcement exists that television exposure seems to bring about a particular behavioral or cognitive response. Consequently, the argument goes, television should be seen as triggering predetermined response tendencies, rather than as an independent source of influence on a child's life, while parents—and other components of a child's social environment—should be seen as playing a much more integral role in the process of effects than is usually thought to be the case.

This position is examined in greater detail through a brief review of pertinent findings from the literature on television effects. The discussion focuses first on what are usually termed "behavioral" effects, i.e., effects on aspects of children's behavior which could, in principle, be observed directly; and, second, on a class of effects whose overt behavioral correlates are less easy to specify—or, at least, to measure—namely, television's contribution to children's beliefs about the real world. Following this discussion, the position under examination here will be linked to a broader, "macro-social" view of the joint role of parents and television in children's lives.

TELEVISION AND CHILDREN'S OBSERVABLE BEHAVIOR

Research on the "behavioral" effects of television has had two main subjects, namely, aggression and "pro-social behavior" (helping, sharing, etc.). Because of its long history and the variety of complications explored in the course of that history, research on aggression is the most convenient focus for this discussion. The prototypical experimental studies on visually-mediated aggression were concerned with demonstrating the possibility that exposure to such aggression could increase the otherwise-obtaining aggression levels of young audience members. In the canonical version of this kind of experiment (e.g., Bandura et al., 1963), differences in average levels of aggression between children who had, and children who had not, seen a particular violent movie or TV program were treated as evidence that films or television can cause children to be violent. In particular, children's imitations of "unusual" kinds of aggression were taken as indications that children can acquire a repertory of aggressive behavior purely by exposure to a visual presentation, without any direct environmental reinforcement. In other words, it was argued that here we had a case of behavioral modification through "vicarious reinforcement," i.e., through observation of the consequences of this behavior for someone other than the acquirer. The implication of this kind of interpretation is that television is a potentially dangerous device which *by iteslf* can turn an otherwise peaceful boy or girl into a nasty little aggressor— without any immediate ("non-mediated") human involvement.

This way of looking at the results of these experiments runs counter to a position which is usually associated most directly with "strict" behaviorism. According to this alternative position (see Gewirtz, 1969, pp. 159-160; Skinner, 1953, pp. 119–122), learning from a mediated presentation cannot occur without direct environmental reinforcement of the behavior to be acquired. Do the violence studies contradict this principle or not? The first thing to keep in mind in answering this question is that the child who enters the "violence laboratory" is obviously not coming in out of a void. He/she has a past history, in the course of which certain forms of aggression will inevitably have been exposed to environmental conditioning. The central question, therefore, is this: To what extent is the aggressive behavior being measured in the "violence laboratory" part of a *new* class of behavior (from the implicit "perspective" of the child's behavioral system), as opposed to a member of the class of aggressive behavior already acquired? The TV-violence experimenters have argued for the former of these two alternatives—that, for example, strangling an inflated plastic doll with a hula-hoop is unlikely to have been part of a previously-reinforced response-class. However, this kind of question cannot be settled purely on the basis of externally-perceived similarity or dissimilarity between previous aggression and the kind of aggression measured in the laboratory. Empirical evidence is needed on what constitutes a single (*implicit*) response-class for the child itself, and much of this evidence supports the more orthodox behaviorist position.

To begin with, studies in which the criterion measure of aggression was deliberately made to appear *different* from the on-screen behavior have been no less successful in establishing a link between the two. Although some investigators have invoked various hypothetical mechanisms other than imitation (e.g., "instigation," in the terminology of Liebert and Baron, 1972) to account for this link, it seems more parsimonious to broaden the boundaries of a pre-existing response-class ("aggressive behavior") than to invent new— and otherwise uncalled-for—learning processes.

A second piece of evidence in favor of the more conservative interpretation of the violence studies is that, in those cases in which researchers have explicitly accounted for subjects' pre-existing aggressive tendencies (e.g., Stein and Friedrich, 1972; Friedrich and Stein, 1973; Parke et al., 1977), the "effects" of exposure to mediated aggression were most pronounced among those subjects who were most aggressive to begin with. In other words, postexposure aggression was associated with degree of previous positive reinforcement of aggression. What these studies cannot tell us, of course, is what happens in the absence of *any* previous environmental conditioning of the criterion behavior (cf., Bandura, 1969).

The type of environmental conditioning with which this paper is most directly concerned is that which occurs through parent-child interaction; and in this regard there are several studies which support the notion that children's responses to televised aggression are conditioned by the family environment. In particular, there is evidence that the relationship between children's (or adolescents') aggressive behavior and their exposure to televised violence varies with their parents' degree of emphasis on nonaggression (McLeod et al., 1972a, p. 238; 1972b, p. 312), with the extent to which a child has a clear understanding of family's attitudes towards aggression (Dominick and Greenberg, 1972, p. 323), and with the degree and kind of aggression entailed in parental disciplinary practices (Korzenny et al., 1979).

In general, then, there is a variety of evidence in favor of the view that children's responses to televised violence should be seen as depending on previous environmental reinforcement of aggression and, in particular, on parent-child interaction bearing upon aggression. In other words, a good argument can be made that the process of "media effects" in this area involves parent-child interaction in almost *all* cases, rather than simply in those— perhaps rare—instances in which parents make an explicit attempt to monitor their children's exposure and response to aggression on television. This is not to say, of course, that such *explicit* parental involvement in their children's relationship with television is not a phenomenon which may have its own independent consequences (cf., Hicks, 1968; Grusec, 1973; Brown and Linne, 1976) and which, in any case, is worthy of study in its own right (cf., Lull, 1980a; 1980b; Messaris and Sarett, 1981). What *is* being emphasized here, though, is that the parent-child components of family processes may well be an integral part of "television's effects," regardless of whether these processes are ever explicitly directed toward television.

The above argument with regard to experimental studies of television violence can be extended, in principle, to the only other area in which there is substantial research on television's effects on children, namely, the area of "pro-social effects." The kind of behavior examined in studies of this variety (e.g., helping other children, and sharing things—see Coates et al., 1976; Friedrich and Stein, 1973; Sprafkin et al., 1975; Sprafkin and Rubinstein, 1979; Stein and Friedrich, 1972) is clearly continuous, as a class, with behavior which must have received previous reinforcement (positive or negative) for any subject in experiments on these issues. Consequently, here too existing research cannot be taken as evidence that visual media are capable, in and of themselves, of causing certain kinds of behavioral change in children, and what was said previously about the need to examine family processes in conjunction with media use can be reiterated here.

TELEVISION AND CHILDREN'S BELIEFS

To date, research on how—if at all—television may contribute to children's beliefs about reality is not as extensive or as intensively focused on a single paradigm as research on more overt "behavioral" effects, but there is at least one body of work in this area which has been subjected to enough scrutiny to provide some empirical basis for the present discussion. The work in question is that of Gerbner, Gross, and their colleagues, who have periodically examined young people's beliefs in conjunction with frequencies of television viewing (e.g., Gerbner et al., 1979). The general assumption behind this body of work is that dramatic network programming presents viewers with an aggregate image which differs in various particulars (e.g., the proportional representation of various demographic strata, and the frequency of violence and illegal activity) from the "corresponding" aspects of reality; and that, the more television a person watches, the more he/she should come to believe in this "television" version of what the real world is like.

In examining the relationship of this kind of "effect" to family environment, the first thing to note is that the expected overall associations between television viewing and beliefs in a "television-like" world evaporate—from certain samples—when they are examined in the presence of simultaneous controls for certain audience-demographic variables (see Hirsch, 1980; Hughes, 1980; also responses to the above in Gerbner et al., 1980b, 1981). The resulting question, then, is whether the postulated effect does not occur at all or whether it can be specified as occurring under particular conditions. Gerbner, Gross, and their colleagues have presented convincing evidence in favor of the latter view. A good example of this kind of evidence revolves around their assumption that viewers' responses to the "exaggerated" amount of violence on television should be to overestimate the chances for violence in their own lives. In an independent test of this assumption, Doob and MacDonald (1979) claimed that the initial appearance of such a relationship between television exposure and belief was artifactual, and that living in a high-crime neighborhood, which is positively correlated with frequency of television viewing, is the actual cause of the overall (uncontrolled) relationship. However, in a further investigation of these and other findings, Gerbner et al. (n.d.; 1980a) have shown that the control on type of neighborhood may indeed result in a weakening of the association in some subgroups of respondents, but actually strengthens the association among those who live in high-crime neighborhoods. This finding argues, then, against a simple hypothesis of unconditional television effects and in favor of the notion that, here too, the "effects" of the medium depend on viewers' "non-mediated" experience with regard to certain issues. In other words, the appropriate view of television's role is "reduced," by this kind of evidence, to that of amplifier of beliefs which have previously been reinforced in one's environment.

This situational augmentation—or, in fact, determination—of the relationship between television viewing and views about the prevalence of real-life violence has been observed among children as well as adults (Gerbner et al., 1979). No doubt a considerable part of the environmental reinforcement of such beliefs among both age groups comes from direct experience of victimization. At the same time, however, it seems almost inevitable that much of this reinforcement must also come through other interpersonal means, which, in the case of children, presumably include varying amounts of parental warnings, advice, reprimands about risks taken, evidence of anxiety, relief, etc. Unfortunately, there do not appear to be any available data permitting one to assess the contribution of this specific environmental component to the television/fear-of-victimization relationship. It may be worth noting, however, that, in a study assessing children's beliefs about *other* aspects of reality as presented on television (i.e., not about crime), Greenberg and Reeves (1976) found that children's beliefs were associated more strongly with parents' and friends' opinions than with their direct experience of the situations themselves.

More generally, there is not much empirical evidence on the degree to which parent-child interactions (*other* than explicit discussions of television) may condition the relationship between television viewing and children's beliefs. The only direct evidence appears to be the finding, by McLeod et al. (1972b, p. 296) of a relatively greater belief in the truth value of televised portrayals of reality among children whose parents placed a simultaneous high emphasis on what these investigators call "socio-orientation" (i.e., conformity to established authority) and "concept-orientation" (i.e., self-determination of thought and action). Any conclusion with regard to the role of parents in this general area of "television's effects" must be tentative, then, since the evidence is incomplete and the argument circuitous. As with the case of "behavioral effects," however, it should be emphasized here too that explicit involvement of parents in their children's use of television may be viewed as an additional means of conditioning children's responses to the medium and is obviously worth studying in its own right. Evidence that this kind of explicit involvement "works" can be found in a study by Gross and Morgan (1980).

MACRO-SOCIAL IMPLICATIONS OF THE ROLE OF PARENTS IN CHILDREN'S RESPONSES TO TV

The intent of what has been said thus far has been to argue that parental conditioning of "television's effects" on children may be more pervasive than is often imagined. The intent of what follows is to consider the implications of this parental conditioning process for the broader social-communicational process in which parents, children, and television are participants.

A frequent assumption about television's role in the broader social system is that it serves as a means of social-structural regulation. There is hardly anything that one could call systematic evidence in favor of this kind of proposition, but it will be adopted here as a premise for what follows. In other words, it will be assumed that television makes some kind of contribution to the reinforcement of behavioral patterns consistent with viewers' differential positions in the social structure. An implication of this assumption is that various "biases" in television use (selective exposure, selective inter-pretation, and selective post-exposure processing of televised material) serve to adapt the medium's overall stock of "lessons" to the more specific char-acteristics of particular segments of the audience (i.e., groups or strata dif-ferentially located with regard to the total social structure—see Sarett, 1981, for an earlier discussion of this issue). With this implication as a given, the parental conditioning of children's uses of and responses to television may be seen as a part of this more general "biasing" process, i.e., as one of the ways—and, perhaps, the most important one—in which children learn to "extract" from the medium the kinds of information, values, behavioral pre-scriptions, etc., most appropriate for people like themselves (males or fe-males, rich, poor, etc.). A convenient illustration of how this kind of thing may occur is provided by the case of social-class differences in parental influence on children's television use.

Several investigators (e.g., Hyman, 1966) have argued that members of different social classes hold values whose effect on their children may be to enforce continuity of class position. In connection with one version of this kind of theory, Kohn (1977) has demonstrated that occupational experiences and educational background bring about a positive association between social-class level and parents' valuation of intellectual and social independence and adaptability for their children; and, conversely, a negative association be-tween social-class level and parents' valuation of their children's conformity toward existing conditions. Kohn concludes that children who are already advantaged are being supported in behavior which promotes continuing mobility, while less-advantaged children are being supported in behavior which limits mobility. How might these social-class differences in parental attitudes toward their children's behavior affect the specific realm of tele-vision-related behavior? The issue is currently being explored in the context of several ongoing, partly-related research projects (see Messaris et al., 1982; Messaris and Thomas, 1981; Sarett, 1981). A common hypothesis being tested in a variety of forms in these projects is that family environments at higher social-class levels are relatively more likely to condition children to deal with television as a tool for the broadening of perspectives and for the facilitation of flexibility in the face of novelty. More specifically, parents of higher social-class position should be more likely to encourage—explicitly or implicitly—a self-consciously "information-extraction" attitude toward television viewing and an emphasis on breadth and novelty in program selection, in the types of people and situations made accessible for observation through the medium, and in the kinds of material chosen for post-exposure "processing" (in chil-dren's television-based play, through reading, etc.).

Support for these propositions has come from a variety of sources. A positive association between social-class level and explicit parental use of television as an informational catalyst has been reported by Martin and

Benson (1970), Messaris, et al. (1982), and Messaris and Thomas (1981). The latter study also found some tentative evidence that parents and children of higher social-class level are more likely to have discussions with each other about unfamiliar (from the child's perspective) people or circumstances encountered on television. Consistent with these findings are the results of two studies indicating that middle-class children have a better understanding of other-class television characters or situations than working-class children do (Newcomb and Collins, 1979; DeFleur and DeFleur, 1967). Other relevant findings are described in a study by Sarett (1981), whose observations of children's television-related fantasy play indicate that the play of upper-middle-class children is more likely to elaborate on televised themes of exploration, encounter with novel situations, etc. With regard to this area of post-exposure "processing" of televised material, another source of relevant evidence is a study of Werner (1975), which indicates that parents of higher social-class level are more likely to promote their children's reading of books related to television programs. Finally, indirect evidence on these issues is also provided by the work of Chaffee, McLeod, and their associates, who, while not concerned with social class directly, found that the difference in parental values which Kohn had observed to be associated with class level is also associated with an information-vs.-entertainment dimension in the character of children's television-program preferences (Chaffee et al., 1971).

There seem to be several respects, then, in which parents of higher social-class level condition children to use television in ways more conducive to the broadening of intellectual perspective, to flexibility in the face of novelty, etc. If one accepts Kohn's general argument about the ultimate consequences of social-class differences of this sort in children's behavior, one can interpret these findings as indicating that certain social-class differences in parental behavior may lead children to use television in ways which contribute to the perpetuation of their class positions.

Whether or not this particular conclusion is justified, however, is not the crucial issue for present purposes. The primary aim of the preceding argument has been to illustrate one possible way in which intra-family processes might play a role in the *hypothetical* broader social process through which television contributes to social-structural continuity. In other words, the purpose of this section of the paper has been to argue for the potential importance of family processes with regard to the more "macro-social" effects of television, rather than simply with regard to the more "individual-level" effects discussed in the preceding two sections.

CONCLUSIONS

The central theme of this paper has been that the process through which television influences children's lives appears to include, as an inextricable component in most cases, the interaction between children and their parents. More specifically, it was argued that the "behavioral effects" which existing research has linked to television were almost certainly contingent on some degree of previous parental conditioning of the types of behavior in question; that a similar, though much weaker, case can be made with regard to television's alleged effects on children's beliefs; and, finally, that parental conditioning may be an important mechanism through which television's messages are "tailored" to suit the prescribed social roles of particular categories of young viewers. The implication is that research concerning television's effects on children may have to control for many more facets of a child's family background than is typically the case, troublesome and costly though this kind of procedure may be.

A further implication of this paper's argument concerns those people, both inside and outside the research community, whose primary interest in any discussion of children and television has to do with allocating blame and devising countermeasures for the medium's putative pernicious influence on the immature. As Liebert et al. (1977) have pointed out, variants of the kind of argument advanced above have occasionally been used by TV-industry apologists in efforts to transfer blame from the industry to parents themselves. In view of such polemics, it may be worth stressing the obvious point that parental behavior itself can hardly be immune to the broader social forces which also shape television in its capacity as a mass medium. This point should be taken as implicit in the preceding discussion of social-class differences. To restrict one's focus to the individual level—to blame individual parents, in other words, for the many ills that are more typically blamed on television—is merely to substitute one form of myopia for another.

REFERENCES

BANDURA, A. (1969). Social-learning theory of identificatory processes. *In* D.A. Goslin (Ed.), "Handbook of Socialization Theory and Research." Chicago, IL: Rand McNally.

BANDURA, A., ROSS D., and ROSS, S. (1963). Imitation of film-mediated aggressive models. *Journal of Abnormal and Social Psychology 66,* 3–11.

BROWN, J.R., and LINNE, O. (1976). The family as a mediator of television's effects. *In* R. Brown (Ed.), "Children and Television. Beverly Hills, CA: Sage.

CHAFFEE, S.H., MCLEOD, J.M., and ATKIN, C.K. (1971). Parental influences on adolescent media use. In F.G. Kline and P. Clarke (Eds.), "Mass Communications and Youth: Some Current Perspectives." Beverly Hills, CA: Sage.

COATES, B., PUSSER, H.E., and GOODMAN, I. (1976). The influence of "Sesame Street" and "Mister Rogers' Neighborhood" on children's behavior in the pre-school. *Child Development 47,* 138–144.

CORDER-BOLZ, C.R. (1980). Mediation: the role of significant others. *Journal of Communication 30* (No. 3), 106–118.

CORDER-BOLZ, C.R., and O'BRYANT, S. (1978). Can people affect television? Teacher vs. program. *Journal of Communication 28* (No. 1), 97–103.

DeFleur, M.L., and DeFleur, L.B. (1967). The relative contribution of television as a learning source for children's occupational knowledge. *American Sociology Review, 32,* 777–789.

Dominick, J.R., and Greenberg, B.S. (1972). Attitudes toward violence: The interaction of television exposure, family attitudes, and social class. *In* G.A. Comstock and E.A. Rubinstein (Eds.), "Television and Social Behavior, Vol. 3, Television and Adolescent Aggressiveness." Washington, DC: U.S. Government Printing Office, 1972, 314–335.

Doob, A.N., and MacDonald, G.E. (1979). Television viewing and fear of victimization: Is the relationship causal? *Journal of Personality and Social Psychology* 37, 170–179.

Friedrich, C.K., and Stein, A.H. (1973). Aggressive and prosocial television programs and the natural behavior of preschool children. *Monographs of the Society for Research in Child Development,* 38(No. 4). (Serial No. 151.)

Gerbner, G., Gross. L., Morgan, M., and Signorielli, N. (n.d.) "Television Viewing and Fear of Victimization: Specification or Spuriousness?" Philadelphia, PA: Annenberg School of Communications, University of Pennsylvania.

Gerbner, G., Gross, L., Morgan, M., and Signorielli, N. (1980a) The "mainstreaming" of America: Violence profile No. 11. *Journal of Communication 30,* (No. 3), 10–27.

Gerbner, G., Gross. L., Morgan, M., and Signorielli, N. (1980b) Some additional comments on cultivation analysis. *Public Opinion Quarterly 44,* 408–410.

Gerbner, G., Gross, L., Morgan, M., and Signorielli, N. (1981). A curious journey into the scary world of Paul Hirsch. *Communication Research 8,* 39–72.

Gerbner, G., Gross, L., Signorielli, N., Morgan, M., and Jackson-Beeck, M. 1979). The demonstration of power: Violence profile No. 10. *Journal of Communication 29* (No. 3), 177–196.

Gewirtz, J.L. (1969). Mechanisms of social learning: Some roles of stimulation and behavior in early human development. *In* D.A. Goslin (Ed.), "*Handbook of Socialization Theory and Research.*" Chicago, IL Rand McNally.

Greenberg, B.S., and Reeves, B. (1976). Children and the perceived reality of television. *Journal of Social Issues 32* (No. 4), 86–97.

Gross, L., and Morgan, M. (1980). Television and enculturation. *In* J. Dominick and J. Fletcher (Eds.), "Broadcasting Research Methods: A Reader. Boston, MA: Allyn Bacon.

Grusec, J.E. (1973). Effects of co-observer evaluations on imitation: A developmental study. *Developmental Psychology 8* (No.1), 141.

Hicks, D.J. (1968). Effects of co-observer's sanctions and adult presence on imitative aggression. *Child Development 39,* 303–309.

Hirsch, P. (1980). The "scary world" of the nonviewer and other anomalies: A reanalysis of Gerbner et al.'s findings on cultivation analysis, Part I. *Communication Research 7,* 403–456.

Hughes, M. (1980). The fruits of cultivation analysis: A reexamination of some effects of television watching. *Public Opinion Quarterly 44,* 287–302.

Hyman, H.H. (1966). The value systems of different classes: A social psychological contribution to the analysis of stratification. *In* R. Bendix and S.M. Lipset (Eds.), "Class, Status, and Power," 2nd ed., New York: Free Press.

Kohn, M.L. (1977). "Class and Conformity. A Study in Values," 2nd ed., Chicago, IL: University of Chicago Press.

Korzenny, F., Greenberg, B.S., and Atkin, C.K. (1979). Styles of parental disciplinary practices as a mediator of children's learning from antisocial television portrayals. *Communication Yearbook 3,* 283–293.

Liebert, R.M., and Baron, R.A. (1972). Short-term effects of televised aggression on children's aggressive behavior. *In* J.P. Murray, E.A. Rubinstein, and G.A. Comstock (Eds.), "Television and Social Behavior, Vol. 2, "Television and Social Learning." Washington, DC: U.S. Government Printing Office.

LIEBERT, R.M., COHEN, L.A., JOYCE, C., MURREL, S., NISONOFF, L. and SONNENSCHEIN, S. (1977). Effects of television: Predispositions revisited. *Journal of Communication 27* (No.3), 217–221.

LULL, J. (1980a). Family communication patterns and the social uses of television. *Communication Research 7*, 319–334.

LULL, J. (1980b). The social uses of television. *Human Communication Research 6*, 197–209.

MARTIN, C.A., and BENSON, L. (1970). Parental perceptions of the role of television in parent-child interaction. *Journal of Marriage and the Family 32*, 410–414.

MCLEOD, J.M., ATKIN, C.K., and CHAFFEE, S.H. (1972a). Adolescents, parents, and television use: Adolescent self-report from Maryland and Wisconsin samples. *In* G.A. Comstock and E.A. Rubinstein (Eds.), "Television and Social Behavior, Vol. 3, Television and Adolescent Aggressiveness." Washington, DC: U.S. Government Printing Office.

MCLEOD, J.M., ATKIN, C.K., and CHAFFEE, S.H. (1972b). Adolescents, parents, and television use: Self-report and other report measures from the Wisconsin sample. *In* G.A. Comstock and E.A. Rubinstein (Eds.), "Television and Social Behavior, Vol. 3, Television and Adolescent Aggressiveness." Washington, DC: U.S. Government Printing Office.

MESSARIS, P., KERR, D., and SOUDACK, A. (1982). "Social Class, Family Communication Patterns, and Mothers' TV-related Comments to Their Children." Paper presented to the International Communication Association, Boston.

MESSARIS, P., and THOMAS, S. (1981). "Social-Class Differences in Mother-Child Discussions about Television." Paper presented to the Speech Communication Association, Anaheim.

MESSARIS, P., and SARETT, C. (1981). On the consequences of television-related parent-child interaction. *Human Communication Research 7*, 226–244.

NEWCOMB, A.F., and COLLINS, W.A. (1979). Children's comprehension of family role portrayals in televised dramas: Effects of socioeconomic status, ethnicity, and age. *Developmental Psychology 15*, 417–423.

PARKE, R.D., BERKOWITZ, L., LEYENS, J.P., WEST, S.G., and SEBASTIAN, R.J. (1977). Some effects of violent and nonviolent movies on the behavior of juvenile delinquents. *Advances in Experimental Social Psychology 10*, 135–172.

PRASAD, V.K., RAO, T.R., and SHEIKH, A.A. (1978). Can people affect television? Mother vs. commercial, *Journal of Communication 28* (No. 1), 91–96.

SARETT, C. (1981). "Socialization Patterns and Preschool Children's Television and Film-Related Play Behavior." Unpublished dissertation, University of Pennsylvania.

SKINNER, B.F. (1953). "Science and Human Behavior." New York: Free Press.

SPRAFKIN, J.N., LIEBERT, R.M., and POULOS, R.W. (1975). Effects of a pro-social televised example on children's helping. *Journal of Experimental Child Psychology 20*, 119–126.

SPRAFKIN, J.N. and RUBINSTEIN, E.A. (1979). Children's television viewing habits and prosocial behavior: A field correlational study. *Journal of Broadcasting 23*, 265–276.

STEIN, A.H., and FRIEDRICH, L.K. (1972). Television content and young children's behavior. *In* J.P. Murray, E.A. Rubinstein, and G.A. Comstock (Eds.), "Television and Social Behavior, Vol. 2, Television and Social Learning." Washington, D.C: U.S. Government Printing Office.

WERNER, A. (1975) The effects of television on children and adolescents: A case of sex and class socialization. *Journal of Communication 25* (No.4), 45–50.

18

Television as an Acculturation Resource In the Third World: Mexico— A Case Study

Susan Christol
Department of Speech
University of California, Santa Barbara
Santa Barbara, California 93101

The mass media have frequently been accorded an important role in social change. Mass communication takes a variety of forms, and together form and content have the potential to function as powerful social-structuring forces. The first cave paintings, the early Mayan codices, the Gutenberg printing press, and today's electronic media have all altered the societies in which they developed. This century's media technology has revolutionized the process by which information is disseminated throughout the world.

Within the last 30 years, the relationship between communication and national development has attracted many scholars in communication, anthropology, economics, and sociology to study issues of concern related to the development of the Third World. Analyses have been conducted from various theoretical perspectives, with the level of analysis ranging from the macro to the micro social unit. Despite these studies, existing theoretical models remain problematic. As Merril (1976, p.187) points out, "We are still in a period of unsynthesized case studies, theoretical dialogue and splintered speculation about this whole area."

Most writers agree that the media do facilitate change in the less developed countries, although the *degree* to which this is true is undergoing reconsideration. Change in the context of development has often been regarded as a shift from traditional to modern society. Much difficulty has arisen in the determination of what modernization signifies. Depending on one's ideological framework, the march toward modernity may herald a better way of life for inhabitants of less-developed countries or, alternatively, can be viewed as a mechanism for the industrialized world to turn less-developed nations into suppliers of resources and consumers of modern goods.

This dichotomy of perspectives is clearly represented in the two major theoretical models of development which have evolved. The first is the dominant paradigm of modernization. The second, more recent theoretical framework is the dependency model, which many Latin American communication scholars advocate. Both models, according to Contreras et al. (1976, p.9) lack a firm data base. They note "the ecstacies and horrors of the global village have been considerably portrayed, but never thoroughly documented."

For the most part, the developing nation-state has served as the primary unit of research focus for writers from both perspectives. Those working out of the modernization paradigm have correllated the growth rates of a variety of interrelated factors like urbanization, literacy, industrialization, and mass-communication systems with national development. Dependency theorists have looked at the structure of communication systems in the LDC's in relationship to the global economic picture, and have analyzed the development process in light of the history of capitalist expansion.

Because the major emphasis of study has been on the communication systems rather than individual reception of messages, the degree of a nation's underdevelopment has been measured in quantifiable terms. Scales like UNESCO's minimal set of national media requirements in order to meet desired universal standards of development (10 copies of daily newspapers, 2 TV sets, 5 radio receivers, and 2 cinema seats for every 100 persons) are widely employed and illustrate this emphasis on system as opposed to *audience* study. Dependency critics frequently tabulate the extent of multinational holdings in domestic media institutions to support their position. It is increasingly becoming apparent to communication researchers (Contreras et al., 1976) that to more fully understand the impact of communication growth, the focus should shift to users of the media in order to complement studies done on the groups, institutions, and channels which create and disseminate the messages.

Additional concern has been voiced (Hur, 1981) about the lack of studies on unidirectional flow and its effects on communication growth in developing countries. A 1974 UNESCO study found the estimated ratio of communication flow between Western nations and the Third World was one hundred to one.

This concern is compounded by the knowledge that it is cheaper to import foreign programs than it is for developing nations to produce their own, thus effectively constraining growth of domestic television industry. Several writers have suggested that even when local programming becomes competitive, it merely copies imported counterparts, shaped by creators schooled in the conventions presented by imported models, and demanded by audiences weaned on imported products (Elliot and Golding, 1974; Contreras et al, 1976; Beltran, 1979).

The effects of cross-cultural broadcasting can only remain speculative until comprehensive research has been done which investigates how members of one culture accommodate the messages created in a differing cultural context.

Recent inquiry into the existing theoretical models of communication and development and an increased role for Third World scholars has led a variety of writers (Galjart, 1971; Beltran, 1976; Bordennave, 1976; Ganju, 1981) to identify socio-economic status as a crucial variable in understanding the effects of mass-media consumption in the developmental context. Increasingly, the simplistic belief that communications alone can bring about attitudinal and behavioral change, regardless of socio-economic and political conditions, is being challenged.

This discussion illustrates the complex and diverse nature of the issues that surround communication and development as an area of study. Unquestionably, the mass media disseminate new information into traditional societies. It is also clear that the effects are inextricably grounded in social, economic, and cultural structure. This study investigates a single mass medium, television, in the acculturation process. Conceptually, development and acculturation are necessarily linked because development and modernization have become synonymous, with modernization commonly defined in terms of Western (particularly American) goals, values, and standards. Acculturation has been defined as "the study of cultural transmission in process" (Herskovits, 1951, p.525) and essentially is the socialization of a member of one culture into the social values, norms, roles of another culture as a result of prolonged contact. This process may occur intranationally, as in the case of immigrants, or internationally, where one nation/culture adopts aspects of another.

To date, virtually all research studies investigating acculturation via the media have shared a common research method, the survey questionnaire. This has allowed the researchers to study large samples, and, perhaps, feel more secure about the generalizability of their findings. However, it has not permitted an examination of the nature of the acculturation process, or analysis of contextual forces at work during an individual's reception and construction of meaning from messages received.

One area of theoretical concern, patterns of consumption, has been shown to covary with levels of acculturation (Goode, 1963) and has also been related to television use and exposure (Beltran, 1979; Cardonna, 1976; Wells, 1972). Shifts in consumption patterns in the less developed countries as a result of the importation of messages and products from the industrialized world have generated a great deal of controversy. Concern has been voiced that consumerist messages may be more successful in persuading people to drink Coca Cola than educational broadcasts are in bringing about the adoption of more positive nutritional practices (McAnany, 1980). Shore (1980) points to the distinction between implicit and explicit commercial media content, the implicit message for audience members in the LDC's often being that the purchase of advertised goods is more "modern" and therefore better.

This study uses an ethnographic methodology to investigate the *process* by which acculturation, particularly along the dimension of consumption patterns, is taking place via television exposure. Because observational studies provide insight into a wide range of behavior and attitudes, issues like familial roles, age, and attitudes toward the U.S. which have also been shown to relate to media and acculturation (Coldevin, 1979; Christol, 1981; Kahl, 1968; Tharp et al., 1968) will be addressed briefly in the study as well.

Through observation and interviews with low income and middle income families in the southern Mexican town of San Cristobal de las Casas, Chiapas, the study uncovers, in a natural setting, some basic issues related to the question of how social class mediates television messages in a developmental context. Ganju (1981, p.12) has written "The mass media by themselves cannot bring about change which requires certain resources, facilities and conditions." If this is the case, the question remains to what extent social class context influences the way in which television content is processed.

For some time, mass-communication research in the developed countries has pointed to a model of media influence stressing limited and indirect effects (Klapper, 1960). Interpersonal communication channels have been ascribed a more direct role in bringing about attitude and behavior change (Katz and Lazarsfeld, 1955; Schram, 1973). The relationship between mass communication and interpersonal communication channels has formed the basis of much communication research. Schram (1973) concludes that the mass media function to direct attention and stimulate interpersonal discussion. The work of development communication researchers (Rogers, 1973) tends to support the primacy of interpersonal communication over the media in diffusing innovations and affecting the adoption of them. However, as Korzenny et al. (1981, p.2) point out, "It is the interaction between exposure to external communication channels and internal system connectedness which account for the power of interpersonal channels." In a development context, where access to new information is particularly limited, the importance of looking at the interaction of mass media and interpersonal communication networks seems clear.

The uses and gratification paradigm of mass communication asserts that individual needs, both social and psychological, determine media use patterns and responses to content (Blumler, 1979; Katz et al., 1974) Integral to this paradigm is the concept of the active audience, which assumes that the media behavior of individuals is purposeful and that varying degrees of utility, intentionality, selectivity, and imperviousness to influence are at work. One might suppose that an individual's cultural identity, personality, and the social (and situational) context of viewing, would predispose how that individual uses television.

Communication scholars have found that television is used by individuals as a social resource, a medium which has the potential to gratify needs. Lull (1980a, p.5) suggests that "TV and other mass media, rarely mentioned as vital sources in the construction or maintenance of interpersonal relations, can be seen to play a central role in the methods which families and other social units employ to purposefully interact within their own special realities." Other writers providing an institutional analysis have identified the mass media as powerful social-structuring forces. Schiller (1976, p.3) has written that mass communication "defines social reality and thus influences the organization of work, the character of technology, the curriculum of the education system, and the use of free time—actually the basic social arrangements of living." If we assume television in some ways has the power to structure society, and if individuals actively use it as a social resource, this leads to an interesting question. Do the ways individuals gratify needs change as a result of exposure to a differing cultural "grammar of gratification"?

Gerbner's conceptualization of cultural indicators has implications for cross-cultural broadcasting that are useful. Building theory which is grounded in empirical data (Gerbner et al., 1973, p.565) he asserts that symbolic messages transmitted through television provide the viewer with cultural indicators which collectively cultivate notions about "What is? (public assumptions about existence), What is important? (context of priorities), What is right? (point of view, values) and What is related to what? (structure of associations between individuals and things)." When two cultures share different perceptions about what is important, right, etc., might not television exposure to differing or even contrary values change or modify in some way the receiving culture's norms?

Pingree and Hawkins (1981, p.77) write that "one of the most promising approaches to studying the influence of television on culture starts with the hypothesis that information learned from the mass media is incorporated into individual's conceptions of social reality, and presumably guides further learning and behavior." This assumption guides the line of inquiry of the present study.

Traditional empirical studies (Deutschman, 1961; Inkeles and Smith, 1974; Kahl, 1968; Lerner, 1958; Rogers, 1965) that consider the media's role in development have not distinguished between domestic and imported media sources nor between various media forms. A limited number of studies, however, have recently focused on the television medium and have looked specifically at the influence of imported programming. That this type of research has occurred only lately is in part due to the fact that television is a recent arrival in most less-developed countries, and has not achieved widespread penetration. Imported programming effects are a natural source of investigation because American programs form the bulk of Third World television broadcasting (Nordenstreng and Varis, 1974).

Other important reasons exist for focusing on the television medium. It has been suggested (Korzenny et al, 1980) that radio, as a verbal medium, may be more likely to generate discussion among viewers in a social context than do the print media. It seems reasonable that this assumption holds for TV as well. Like radio, television participation does not require literacy on the part of the viewer. Unlike radio, television provides visual imagery; modes of behavior, character roles, details of dress. Ways of living are precisely articulated by program creators. Critics and advocates of TV's role in the Third World concur that it provides images of an alien world unlike any other mass medium.

Hornik's (1977) three year panel study of El Salvadoran junior high school students examines the relationship between hours of media exposure (TV, radio, newspapers, magazines, cinema) and media ownership (TV, radio, magazines) to educational aspirations, occupational aspirations, and openness to change. He found the television ownership and exposure variable to be more useful than the other media variables because of television's novelty, and because its content presented an image of the world most unlike the recipients' own. Increased television exposure was related to increased educational and occupational aspirations and decreased desire for urban life. The author notes that junior high students are a special sample of the population, and refrains from generalizing to a broader group.

Especially important for the present study is Hornik's theoretical synthesis of the active, selectively perceptive audience model with the model which ascribes to the mass media a social-structuring capacity (maintaining the status quo or offering a new one). He interprets his findings as indicative of the audience's ability to reject messages inconsistent with their perceived reality, but also asserts that new aspirations will be fostered by exposure to television content when an individual's environment can reinforce and support such expectations (Hornik, 1977, p. 387). He uses his support of the active audience model to challenge Lerner's (1958) widely accepted theory of a "revolution of rising frustrations," where wants generated by the media outstrip the means to supply them.

Another study of television effects done in a development context is Coldevin's (1979) analysis of "electronic colonialism" in the Canadian Arctic. Coldevin studied an Eskimo community which had received regular Canadian Broadcasting Company programming via satellite for two and a half years. Normal fare—*Cannon, Police Story, Six Million Dollar Man*, etc.— with only one weekly Eskimo program. Coldevin compared the extent of traditional cultural replacement among the community's adult and adolescent population, and among visiting settlement students from media-isolated areas. The subjects' responses to questions on the following dimensions served as indicators of the extent of acculturation: television exposure patterns, most and least preferred programs, national unit information, international and national issue identification, travel aspirations and preferred employment locations, and predominant leisure time activities. The findings showed the "TV town" adolescents demonstrated a higher acculturation profile than the settlement students, and both adolescent groups scored higher on acculturation levels than did the "TV town" adults. The author concludes "television represented a major foreign acculturation agent injected into an emergent transitional society." (Coldevin, 1979, p.116).

Several cross-cultural broadcasting studies conducted in developed nations have also pointed to a significant role for television as an agent of change. Tsai (1970) looked at the effects of American television programs on the attitudes of Formosan children. The relationship between specific cultural values and television habits was investigated. A measurement instrument was developed based upon the work of Kluckhorn and Strodtbeck (1961, p. 231), who hypothesized that there are five problems considered fundamental to all human groups: "1) what is the character of innate human nature? 2) what is the relation of man to nature (and supernature)? 3) what is the temporal focus of human life? 4) what is the modality of human activity? 5) what is the modality of man's relationship to other men?" In some ways these are reminiscent of Gerbner's cultural indicators. Tsai's questionnaire posed questions which assumed that there are value orientations to Kluckhohn's typology that are culturally specific, and that "if they could be measured the result would constitute an index of the fundamental attitudes of the culture."

His population consisted of 160 Formosan 12-year-olds, half of whom had been exposed to American TV programming for 2 years, and half of whom had not been exposed. Tsai found no significant difference between fundamental value orientations of the two groups. However, specific attitudes to items, like preference for travel locations, American clothing, and music, did correlate significantly with American program viewing. He suggests that there may be several reasons for the lack of significant value change findings. First, the TV-viewing subjects may not have been exposed to American programming long enough for it to affect change. Second, the measurement instrument may not have tapped the construct of value change effectively.

Pingree and Hawkins (1981) found that Australian children's viewing of American programs contributed more to their conceptions of social reality (especially in terms of violence and meanness) than did local or other imported programs. Barnett and McPhail (1979) investigated the effects of American television on Canadian national identity and found frequency of American TV viewing clearly related to individuals' national identity orientations. The more U.S. programming viewed by Canadians, the less they perceived of themselves as Canadian and the more they perceived of themselves as Americans.

Not all cross-cultural broadcasting studies demonstrate American program viewing has effects on foreign populations. Sparkes (1977) found little attitudinal difference on the part of Canadian viewers watching televised American news programs. According to Payne (1978), U.S. program viewing contributes minimally to Icelandic children's perceptions and attitudes regarding the U.S. As Hur (1981) notes, the inconsistency in the findings of cross-cultural broadcasting studies may be the result of a variety of factors, including population sampling, reliability and validity of effects measures, and differences among foreign populations. It should also be noted that the studies look at effects along different dimensions, some of which may be subject to influence more than others. The preponderence of surveys as a methodological tool, and the fact that inconsistent findings are possibly due to measurement problems, points to the need for other methodological approaches in the area of cross-cultural broadcasting. One of the key interests of this researcher is the *process* involved in acculturation via television; thus an observational study of two families, augmented by a survey of a larger sample of the population, forms the basis for this work.

Because this is an exploratory field study, the results will be discussed in a non-hypothesis testing manner. Instead, the following research questions guided the inquiry:

(1) How do family members of differing social class *perceive* the culture-laden television messages they receive through cross-cultural broadcasting?

(2) How do family members of differing social class *use* the messages they receive?

(3) Is there a convergence of imported values, or is social class differentially mediating the message?

(4) How do interpersonal communication channels work together with television to facilitate acculturation?

(5) Do low income "no TV" families, low income "TV" families and middle income "TV" families demonstrate similar or dissimilar consumption patterns and attitudes?

The family was chosen as the unit for observational analysis for several reasons. Deutschman's (1973, p.34) study of mass media use in a Columbian village led him to suggest looking at the family unit as "receiver," rather than the individual, because media messages could be received by one family member and then passed along through interpersonal channels to other members, "thus raising the knowledge of all." Various ethnographers (Anderson et al., 1979; Frazer and Reid (In press); Reid, 1979; Lewis, 1959, 1965; Lull, 1976, 1980a, 1980b), have also done family studies. The ethnographic method lends itself well to family studies because, as Lull (1980b, p.3) states, "the family, television's primary audience, is a natural unit for this kind of analysis. Through ethnographic inquiry, the researcher can study actual communicative contexts and ways in which media experiences enter the lives of family members." Since the family institution is recognized as a powerful socializing agent and provides a micro-social unit, including members of different sexes and age groups, it seems logical to look at the family as a unit, as well as at individual family members, when investigating the acculturation process.

RESEARCH SETTING

The data was collected during a three week period in the town of San Cristobal de las Casas, Chiapas, Mexico. San Cristobal (pop. 40,000) and its environs have a very low standard of living compared with Mexico as a whole. The region's remoteness and mountainous topography, together with its large indigenous Indian population, have impeded its entry into mainstream development. There is no industry in San Cristobal, and the town functions as a marketing center for the surrounding agricultural area. Although television broadcasts began as early as 1950 in the more developed regions of Mexico, San Cristobal did not receive television broadcasts until 1967.

The town has a small commercial center surrounding the main plaza, an extensive open market area, and is divided into various barrios (neighborhoods), each grouped around a church. The barrios are well-demarcated both socially and economically, and each tends to contain a population which is homogeneous in both income and status.

METHOD

The survey was conducted in the week prior to the observational period. The interview respondants were female heads of household selected randomly from each of 10 of the city's barrios. Females only were interviewed for the following reasons: as a control for sex differences, because women tend to be the primary purchasers of low cost goods, and because changes in women's roles along the traditional-modern continuum are more dramatic than men's.

Survey data was collected for three groups: lower-class TV families, middle-class TV families, and non-TV families. The non-TV group is collapsed (lower and middle class), because it was assumed few middle-class families could be located that do not possess a television. Ten respondents from each of the three groups were interviewed with interviews lasting approximately one hour.

Local informants provided the initial contact with television-owning families who indicated a willingness to participate in an observational study. The observation was described as part of a study on different families and their communication patterns. High-income families were excluded because it was assumed that families of this status are fully modern. Two families were selected as representative of lower-class and middle-class status based upon indicators suggested by Castro, et al. (1980) and verified by local sources.

The lower-class family had eight family members residing in a three-room house, and lodging for the researcher could not be realistically provided. For this reason, the researcher resided for two weeks with the middle-class family, the Cuevas. The first week was spent observing and participating in family activities in the Cuevas household. The second week, the researcher went to the home of the lower-class family (Ramirez) each morning and left each evening at bedtime. Family members in both households were directed to behave as they normally would, and not to vary their behavior or schedules. During the first day, family histories, demographic information, and descriptions of the physical environment were recorded in written form. Family members thus became accustomed to note taking, which was done as unobtrusively as possible. On the final day of the two week period the female head of household in each family was administered the same questionnaire used in the survey, to gain comparative data. All family members were asked the extent to which the researcher's presence altered their behavior or that of others during the stay, and were debriefed as to the actual intent of the study.

FINDINGS AND DISCUSSION

A thorough analysis of the data collected is presently being conducted. Statistical analyses have not been completed. However, a preliminary analysis of the ethnographic data and descriptive information provided in the responses to open-ended questions posed in the interviews point to the emergence of some well-defined trends.

The observational data suggest an appreciable difference in the television exposure patterns of the two families. These differences are no doubt partially due to differences in their daily schedules. A manual laborer, Carlos Ramirez (40) leaves the house early each morning, returning by six or seven in the evening. His wife Rosa (34) spends her days cooking, cleaning, washing clothes, shopping, and caring for her new baby and her other five children (aged 3, 5, 6, 10, 12). The Ramirez family's TV viewing habits are as rigorously structured as their daily schedules. Their black and white television set, located in the living room (doubling as parents and baby's bedroom), was not turned on in the evenings until Carlos returned home. On four of the seven afternoons observed, the children watched cartoons, a children's program, and *Happy Days* before dinner. No viewing occurred at dinner time, when the family ate and conversed. Evening viewing was composed of telenovellas (soap operas) and Mexican variety shows. Carlos occasionally stayed up to watch the news at ten but the family did not watch the American programming that followed. Rosa told me that they did not watch American programs because they were too difficult to understand. This notion was frequently expressed by other lower-class women. Often illiterate, lower-class men and women found subtitled programs problematic, but they expressed difficulty even with dubbed shows. The Ramirez family watched TV an average of four hours a day.

The Cuevas, on the other hand, watched considerably more television. They owned two portable sets that often accompanied family members into different rooms. Unlike the Ramirezes, who generally viewed as a family unit, the Cuevas demonstrated more individual viewing. Roberto Cueva (50) is a truck driver for a government-controlled company. He is on the road for several days at a time, and at home for similar intervals. TV viewing in the Cueva household began as early as 11 a.m. and as late as 4 p.m., the average number of viewing hours was 7½ during my stay. The set(s) were generally turned on by Roberto, his son Ricardo (29), or the two younger children, Antonia (7) and Miguel (4), although Angela (49) and her older daughters (27, 25, 24, 22, 19) frequently joined the viewing. An extended family situation, (Miguel and a 6-month-old baby were children of two of the daughters), 11 family members resided in the Cueva's six-room home.

There is only one TV channel received in San Cristobal. The Cuevas watched TV fairly consistently throughout the day, often at dinner time, and usually until twelve or one at night. Unlike the Ramirezes, they made a point of watching the American programming available to them, and on several occasions told me I was lucky to be able to watch "good" TV all the time.

The survey data supports the observation that middle-class families watch more TV than do lower-class families. This is quite possibly because middle-class families have more leisure time, more convenience items like cars, washing machines, etc., and have to spend less time engaged in subsistance and daily living chores. The concept of *time* and the amount of it available to watch television consistently surfaced in the interview data. Lower-class women frequently mentioned that they didn't have the time to watch television. After his wife's interview, one man commented that "the people on TV don't ever work, they just sit around. Their life is better than ours."

The survey also supports the observation that men in both groups watch more TV than do their wives. Children, not surprisingly, are the heaviest viewers in both groups.

As well as differences in exposure patterns, the families differed some-what in their *use* of televised content. In both the observed families and in interview responses, the lower-class individuals indicated they primarily used television as a learning instrument—a source of new information. Middle-class viewers reported using TV more for entertainment than learning. Of course middle-class individuals have greater access to additional sources of information than do lower-class individuals. However, middle-class individuals watch more news and public affairs programming than do lower-class families. This suggests that self-assessed use of television for either learning or entertainment does not necessarily coincide with what might be assumed entertainment vs. informational program selection.

The ethnographic data clearly suggests learning from television content is occurring in both groups. Children in both families were observed mouthing the words of frequently shown commercials, repeating phrases uttered by characters on the screen, and singing along with songs and jingles. They were familiar with various cartoon characters, knew their names, roles in the storyline, and their appropriate behavior. *Happy Days* was on every day at 5p.m., and the older boys, particularly in the Ramirez family, would often mimic behavior (dancing, fighting) portrayed in the show. TV referents appeared in behavior outside of the televiewing context as well. In a game of catch with some friends, Antonia labeled her friend "Mujer Bionica" (Bionic Woman) after a noteworthy throw.

Adults also appeared to be actively engaged in learning from TV. Quite often television content prompted discussions when new information was transmitted. Ricardo was observed instructing his younger cousin in how to obtain and use a credit card, after being cued by a "Bancomer—Symbol of the new generation" commercial. In the same interaction where the two men were watching an American football game, they read aloud and identified sponsors whose signs were placed alongside the playing field. Ricardo's cousin was able to demonstrate knowledge of consumer items by citing products supplied by the various companies. Ricardo in turn proceeded to identify car makes and models that appeared on the screen. It seems apparent that this kind of knowledge was valued. The exchange between the cousins did not escape Miguel and Antonia, who in a later viewing context began identifying objects aloud in a similar fashion.

Such obvious learning was not as clearly evidenced among the parents in the Ramirez family. The novellas they watched were more likely to prompt comments related to the plot, and behavior of the characters. *Las Tandas del Treize*, a variety show, elicited comments about the quality of singing, how pretty the set was, and how accomplished the dance numbers were. Quite frequently songs on this program were sung in English, but no translations were ventured or phrases repeated. This contrasts the repetition of phrases like instant replay, touchdown, and playoff and discussion of their meaning by Ricardo and his cousin while watching the American football game.

One of the interview questions asks if individuals think having material possessions brings happiness, or if happiness depends on other things. Responses from middle-class individuals indicated they saw the acquisition of things like cars, stoves, and refrigerators as indispensible and necessary for a happy life. Lower-class respondants tended to cite health, family togetherness, etc., as most important for happiness. This finding seems to reinforce Hornik's refutation of Lerner's "Revolution of Rising Frustrations" hypothesis by suggesting that instead of individuals' wants outstripping their means, they ignore those messages they cannot act upon. It seems possible that the light American program viewing by the lower-class families is in some ways a rejection of a lifestyle seen as unobtainable. Middle-class families, on the other hand, clearly have aspirations which coincide with the world portrayed through American television.

Attempting to ascertain views towards traditional versus modern sex roles, one interview question asked whether married women should be able to work outside the home. All of the middle-class respondents answered yes, and comments such as "both should work to get ahead and have a better life" are typical. The majority of lower-class TV respondents also answered this question affirmatively, but the non-TV wives overwhelmingly thought a woman's place is in the home. Further interpretation of the data is necessary, but it is possible that while "modern" consumer information and patterns are processed and adopted, based on the individual's ability to buy, value changes, like that of women's roles (which are not directly linked to financial status) may be more susceptible to influence regardless of social class. However, sex role identity may be a unique case.

In one interaction, two of the Cueva daughters and a friend were watching a *Happy Days* episode about dating. They remarked on the freedom American girls have in such contexts. They asserted that this system was much better than theirs. One lower-class woman commented that Mexican women should use the American women seen on TV as positive examples of independence and self-reliance.

This discussion constitutes a preliminary analysis of the collected data. However, it seems to suggest that the study may shed some light on the processes by which individuals use television as an acculturation resource.

REFERENCES

ANDERSON, J.A., TRAUDT, P., ACKER, S., MEYER, T., and DONOHUE, T. (1979). "An Ethnological Approach to a Study of Televiewing Settings." (Paper presented to the Western Speech Communication Association, Los Angeles, CA.)

BARNETT, G.A., and MCPHAIL, T.L. (1979). "Media/Cultural Imperialism: The Effects of U.S.

TV on Canadian Identity." (Paper presented at the International Communication Association, Philadelphia, PA.)

BELTRAN, L.R. (1976). Alien premises, objects, and methods in Latin American communication research. *Communication Research 3*, 197–234.

BELTRAN, L.R. (1979). TV etchings in the minds of Latin Americans: Conservatism, materialism, and conformism. *Gazette 24* (No. 1), 61–85.

BLUMLER, J.G. (1979). The role of theory in uses and gratifications studies. *Communication Research 6*, 9–36.

BORDENAVE, J. (1976). Communication of agricultural innovations in Latin America: The need for new models. *Communication Research 3*, 135–154.

CARDONNA, E.DE. (1975). Multinational television. *Journal of Communication 25* (No. 2), 122–127.

CASTRO, B., HAKANSSON, J., and BROKENSHA, D. (1980). "Indicators of Rural Inequality." Unpublished manuscript, University of California, Santa Barbara.

CHRISTOL, S. (1981). Television and the acculturation process: An ethnographic investigation. (Paper presented at the Western Speech Communication Association, San Jose, CA.)

COLDEVIN, G. (1979). Satellite television and cultural replacement among Canadian eskimos—adults and adolescents compared. *Communication Research 2*, 115–133.

CONTRERAS, E., LARSON, J., MAYO, J.K., and SPAIN, P. (1976). "Cross-Cultural Broadcasting." Paris: UNESCO. (Reports and Papers on Mass Communications, No. 77.)

DEUTSCHMANN, P. (1973). The mass media in an underdeveloped village. *Journalism Quarterly 40*, 27–35.

ELLIOT, P., and GOLDING, P. (1974). Mass communication and social change: The imagery of development and the development of imagery. *In* E. de Kadt and G. Williams (Eds.), "Sociology and Development," pp. 229–254. London: Tavistock Publications.

FRAZER, C.F., and REID, L. (In press). Children's interaction with commercials. *Symbolic Interactionism*.

GALJART, B. (1971). Rural development and sociological concepts: A critique. *Rural Sociology 36*, 31–41.

GANJU, V. (1981). "Communication and Development: 'Context' as a Critical Element in the New Paradigm." (Paper presented at the International Communication Association, Minneapolis, MN.)

GERBNER, G., GROSS, L.P., and MELODY, W.H. (1973). Toward cultural indicators: The analysis of mass mediated public message systems. *In* G. GERBER, L.P. GROSS, and W.H. MELODY (Eds.), "Communication Technology and Social Policy: Understanding the New Cultural Revolution." New York: John Wiley and Sons.

GOODE, W.J. (1963). "World Revolutions and Family Patterns." London: Free Press of Glencoe.

HERSKOVITS, M. (1951). "Man and His Works." New York: Alfred A. Knopf.

HORNIK, R. (1977). Mass media use and the "revolution of rising frustrations:" A reconsideration of the theory. *Communication Research 4*, 387–414.

HUR, K. K. (1981). "The Cultural Impact of Television Entertainment about the 'Other Culture.'" (Paper presented to the San Diego Conference on Culture and Communication, San Diego, CA.)

INKELES, A., and SMITH, D.H. (1974). "Becoming Modern: Individual Change in Six Developing Countries." Cambridge, MA: Harvard University Press.

KAHL, J. (1968). "The Measurement of Modernism." Austin, TX: University of Texas Press.

KATZ, E., BLUMLER, J.G., and GUREVITCH, M. (1974). Utilization of the mass media by the individual. *In* J.G. BLUMLER and E. KATZ (Eds.), "The Uses of Mass Communication: Current Perspectives on Gratification Research." Beverly Hills, CA: Sage.

KATZ, E. and LAZARSFELD, P.F. (1955). "Personal Influence: The Part Played by People in the Flow of Mass Communications." Glencoe, IL: Free Press.

KLAPPER, J.T. (1960). "The Effects of Mass Communication." Glencoe, IL: Free Press.

KLUCKHOHN, F.R., and STRODTBECK, F.L. (1961). "Variations in Value Orientations." Elmsford, NY: Row Peterson.

KORZENNY, F. ARMSTRONG, G.B., and GALVAN, T. (1980). "Mass Communication, Cosmopolite Channels, and Family Planning Knowledge, Attitudes and Practice among Rural Villagers in Mexico." (Paper presented at the International Communication Association, Acapulco, Mexico.)

LERNER, D. (1958). "The Passing of Traditional Society." Glencoe, IL: Free Press.

LEWIS, O. (1959). "Five Families." New York: Basic Books.

LEWIS, O. (1965). "La Vida." New York: Random House.

LULL, J.T. (1976). "Mass Media and Family Communication: An Ethnography of Audience Behavior." Unpublished dissertation, University of Wisconsin, Madison.

LULL, J.T. (1980a). Family communication patterns and the soical uses of television. *Communication Research 7*, 319–334.

LULL, J.T. (1980b). The social use of television. *Human Communication Research 6*, 197–209.

MCANANY, E. (Ed.) (1980). "Communications in the Rural Third World." New York: Praeger.

MERRIL, J.C. (1976). Media and national development. In H.D. Fischer and J.C. Merril (Eds.), "International and Intercultural Communication." New York: Hastings House.

NORDENSTRENG, K., and VARIS, T. (1974). "Television Traffic—A One-Way Street." Paris: UNESCO. (Reports and Papers on Mass Communications, No. 70.)

PAYNE, D.E. (1978). "U.S. TV in Iceland: A Synthesis of Studies." (Paper presented to the International Communication Association, Chicago, IL.)

PINGREE, S., and HAWKINS, R. (1981). U.S. programs on Australian television: The cultivation effect. *Journal of Communication 31* (No. 1), 97–105.

REID, L.N. (1979). Viewing rules as mediating factors of children's responses to commercials. *Journal of Broadcasting 23*, 15–26.

ROGERS, E.M. (1965). Mass media exposure and modernization among Columbian peasants. *Public Opinion Quarterly 29*, 614–625.

ROGERS, E.M. (1973). "Communication Strategies for Family Planning." Glencoe, IL: Free Press.

SCHILLER, H.I. (1976). "Communication and Cultural Domination." White Plains, NY: International Arts and Sciences Press.

SCHRAMM, W. (1973). Channels and audiences. In I. de Sola Pool, F.W. Frey, W. Schramm, N. Macoby, and E.B. Parker (Eds.), "Handbook of Communication," pp. 116–140. Chicago, IL: Rand McNally.

SHORE, L. (1980). Mass media for development: A reexamination of access, exposure, and impact. In E. McAnany (Ed.), "Communication in the Rural Third World." New York: Praeger.

SPARKES, V. (1977). TV across the Candian border: Does it really matter? *Journal of Communication 27* (No. 4), 40–47.

THARP, R.G., MEADOW, A., LENNHOFF, S.G., and SALLERFIELD, D. (1968). Changes in marriage roles accompanying the acculturation of the Mexican-American wife. *Journal of Marriage and the Family 30*, 404–412.

TSAI, M.K. (1970). Some effects of American television programs on children in Formosa. *Journal of Broadcasting 14*, 229–238.

WELLS, A. (1972). "Picture-tube Imperialism? The Impact of U.S. Television on Latin America." New York: Orbis.

19

The Role of the Mass Media And Other Socialization Agents In The Identity Formation of Gay Males

SEAN O'NEIL
Annenberg School of Communication
University of Pennsylvania
Philadelphia, Pennsylvania 19104

Homosexuality is a subject largely ignored by our cultural institutions. When socializing agents do address it, the messages are usually negative. When an individual is experiencing homosexual feelings, the meaning attached to such thoughts must be defined through interaction with his or her environment. A self-label can not be applied until some conception of homosexuality is (a) appropriate to the respondent's feelings and experiences and (b) at least partially acknowledged by the respondent's environment.

The possibility that the mass media influence our view of the world—that is, teach values, expectations, and especially norms of behavior—has inspired a variety of attempts to identify and measure the consequences of symbolic messages. (cf., Gerbner and Gross, 1975; Schwartz-MacDonald, 1977) The specific case of homosexuality should be particularly illustrative of the media's socializing powers, as so few other agents address the lifestyle.

This study explores, through interviews with male homosexuals, the ways in which the mass media and other agents of socialization affect their (a) notions or conceptions of homosexuality, (b) feelings or suspicions of their own homosexuality, (c) actual relevant experiences, and (d) eventual self-labeling as "gay." Unfortunately, the sample is atypically well-educated, middle class, and white, so care must be taken when generalizing from the data. However, the examination does elaborate upon the ways that people assess their beliefs and actions, and ultimately attach some meaning and label to them.

Sample and Interviewing Instrument

Forty gay, male respondents were recruited for this study, either through the individual contacts or through gay organizations. The sample was evenly divided between men under 25 years of age and those over 40. As noted earlier, the sample was predominantly white (37 subjects), well-educated (75% having at least an undergraduate degree), and middle class (80% middle or upper-middle, 20% working class.) Although other demographic data were recorded, the sample's general homogeneity probably caused there to be no real differentiating patterns on the basis of religion, SES, area of origin, or education. A pilot study yielded a flexible (open-ended) interview format.

MASS MEDIA USAGE

Thirty seven of the forty respondents (92.5%) recalled encountering mass-mediated messages during sexual identity formation. Sixty percent of the older group and 70% of the younger group recalled actually seeking mass-mediated messages. The older group sought information almost as much as the younger group, although messages were less frequently available.

The actual *existence* of relevant messages proved more important than the specific medium of origin or the content itself. The general lack of relevant messages in other socializing agents affected this pattern of citing any and all discovered messages, whether they were read in a book, seen on television, portrayed as fiction, or a written medical diagnosis.

The media which were attended to most frequently were, in order, books for both groups, erotic/pornographic books, magazines or newspapers for both groups, legitimate newspapers for both groups, magazines and television for the younger group only, movies and theatre for both groups, and finally, gay-oriented media (books, newspapers, and magazines) for the younger group only.

Conventional methods for seeking information in our society, especially with such a taboo subject, explain the popularity and feasibility of such anonymous and available media as books and newspapers, which would not incriminate the respondents. The older respondents, in particular, were effected in their information-seeking in that mainstream medium (e.g. television) and specialized media (e.g., gay magazines) were either not available or amenable to any publicity regarding homosexuality.

The messages that *were* found were viewed as predominantly "negative," with 72.5% of the sample (both young and older) recalling such content. Erotic messages were encountered by 55% of the sample (again, equally distributed among younger and older respondents). Mixed messages (e.g., a "negative" message that still proved helpful in reducing the respondent's feelings of isolation) were encountered by 7 of the younger respondents and 3 of the older respondents. Neutral but relevant messages were encountered by 4 of the younger group and 5 of the older group. Lastly, 8 younger and 4 older respondents met with totally positive messages, and these messages proved instrumental in an earlier application of the label "homosexual."

The role of the media as well as other socializing agents is summarized in the next four sections:

NOTIONS

General notions about homosexuality actually began when the typical social forces in the respondents' lives (e.g., school, friends, family) began publicly defining heterosexuality as the only legitimate lifestyle. The lack of options in sexual behavior was clearly outlined, verbally and nonverbally, by all message channels, but most particularly by family and peers.

When initial feelings of homosexuality surfaced, half of the older group had little or no means of relating their thoughts to this label, while all of the younger respondents were able to relate their ideas to this concept. Most members of the older group first conceptualized homosexuality in terms of the effeminate, limpwristed stereotype. While the majority of the younger respondents also began with the stereotypical image, 8 younger respondents *did* remember starting with a more clinical definition of homosexuals as men who have sex with or love other men.

FEELINGS

These initial notions (as described above) were generally negative and, interestingly, were not usually related by respondents to their initial feelings and experiences. Therefore, the amount of time between initial homosexual feelings and/or experiences and self-labeling as gay averaged a relatively lengthy eight years.

Initial feelings surfaced for both age groups at approximately age 13. The origin of such feelings was largely due to sexual arousal during social interaction with peers. During adolescence, all of the respondents recalled pressure for developing romantic interests in girls. As these messages continued, the newly-recognized homosexual feelings evoked considerable anxiety and questions about their origin, meaning, and consequences.

The assessed femininity of the respondent by himself and his environment did not seem to affect the timing of self-labeling. Forty-five percent of the older group and 60% of the younger group remember being subjected to derogatory comments, but still, these respondents did not apply the homosexual label to themselves any earlier than the others; however, those respondents who had been taunted did tend to consider their femininity as "one more difference" from their peers, whereas the respondents who were not so singled out actually recalled a greater need to explain their feelings of "difference." Of the total sample, however, 83.5% recalled derogatory comments about others during this time period and definitely recognized an intense aversion by their environment to "sissies," "faggots," and "queers."

The majority of respondents tended to feel guilty because of their feelings, and both age groups understood that such thoughts should be hidden. Many of the older respondents understood their feelings as pathological, whereas many of the younger respondents had encountered information, especially from the media, depicting homosexuality as "just a phase."

Experiences

The responses to these early feelings did not result in discussions with doctors, clergymen, or teachers. Also, gay places and/or people were not sought out or discovered, as their accessability was limited and fear of discovery was great.

Fifty percent of the respondents recalled discussions about homosexuality with or by their families, and 50% recalled discussions with friends. (Twelve of the 20 respondents who recalled family discussions were also among the 20 respondents who recalled friend discussions). The older group recalled fewer discussions in general and those that did occur were consistently rated as negative. The familial discussions for the younger group were predominantly negative; however, half of the friend discussions were positive for the younger group and led to less stereotypical conceptions.

Sixty percent of the older group and 80% of the younger group actually saw "homosexuals" during this time. They were usually other students in school or adults in their neighborhood. Their homosexuality was known to the respondents because of (a) their appearance, (b) their club or job association, and (c) rumors by peers. They tended, again, to be stereotypically described and sustained the respondents' unwillingness to define themselves as gay.

The average age of the group's first sexual experience was 14 for the older respondents and 13 for the younger ones. This experience might have been most significant in terms of explaining the "difference," but it was often consciously ignored until it happened again, at which time some definition was needed. Forty-five percent of the older group and 20% of the younger group began psychotherapy as a result of these experiences, and most of the older respondents reported traumatic accounts of psychotherapeutic methods used to change or cure their "problem." The younger group's experiences in therapy were usually positive, with acceptance of their homosexuality the result.

Mass media were most often the means by which respondents could legitimize and learn about their experiences, even though the mass media usually presented negative images. Also, the mass media socialized the respondents with respect to roles and relationships for homosexuals, while reinforcing the cultural stereotype. However, as the respondents grew more certain of their sexuality, they reported using selective behavior in terms of what they might "use" from these media portrayals. Many respondents, especially from the older group, held negative self-perceptions for years until they had constructed a lifestyle with other gay friends, lovers and institutions.

LABELING

The research indicates that age was the most important variable for the length of time between earliest feelings or experiences and subsequent labeling. (Younger respondents averaged 5 years and the older group 13 years). Six younger respondents (and none of the older respondents) labeled themselves "gay" before any sexual interaction with other males. The increase in public visibility of homosexuals, including increased attention by the mass media to homosexuality and the emergence of specifically gay-oriented media, helps to explain the early-labeling phenomenon for these younger respondents. The rest of the respondents were divided evenly, with 17 (10 older and 7 younger) having sexual experiences before sexual feelings or questions, and 17 (10 older and 7 younger) having suspicions from sexual feelings and then actual sexual experiences. Interestingly, the group who reported homosexual experiences before homosexual feelings also reported the longest time period between initial experiences and labeling: 14 years for the older group and 5.8 years for the younger group. The group whose feelings preceeded their experiences reported an average of 11 years (older group) and 5 years (younger group) between initial interactions and self-labeling.

As the two processes of identity development and homosexual-image training continued, their connections occurred at different times depending on the amount of (a) information encountered, (b) experiences and feelings surfacing, (c) perceived success of acting on feelings, and (d) perceived interpretations of these feelings and experiences by external events. The intensity of the labeling process was not age specific, as it depended heavily on the experiences of each respondent with his environment.

CONCLUSION

Clearly, this study was designed to illuminate processes rather than to develop statistically projectable findings. The development of a gay sexual identity included two related processes that eventually connect and interact to form the self identity: (a) the personal feelings of arousal recognized at approximately age 13 and (b) the socialization of what a homosexual is, according to various agents in one's environment.

The effects of the media did not differ between the two age groups for the significant functions listed below: (a) Legitimating (in that homosexuality and that homosexuals do indeed exist), (b) Reinforcement (media images tended to support stereotypes from other sources), (c) Identification (although stereotypical, enough information is relevant to the respondent to correspond to his own feelings and experiences), (d) Eroticism (sexual pleasure and/or questions derived from subject matter or pictures), (e) Image Training (how homosexual roles and relationships are taught as well as how such a lifestyle is negatively evaluated by our culture), and (f) Instigation of Subsequent Interaction (discussions with other relatives, friends, or peers regarding the mass-mediated message or related issues).

This paper has illustrated some aspects of how the media can socialize an audience, especially when other agents do not address particular subjects. The power of the media to influence the way we perceive not only our world, but ourselves, is clearly indicated by the instrumental role of media in gay-male sexual identity. The media, in combination with other socializing agents, are undoubtedly a potent influence for cultivating and maintaining images which shape our beliefs, actions, and self-perceptions.

REFERENCES

GERBNER, G., and GROSS, L.P. (1975). The world of television: Towards cultural indicators. *Intermedia* 3 (No. 3).

SCHWARTZ-MACDONALD, S. (1977). "Learning about Crime: Conceptions of Crime and Law Enforcement as They Relate to Use of Television and Other Information Sources." Unpublished Dissertation, University of Pennsylvania.

20

Is That All There Is To Love?:
Values and Program Preference*

OSCAR H. GANDY, JR.
School fo Communications
Howard University
Washington, DC 20069

Graham Murdock and Peter Golding have argued for the development of an analysis of mass media and social class relations which would start from a "concrete analysis of economic relations and the ways in which they structure both the processes and results of cultural production" (Murdock and Golding, 1979, p. 18; Golding and Murdock, 1978). Such an analysis would begin quite properly with a description of the communications industry, its structure of ownership and control, and the normative influences which guide the work of media professionals. The most troublesome part of such an analysis would be the establishment of a clear perspective on the interaction between economic and ideological forces as revealed in the marketplace.

While the business of mass communication is the production of content for sale, at the same time the business of mass communications is the production of audiences for sale to advertisers. Both are driven by the need to maximize profits through the maximization of audience size. And, as Murdock and Golding (1979, p. 40) suggest, "in seeking to maximize this market, products must draw upon the most widely legitimated central core values while rejecting the dissenting or incompatible objection to a ruling myth. The need for easily understood, popular, formulated, undisturbing, assimiliable fictional material is at once a commercial imperative and an aesthetic recipe."

The process through which audiences are produced for television pro-

*The author's work on this project was supported in part by a grant from the University-Sponsored Faculty Research Program in the Social Sciences, Humanities and Education, 1979–80, in the Office of the Vice President for Academic Affairs at Howard University.

grams is complex and not well understood. The production of audiences is not synonomous with the production of a given program. Audience Production Functions (APF), as an approach which seeks to specify the links between program attributes and audience size, has so far been limited to examining the independent and additive contribution of program violence to the size of the national television audience as estimated by the A.C. Nielsen Company (Gandy, 1979, 1980; Gandy and Signorielli, 1979, 1981). These studies have suggested that program violence, which might be appropriate and productive of audience shares for action-adventure programs, may be inappropriate and counter productive when used in situation comedy. They suggest as well that there might be something less than open competition between program sources seeking to maximize total audience size. Instead, it is suggested that networks may choose to specialize on a given evening and maximize the production of more homogeneous audience groups to better suit the needs of advertisers of specialized products.

To some degree, the ability of the programmer to produce a more homogeneous audience is dependent upon the existence of a group-specific preference for certain program attributes (or their combination). While accepting the existence of such tastes and preferences on little more than face value, scholars associated with the "uses and gratifications approach" continue to debate the social genesis of those preferences and the utility of such measures as predictors of media behavior.

That is, while it is clear that there are differences between black and white viewers, in that blacks prefer, or are more likely to choose a program with black characters (Allen, 1980), (and we might conclude with Blumler that such choice is made on the basis of the ability of those characters to "speak to the condition" of the audience — Blumler, 1979), it is also clear that there are more whites than blacks in the audience for *Good Times*, despite the fact that there are no white characters. While race, sex, or ethnic-group membership may lead to the sharing of common experiences, and these demographic variables may "stand for" the experiences they are associated with, for such an approach to provide meaningful insight into the audience production process, it would have to be based upon more basic, universal constructs.

Numerous studies have pursued audience behavior from a functionalist perspective. People sought media for information, for entertainment, for relaxation, even for companionship or a way to avoid the problems of the day (Blumler and Katz, 1974). Unfortunately, for those studies that sought to link functional categories of media use to particular media content, the conclusions of David Swanson (1978, p. 12) are hard to avoid: "almost any message content can serve almost any use or provide almost any gratification to almost any sort of person in almost any circumstances."

This study represents an attempt to go beyond motivations to personal values as the base from which motivations and preferences emerge. Without attempting to speculate on the social basis for values, this initial study is limited to the examination of the association between values and television program preference.

HUMAN VALUES AND BEHAVIOR

Milton Rokeach (1973, p. 6) defines a value as "an enduring belief that a specific mode of conduct or end-state of existence is personally or socially preferable to an opposite or converse mode of conduct or end state of existence." He suggests further that a value system is "an enduring organization of beliefs concerning preferable modes of conduct or end-states of existence along a continuum of relative importance." Values are important as functional aides in that they are used as personal standards which are helpful in making choices, arriving at decisions, or resolving personal conflict. Rokeach (1973, p.24) suggests that "values are guides and determinants of social attitudes and ideologies on the one hand and of social behavior on the other."

In order to test the hypothesized relationship between value systems and social behavior, Rokeach has over the years applied his Terminal and Instrumental Values to the task of differentiating between groups on the basis of their religion, political philosophy, academic majors, social class, sex, and race. Others have used his methods to differentiate between buyers of Fords and Chevrolets.

The method is quite straightforward, which explains, perhaps, its popularity with the community of behavioral scientists. After some modification, Rokeach has arrived at a list of 18 Terminal and 18 Instrumental Values. Terminal values, which refer to end-states, are both personal and social, that is, important to the individual or to the society. Instrumental Values, which are descriptive of modes of conduct or attributes, are concerned with morality or with competence. Subjects are presented with either lists of values, to which they assign ranks, or they are provided with cards to sort (or gummed labels) according to their importance. Depending upon the number of subjects performing the sort, Rokeach uses either the mean or median ranks for each value to differentiate between populations. With a small number of cases, Rokeach suggests that a t-test is a sensitive measure of difference between groups.

A STUDY OF DORMITORY RESIDENTS

In 1979, students in an undergraduate research methods class administered surveys to dormitory residents as part of a class exercise. A systematic sampling method identified every fifth room from a list of rooms in each dormitory. These rooms were systematically divided among the student-interviewers, and in all 227 interviews were completed, 179 having responses for all items.

The survey instrument sought information about the media usage of dormitory residents, such as the number of hours of television watched during the week and over the weekend, and whether they used *TV Guide* or other program selection aids, as well as information about their major, grade point average, and year in school.

Eight items were included which sought to describe their reasons for watching television. Respondants were asked to indicate the degree to which a statement applied to them on a scale ranging from "a lot" to "not at all."

Next, respondents were presented with a list of 62 prime-time television programs, excluding sports and "movies of the week," and were requested to select and rank order the ten programs they liked the most.

Finally, respondents were presented with the Rokeach Value instruments. The Terminal Values were described as "Goals . . . those things which we value in life, which stand as goals or targets we hope to attain or achieve." The Instrumental Values were described as "Instruments . . . personal qualities which are valued in friends, mates, and you would like to develop for yourself, and have others see you as." The Values were listed on questionnaires in two groups, and respondents were asked to rank these values from 1-18 in order of importance to them, with 1 as the most important, and 18 as the least important.

FINDINGS

The population was heavily female (70.6%); more than 60% were underclass, with only a single graduate student. Students averaged slightly more than 6 hours of televiewing Monday through Thursday, and 7.3 hours between Friday afternoon and Sunday evening. The greatest proportion of respondents indicated that the statement "I watch TV because it helps me to unwind, relax, or calm down" described them "a lot" (21.8%). Only 3.1% felt similarly described by the statement "I watch TV because it helps me to forget my problems."

Men and women respondents were compared on all variables. Table 1 reports the variables on which there was a significant difference between male and female residents. Males did not differ significantly from females in terms of the amount of viewing, gradepoint average, use of program guides, or on 7 out of 8 uses and gratifications measures. Females were, however, more likely to report using television for companionship ($t = 2.29$, $p = .024$, two-tailed).

TABLE 20.1   Comparison of Male and Female Dorm Residents

| | Group Means | | |
Programs	Males	Females	t
Eight is Enough	28.64	20.29	− 5.98***
Dallas	23.87	18.85	− 2.69**
Shirley	29.89	27.95	− 2.11*
California Fever	31.00	29.98	− 2.47*
Bad News Bears	31.00	30.18	− 2.26*
The Jeffersons	20.64	16.38	− 2.19*
Buck Rogers	26.98	29.90	2.32*
The Waltons	30.28	28.77	− 2.02*
Three's Company	28.28	24.95	− 2.55*
One Day at A Time	29.07	26.20	− 2.52*
The Incredible Hulk	24.01	28.23	2.62**
Real People	25.15	28.20	2.06*
Terminal Values Self Respect	4.85	3.51	− 2.25*
Social Recognition	12.13	13.89	2.80**
Instrumental Values Imaginative	10.68	12.77	2.72**

*p = lt.05
**p = lt.01
***p = lt.001

There were however, several differences between males and females in the ratings assigned to programs. These differences were generally related to the least popular programs, with males tending to give the lowest ratings. The exceptions to this pattern were those programs heavy on violent action, like *Buck Rogers* and the *Incredible Hulk*.

Males rarely differed from females in their rankings of Rokeach's values. Women placed a somewhat higher value on self-respect, while men placed higher value on social recognition. On the instrumental values, men placed a slightly higher value on imagination.

The sensitivity of Rokeach's values to the issues of the times may be reflected in the differences between this population and the national (NORC) sample taken in 1968. The most important Terminal Value for both men and women in 1968 was a world at peace. It was 14th for both men and women in this sample. Surprisingly, considering that these respondents were students at a traditionally and predominently black insitution, freedom and equality were ranked around 6th and 11th for the dorm residents, but around

3rd and 9th for the national sample. Blacks in the 1968 sample ranked equality 2nd and freedom 3rd in 1968 (Rokeach, 1973, pp. 52-70). Honesty remains the number one instrumental value for both sample populations.

PROGRAM RATINGS

With 62 program options, programs could not be ranked easily according to preference. Those programs not ranked in the top ten were assigned a default value, the midpoint of the list (31). In this way, it was possible to treat respondent scores in a number of ways. The first, reported in Table 2, treats ranking as a simple choice between rated and nonrated programs. A program which was in a respondent's top ten was considered rated, and a program assigned the median score was considered nonrated. Treating the program's rating as a dichotomous dependent variable, 9 discriminant functions were estimated.[1] These functions were all significant, and the percentage of programs ranked correctly ranged from 59.0 to 69.4%. No variables were allowed to enter the stepwise discriminant function unless they were significant at the .05 level.

The standardized coefficients reflect the relative contribution of each variable to the discriminant function, thus its relative importance in discriminating between two groups of programs (and the people who rate them). For the program *Benson,* the number of hours of televiewing on the weekend was more important as a discriminator than the instrumental value of self-respect. The negative sign of the coefficient for values should be interpreted to mean that the higher one placed self-respect in the list of terminal values, the more likely one was to have placed *Benson* among the top ten programs. Whereas, for *Charlies Angels,* placing a high value on salvation or obedience would decrease the probability of one's having rated that program in the top ten. Of the nine relatively popular programs examined, only *Eight is Enough* has sex as an important discriminating variable. If a respondent was female, the coefficient (.943) suggests that there is a high probability that she put *Eight is Enough* in her top ten.

In two out of the nine programs examined in this way, uses and gratifications variables emerged as the most important discriminators. For *Soap,* watching television because it is thrilling, or provides excitement, is a good predictor of a top ten rating. For *White Shadow,* watching television out of habit it the most important predictor.

It is worth noting at this point that some values turn up in more than one discriminant function, suggesting that as in Rokeach's analysis of the

---

[1]SPSS Version M, Release 9A was used for all statistical analyses.

TABLE 20.2   Variables Discriminating Between Persons on the Basis of Programs Rated as Top Ten Favorites

Programs		% Classified Correctly	Chi-squared
Variables	*Beta*		
BENSON		66.99	14.792***
Hours of Weekend TV	.788		
Self Respect	− .593		
CHARLIES ANGELS		69.42	15.164**
To Pass Time	− .546		
Salvation	.603		
Obedient	.612		
60 MINUTES		65.84	27.637***
Hours of Weekend TV	− .471		
Pleasure	.470		
Clean	.374		
Helpful	− .480		
Obedient	.409		
20/20		67.63	39.593***
Broadminded	− .508		
Polite	− .460		
To Rest	− .426		
Responsible	.441		
Pleasure	.403		
Clean	.380		
Self Controlled	.357		
SOAP		64.15	19.003***
Comfortable Life	.477		
Pleasure	.532		
To Get Excited	.678		
SATURDAY NITE LIVE (Best Of)		62.50	34.278***
Obedient	.679		
Self Respect	.455		
Salvation	.429		
Polite	− .409		
Honest	.443		
Freedom	.361		
WHITE SHADOW		61.35	37.244***
Forgiving	− .381		
Polite	− .361		
Habit	.470		
Information	− .393		
Freedom	.368		
Intellectual	.430		
Obedient	.373		
DIFFERENT STROKES		59.05	8.280*
National Security	.795		
Loving	− .693		
EIGHT IS ENOUGH		65.58	25.110***
Female	.943		
Thrill/Excitement	.482		

*p = lt.05
**p = lt.01
***p = lt.001

Note: negative signs for coefficients for values should be interpreted as a high degree of association. Thus a group rating a program in the top ten, and rating a particular value (Loving) highly as well, would result in a negative coefficient. The opposite would be true for the Uses and Gratification and demographic measures.

importance of freedom and equality to political philosophy,[2] one or more variables may underlie content preferences in some systematic way. Obedient, the variable which is ranked last by both males and females in this sample, emerges as a signficant variable in four out of nine discriminant functions. The sign of the coefficient is positive in all cases, which means that if persons departed from the norm for the sample, and rated obediance as relatively more important as a value, they were less likely to put *Charlies Angels, 60 Minutes, Saturday Nite Live,* or *White Shadow* among their top ten programs.

Pleasure, ranked 12th and 13th by males and females respectively, was a significant discriminator in three functions: *60 Minutes, 20/20,* and *Soap.* Polite, also important in three functions, had a negative coefficient, which is interpreted to mean that persons who placed a high value on politeness were likely to favor *20/20, Saturday Nite Live,* or *White Shadow.*

PREDICTED RANKING

By selecting only those persons who had placed a particular program in their top ten category, stepwise multiple regression was used to identify the most important predictors of variance in program ranking for each of 11 programs. In the analysis reported in Table 3, only the Terminal and Instrumental values were eligible for entry into the multiple regression equation.

Variables which were important in discriminating between top ten and unranked programs were unlikely to emerge as important in this analysis, since members of this subsample were more alike than unlike on those variables.

The amount of variance associated with Rokeach's Terminal and Instrumental Values ranged from 1.6 to 15.1%. The standardized beta coefficients reflect the relative importance of each to the total variance in program ranks assigned by each respondent. The same values rarely appear in more than one program's equation. When they do, as in the case of happiness in the equations for *Soap* and *MASH,* or true friendship in the case of *The Jeffersons* and *White Shadow,* the coefficients are of different signs.

It should also be noted that programs which would ordinarily be grouped together as similar because of their formats, such as situation comedy or news/documentary, are apparently treated differentially by those who place them in their top ten.

60 Minutes, the most popular program for this sample, had only one

---

[2]Rokeach's most impressive analysis involved the discrimination between four political philosophies on the basis of the prominence of two values, freedom and equality in the speeches and writing of socialist, capitalist, fascist, and communist thinkers.

TABLE 20.3   Program Ratings as a Function of Terminal and Instrumental Values
First Three Entrants in Stepwise Multiple Regression

Program	N	Variable	Beta	R^2 Change	F
1 Soap	88	Happiness	.287	.055	7.718**
		Helpful	−.276	.052	6.908*
		Intellectual	−.217	.045	4.488*
2 Mork And Mindy	66	World Peace	−.351	.055	7.587**
		Pleasure	−.261	.057	4.222*
		Polite	−.210	.044	3.249
3 The Jeffersons	103	Capable	−.320	.117	12.176**
		Inner Harmony	−.184	.033	4.043*
		True Friendship	.150	.022	2.713
4 Saturday Nite Live	107	Clean	.334	.080	13.233**
		Self Respect	−.256	.053	8.126**
		Broadminded	.217	.044	5.523*
5 MASH	74	Happiness	−.384	.119	12.067**
		Logical	−.256	.047	5.314*
		Accomplishment	.207	.041	3.641
6 Different Strokes	50	Obedient	.361	.151	8.087**
		Honest	.222	.066	3.023
		Cheerful	.220	.046	2.927
7 Benson	55	Ambitious	.264	.070	3.99
		###			
		###			
8 Fantasy Island	54	Freedom	.373	.102	9.933**
		Self Respect	.363	.120	9.400**
		Self Control	.288	.082	5.981*
9 20/20	101	Logical	.351	.085	13.481**
		Forgiving	.305	.061	9.491**
		Exciting Life	.171	.026	3.146
10 White Shadow	100	Family Security	.235	.063	5.950*
		World Peace	−.214	.032	4.735*
		True Friendship	−.156	.023	2.550
11 60 Minutes	144	Loving	−.236	.047	7.786**
		Salvation	.135	.022	2.56
		Self Control	.130	.016	2.53

*p = lt.05

**p = lt.01

F insufficient to enter

significant variable, loving. As the second most important Instrumental Value for females, and third most important for males, loving was apparently much lower on the lists of those who rated *60 Minutes* highly. For *Benson*, a program with a Black character generally shown as competent and intelligent, only ambitious met the criterion for entry into the equation.

Table 4 reports the three most important predictors of program ratings, but differs from the equations in Table 3 in that uses and gratifications and other descriptive variables were considered along with Values as potential factors. As one might expect, information-seeking as a motivation emerged as an important factor in respondants' rating of *60 Minutes*. The negative sign of the coefficient should be interpreted to mean that as an individual indicated that the statement "I watch TV because it provides me with information I need" described their use "a lot", they were more likely to assign a high rank to *60 Minutes*.

Sex, as a demographic variable, emerges as a predictor of rating for *20/20*. The negative sign of the beta coefficient should be interpreted to mean that women were more likely to give a higher rating to *20/20* than men, once the other variables were held constant.

The number of hours in which one watches television was inversely related to subject's evaluation of *White Shadow*, in that heavy users of

TABLE 20.4   Program Ratings as a Function of Values and Uses and Gratifications
Measures
First Three Entrants in Stepwise Multiple Regression

	Program	*N*	*Variable*	*Beta*	*R²* *Change*	*F*
1	60 Minutes	114	Companionship	.311	.106	12.794**
			Capable	.196	.036	5.119*
			Information	− .162	.026	3.462
2	Saturday Nite Live	90	Clean	.349	.093	12.585**
			Self Respect	− .212	.052	4.725*
			Accomplishment	− .203	.040	4.236*
3	20/20	74	Logical	.395	.103	13.138**
			Forgiving	.249	.078	5.004*
			Sex of Viewer	− .180	.030	2.741
4	The Jeffersons	72	Capable	− .407	.167	15.539**
			Habit	− .247	.050	5.732*
			Salvation	− .236	.056	5.339*
5	White Shadow	77	Family Security	.314	.071	8.437**
			Weekly TV	.280	.056	6.54 *
			Self Control	.241	.056	5.105*

*p = lt.05
**p = lt.01

television were less likely to rate the program highly. On the other hand, Viewers of the *Jeffersons* were more likely to rate the program highly if they were also likely to agree that they watch television because "it has become a habit."

In no case did a uses and gratifications or demographic variable emerge as the most significant contribution to R^2.

DISCUSSION

Rokeach's Terminal and Instrumental Values are useful as discriminators between groups of television viewers in terms of their identification of prime time programs as being in their top ten. These values are reliable predictors of the ratings these viewers assign to these programs. While the traditional uses and gratifications measures also emerge as significant predictors of program value, they do not surpass Rokeach's values for any of the programs examined.

What is most important in terms of our ultimate goal of understanding the role of television program content in the production of audiences and, through them, the reproduction of the dominant ideology, is that the importance of these values varies from program to program, even within broad program types.

Positive coefficients for values are interpreted to mean that persons who rate a value highly also rate a program highly. Does it also mean that characters in the program share their values? That is, does a person rate a program highly because it supports, or reinforces values they hold, or as Blumler (1979, p. 27) suggests when referring to expected gratifications,[3] values people like them are *expected to hold?*

Of course, this analysis suffers from the weaknesses common to most correlation-based studies, the difficulty of assigning temporal order. Do persons watch and then value a program because it reinforces their values, or do they develop values because they happen to like a program which stresses those values?

The work of Gerbner and his colleagues has gone a long way toward generating support for the causal influence of media on social perceptions.[4]

---

[3]Blumler discusses the possibility that gratifications are socially conditioned in that the social environment may *teach* people which "satisfactions people like themselves are expected to derive from their media use."

[4]The Cultural Indicators Project is a long term effort by Gerbner and his associates to "monitor those aspects of our system generating and using bodies of broadly shared messages that are most relevant to social issues and public policy decisions" (Gerbner, 1972, p.5). The annual violence profiles, published each summer in the *Journal of Communication*, focus on one aspect of the message system, and its involvement in the cultivation of social perceptions.

Because the emphasis of their Cultural Indicators Project over the years has been on violence—as a teacher of power (class) relationships—personal values have not been addressed as I suggest they might.

Content analysis of programs should characterize major characters, and perhaps, in summary fashion, entire programs in terms of their emphasis on Terminal and Instrumental values. While it may be the case that all programs share the same value structure, I doubt it seriously. Instead, we would probably find that certain programs stress family security, love, and perhaps true friendship, while other programs emphasize ambition, courage, independence, and responsibility.

The data in this study suggest that audiences differ in their valuation of programs in a manner consistent with their different value structures. Without the benefit of objective measures of the values expressed in those programs, we can only speculate that there is a direct link.

This study does not have direct measures of the frequency with which respondents view particular programs, though one might reasonably assume that the more one values a program, the more one watches it. This assumption would support the present interpretation of the static correlations. Because values are generally considered to be more stable than attitudes and opinions, it is probably less realistic to expect measurable change in values over the length of a television season. A longitudinal study of the sort reported by Himmelweit and Swift (1976) would be most useful in establishing the link between values, preferences, and exposure to content, just as their personality variables were significant predictors of adult preferences for news, sports, and thrillers.

We should recognize that the trend toward more highly-specialized, homogeneous audiences is being accelerated by the expansion of channel capacity in cable television systems, and the likely introduction of thousands of local, low power television stations.[5] This change in the organization and structure of television must result in some change in the manner in which it performs its ideological function. The changing technology of audience production is a vital aspect of that change and should be explored.

At the very least, effort should be taken to replicate this study on less homogeneous populations to see if values are important discriminators for other audiences as well as they are for predominantly black, dormitory residents.

REFERENCES

ALLEN, R.I. (1980). "The State of Communication Research on Black Americans." (Paper presented to Symposium on Minority Audiences and Programming Research, Lenox, MA.)

---

[5]*Broadcasting* (1981) discusses the expansion of broadcast outlets, and predictions of the probable specialization of low power television stations.

BLUMLER, J.G. (1979). The role of theory in uses and gratifications studies. *Communication Research 6*, 9–36.

BLUMLER, J.G., and KATZ, E. (Eds.) (1974). "The Uses of Mass Communications." Beverly Hills, CA: Sage.

Broadcasting. (1981). (March 16), 51–52.

GANDY, O.H., JR. Audience production functions: A new look at the economics of broadcasting. *Media Asia 6*, 170–178.

GANDY, O.H., JR. (1980). "Toward the Production of Minority Audience Characteristics." (Paper presented to Symposium on Minority Audiences and Programming Research, Lenox, MA.)

GANDY, O.H., JR., and SIGNORIELLI, N. (1979). "Cultural Pollution and the Productivity of Violence." (Paper presented to the Association for Education in Journalism Convention. Houston, TX.)

GANDY, O.H., JR., and SIGNORIELLI, N. (1981). Audience production functions: A technical approach to broadcasting. *Journalism Quarterly 58*, 232–240.

GERBNER, G. (1972). "Technology, Society, and Symbols: The Need for Cultural Indicators." (Paper prepared for the International Symposium on Communications: Technology, Impact, and Policy. Philadelphia, PA)

GOLDING, P., and MURDOCK, G. (1978). Theories of communication and theories of society. *Communication Research 5*, 339–356.

HIMMELWEIT, H., and SWIFT, B. (1976). Continuities and discontinuities in media usage and tastes: A longitudinal study. *Journal of Social Issues 32*, 133–156.

MURDOCK, G., and GOLDING, P. (1979). Capitalism, communication, and class relations. *In* J. Curran, M. GUREVITCH, and J. WOLLACOTT (Eds.), "Mass Communication and Society." Beverly Hills, CA: Sage.

ROKEACH, M. (1973). "The Nature of Human Values." New York: Free Press.

SWANSON, D.L. (1978). "The Uses and Gratifications Approach to Mass Communication Research." (Paper presented to the International Communication Association Conference, Chicago, IL.)

21

Functional Analysis of Soap-Opera Viewing: A Comparison of Two Populations

SALLY M. JOHNSTONE
Department of Psychology
University of North Carolina
Chapel Hill, North Carolina 27514

ROBERT C. ALLEN
Department of Radio, Television and Motion Pictures
University of North Carolina
Chapel Hill, North Carolina 27514

In recent years, increasingly more notice has been given to the importance of daytime-serial viewing. Arnold Becker, CBS Vice President for Research, recently estimated that 63% of all American women living in homes with television sets (i.e., 50 million women) are soap-opera viewers, and that the average serial viewer watched ten hours of such programming per week (Lindsey, 1979). Also noted by the industry has been a demographic broadening of the soap-opera audience. While this audience remains predominantly 18-35 year old females, more men, college students, and adolescents have also become viewers (Lindsey, 1979).

Surprisingly, few audience analyses of soap-opera viewing have been conducted since Herta Herzog's pioneering work with radio-serial listeners (Herzog, 1944),[1] and none has examined the attitudes of members of these "new" audience groups: college students, men, adolescents.[2] From a uses and gratifications perspective, this study investigates two largely unexamined

---

[1] A notable exception is Sari Thomas' dissertation (1977).

[2] Ronald J. Compesi (1980) notes "while some recent research has been done on contemporary television serial content very little has been done on television serial audiences." Compesi studied 259 soap opera viewers in Eugene, Oregon. His sample included only viewers of a single program (*All My Children*), however, and the demographics of his sample, drawn entirely from a college community, limits the applicability of his findings to the national audience.

audience groups: residents of *urban* areas (in this case, those residing in the middle-size urban communities of Durham and Raleigh, North Carolina) and *college students* (from the University of North Carolina at Chapel Hill).

METHOD

A random sample of viewers from each of these groups was drawn, using appropriate telephone directories, the respondant being included in the study's sample if he/she answered positively to the question "Do you watch daytime dramatic serials—what we sometimes call Soap Operas?" The affirming respondant was then read a series of gratifications statements to be answered in terms of a 5-point Likert-type scale. The statements were derived from Herzog's work, the gratifications categories suggested by McQuail, Blumler, and Brown, and from preliminary open-ended interviews with student and non-student soap-opera viewers. Respondents also provided demographic information, including age, educational level, marital status, and sex, as well as data regarding viewing "intensity"—number of hours viewed each day and days per week, number of years he/she had been watching, attention to the screen while watching, etc. The interviews were conducted over a five day period in March 1980. Interviews were completed with 260 UNC students and 250 Raleigh-Durham viewers. Only viewers 18 years of age and older were included in the Raleigh-Durham sample.

RESULTS

Questionnaire responses were compiled using SAS (Statistical Analysis System). For comparison, the initial analysis provided demographic information about each of the two samples. These data are summarized in Table 21.1.

As can be seen, both samples were predominantly female. However, the general population sample from the Raleigh and Durham areas was older—more than half of the urban respondents were over 34 years of age, while almost all of the college sample fell between 18 and 21 years old. There were also differences between the two groups' marital and educational status. Most of the members of the city sample were married, and less than half of them had never gone to college, while very few of the college group were married and, of course, all of them had attended college.

The reported television viewing habits differed somewhat between these groups. While most from the city sample reported watching daytime programs *other* than the serials, less than half the college students did. The students also reported watching serials less frequently and rarely watching night-time television.

TABLE 21.1 Demographic Comparisons Between the Two Sample Populations.

	Comparison of Populations	
	Urban Group	College Group
Age	51% over 34 years 40% 19–34 years	22% over 21 years 78% 18–21 years
Sex	86% Female	75% Female
Education	43% College	100% College
Marital Status	59% Married	3% Married
Frequency of Viewing Soaps	73% 3 Days or More	55% 3 Days or More
Frequency of Viewing Other TV	61% Other Daytime 69% Night time (at least 2 hours)	38% Other Daytime 7% Night time (at least 2 hours)
Most Popular Soaps	25% ALL MY CHILDREN 22% GENERAL HOSPITAL	35% GENERAL HOSPITAL 24% ALL MY CHILDREN

Further analysis of the questionnaire responses was performed using the PRINIT method of the FACTOR procedure of SAS. In the Raleigh-Durham sample, there were eight factors with eigenvalues greater than one, which accounted for 58% of the total variance. These eight factors were rotated to the VARIMAX criterion. The same procedure was followed for the college student sample, and nine factors emerged with eigenvalues greater than one, accounting for 61% of the total variance. However, several of these nine had only one loading, so reanalyses were done. The six-factor solution which accounted for 50% of the total variance that best fit the criterion of simple structure was used.

There were five factors in each group that seemed to be comparable. These are listed by factor names, items, and loadings in Figure 21.1. While the factors for each group are all given the same names, it may be noted that the actual items included in these factors are not always identical. Since the highest loaded items are typically the same for both samples, and most of the items relate to the same notions as the factor name indicates, the factors were assumed to be close enough for the comparisons between the two groups to be made. Unusual or unexpected differences in the items on any one factor are discussed below.

In order to make the comparison between the two populations sampled more understandable, the average percent of positive responses (or negative responses in the case of negatively loaded items) was calculated for each factor. These data are graphically presented in Figure 21.2.

The eight factors from the Raleigh-Durham sample included three that were not comparable to any in the college sample. The first of these seemed

FIGURE 21.1   Listing of Factors, Items and Loadings for Both Groups Sampled.

R-D		UNC	
Item	Loading	Item	Loading
FACTOR: Social Function			
I like to discuss what happens on my soap with my friends.	.689	I like to discuss what happens on my soap with my friends.	.638
When my friends miss an episode of my soap, they call me to find out what happened.	.630	I watch soap operas with other people.	.596
If I miss an episode of my soap, I call someone to find out what happened	.598	My close friends are also viewers of soap operas.	.579
I sometimes find myself talking back to the TV set when I watch soaps.	.555	When my friends miss an episode of my soap, I call someone to find out what happened.	.335
viewers of soap operas.	.473		
I watch soap operas with other people.	.451		
When my soap is on, I watch the screen closely so I won't miss anything.	.300		
FACTOR: Time Filler			
Soap operas keep me company during the day.	.681	Soap operas keep me company during the day.	.712
Watching soaps helps to pass the time when I'm by myself.	.638	Watching soaps helps to pass the time when I'm by myself.	.678
I enjoy watching soap opera characters do things I could never get away with.	.317	I have been watching my favorite soap longer than 6 years.	.308
FACTOR: Reality Counseling			
One reason I watch soaps is that they deal with real problems.	.647	You can learn a lot from the ways characters in soaps handle crisis situation.	.649
You can learn a lot from the ways characters in soaps handle crisis situations.	.589	One reason I watch soaps is that they deal with real problems.	
I've learned things about medicine or law from soaps.	.547	The characters and situations in soaps are not that different from real life.	.647
The characters and situations in soaps are not that different from real life.	.505	I've learned things about medicine or law from soaps.	.516
I have learned new ways of helping myself from watching soaps.	.497	I've learned new ways of helping myself from watching soaps.	.493

FIGURE 21.1 *(continued)*

R-D		UNC	
Item	*Loading*	*Item*	*Loading*
FACTOR: Social Function *(continued)*			
I feel closer to some of the characters on my soap than to some of my friends.	.348	Soap operas show what it's like to be rich.	.351
I wish I could trade places with one of the characters.	.307	There is a character on my soap who is a lot like me.	.307
FACTOR: Social Compensatory			
I feel closer to some of the characters on my soap than to some of my friends.	.583	I feel closer to some of the characters on my soap than to some of my friends.	.522
I can miss several days of my soap and it really doesn't matter to me.	−.434	I watch my soap because the people in them are attractive.	.492
I wish I could trade places with one of the characters in my soap.	.363	There is a character on my soap who is a lot like me.	.485
I sometimes find myself talking back to the TV set when I watch soaps.	.339	I wish I could trade places with one of the characters in my soap.	.421
There is a character on my soap who is a lot like me.	.315	Soap operas are a good way to keep up with current styles in clothing.	.404
If I miss an episode of my soap, I call someone to find out what happened.	.309	Soap operas help me forget my own problems.	.399
What is the highest level of educational grade you completed.	−.302	I have learned new ways of helping myself from watching soaps.	.381
		I often find the characters in soaps silly.	−.352
		When my soap is on, I watch the screen closely so I won't miss anything.	.340
		Soap operas show what it is like to be rich.	.312
FACTOR: Intensity			
When my soap is on, I watch the screen closely so I won't miss anything.	.459	If I miss an episode of my soap, I call someone to find out what happened.	.628
I often find the characters in soaps silly.	−.360	I can miss several days of my soap and it doesn't really matter to me.	−.446
If I miss an episode of my soap, I call someone to find out what happened.	.326	How many days each week do you spend some time watching soaps.	.397
FACTOR: Glamor			
Soap operas are a good way to keep up with current styles in clothing.	.524		
I watch my soap because the people in it are attractive.	.502		
Soap operas show what it's like to be rich.	.359		

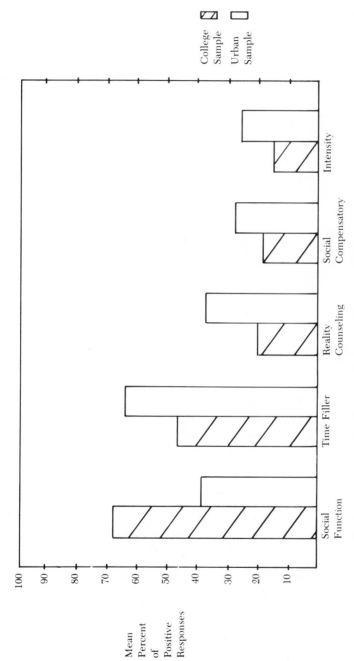

FIGURE 21.2   Comparison of College and Non-College Urban Viewers on Factors
Involved in Soap-Opera Watching

to be a "time" indicator with high loadings for the length of time watching one's favorite soap and number of hours per day watching. The second noncommon factor seemed to be an "old-and-poor" factor. Those attributes contributing to this factor were older age, lower income level, lower educational level and "not wanting to trade places with the characters in the soaps." The final noncommon factor was a "fantasy" factor, for which statements involving clothing styles, attractiveness, and wealth loaded high.

Of the six factors from the college sample, one did not have a counterpart in the Raleigh-Durham sample. This was an "age" factor. It had high loadings from the highest level of school class, age, and length of time watching a favorite soap.

DISCUSSION

The comparison of these two populations of viewers poses a few problems, but also indicates some interesting differences. The problems result from each group defining its own "uses" factors. This is because the factor analysis was done independently on the responses from the two groups. As a result, the items on equivalent factors are not always identical, but they are close enough, in our opinion, to allow the factors to be considered together. The primary differences between these college and urban viewers of soap operas lie in how many in each group seem to "use" the various factors. That is, there are differences in the relative percentages of respondants that are described by each factor.

In addition, there are three factors in the urban group that have no counterpart in the college group. Two of these seem related to age and amount of time available for watching soaps. The third is a "glamor" factor, to whose statements an average of 43% of the urban viewers responded positively. Thus almost half of the urban viewers report "using" soap operas in in a way which is uncharacteristic of college viewers. This distinctively noncollege-viewer "use" of soaps is worth further investigation, in order to understand more about the differences between these two groups of viewers.

Each factor identified by both of these two groups is discussed below. We interpret the factor itself and discuss the problems and differences between each population of respondants. It may be helpful to the reader to refer to the table of common factors and statements which load on each as these factors are discussed.

SOCIAL FACTOR

Individuals for whom soap operas serve a social function tend to focus on the characters from these shows for interactions among their real-life friends.

They gossip about the characters and usually view the shows with other people. These viewers may also "use" the soaps as an excuse to initiate conversations with others. Thus soap-opera watching is seen as a peer-group activity.

While many viewers in both groups reported "using" soap operas in social interaction, this activity was even greater (30% more) among the college students. While we did not question the students directly about this, we can assume that many of them view the serials in dormitory lobbies or other commercial viewing rooms. Consequently, the opportunity for such inter-action may be more available to the students.

However, there may be another reason why more college students than city dwellers use the serials to facilitate social interaction. The college living experience generally involves high-density residences where the student is virtually among strangers, and often apart from his or her family for the first time. For the college viewers, then, soap operas may provide a common experience to use as the basis for more comfortable interactions with ac-quaintances. Most of the city residents, on the other hand, live with their families, and thus, may need to rely less on this pattern of interaction facilitation.

TIME FILLER

The "use" of soap operas as a means to "pass the time" is prominently reported in both groups. The college viewers are a little less likely to report this "use" for the serials than the city viewers. Perhaps, the students' more structured daytime regimens account for this finding.

Among the college viewers, the time-filling function of soap-opera view-ing appears to be most important to those individuals who have been watching the soaps the longest (more than six years). Some of those in the city group who "use" the soaps to "fill time" seem also to enjoy watching the characters engage in activities that the viewers would not engage in. We speculate that the combination of these time-filling and vicarious-enjoyment statements seem indicative of a group of viewers who see their own lives as less exciting than the lives of the soap-opera characters they watch.

REALITY COUNSELLING

Viewers who responded positively to the statements which load on this factor seem to find soap operas to be relatively accurate reflections of real-life situations. Believing soaps to be "realistic," these viewers feel they learn about the world from their soaps and "use" the information they get from the soaps in coping with problems in their own lives.

This function is considerably more important for the city group than for the college audience. The complexity of this function and of the underlying motives for these viewers does not allow us to speculate too much about why the two groups would be so different. Further investigation of this factor seems warranted.

SOCIAL COMPENSATORY AND INTENSITY

The intensity function seems to be a measure of involvement with the soap opera and not actually a described "use." The items that loaded on this function seem to have a great deal of overlap with those that load on the social compensatory function, so the two are discussed together. It seems that the degree of seriousness with which a viewer takes soap-opera watching is related to the extent to which that viewer "uses" soap-opera watching as a vicarious social activity.

These viewers feel closer to the characters than to their friends, would like to trade places with a character, and do not want to miss a single episode. All of the items that are involved with these factors seem to indicate that these viewers share an extreme attitude about the soap opera. It is interesting to note that, while these factors account for the smallest number of viewers in both groups of viewers, there is the smallest difference between the two groups on these factors.

In looking at all of the items that contribute to all the individual factors, there are several items that load on more than one of the factors. The greatest overlap of shared items occurs in the factors involved with reality counselling, social compensation, and intensity. This may imply that these viewers have relatively few opportunities for social interactions and reality testing. Consequently, they learn about the world from watching soaps, derive vicarious social experience from them, and, hence, take their viewing very seriously. It is important to realize that this group of people does not represent the majority of soap-opera watchers. Most watchers are more likely to be described by the time-filling factor or the social-interaction factor.

REFERENCES

COMPESI, R.J. (1980). Gratifications of daytime serial viewers. *Journalism Quarterly* 57, 155–158.

HERZOG, H. (1944). What do we really know about daytime serial listeners? *In* P.F. Lazarsfeld and F.N. Stanton (Eds.), "Radio Research 1942–43." New York: Duell, Sloan, and Pearce.

LINDSEY, R. (1979). Soap operas: Men are tuning in. *New York Times* (Feb. 21), III, 1.

THOMAS, S. (1977). "The Relationship between Daytime Serials and Their Viewers." Unpublished dissertation, University of Pennsylvania.

PART **VI**

TECHNOLOGY

22

The Human Option:
Media Evolution and Rationality
as Checks on Media Determinism

PAUL LEVINSON
Department of Communications
Fairleigh Dickinson University
Teaneck, New Jersey 07666

Like most provocative ways of looking at the world, "media determinism" has meant different things to different researchers. In one sense, this perspective has been used to call attention to the ways that communication systems have made possible great unforeseen changes in our history and culture. One might say, for example, following the leads of Innis (1951), McLuhan (1962), Eisenstein (1979), and others, that the printing press helped make possible the Protestant Reformation by providing a wide and rapid dissemination of Luther's ideas, and, more importantly, by making the Bible itself available to the masses and thus putting teeth in Luther's dictum that people should read the Bible for themselves. Used in this sense, media determinism becomes a search for what McLuhan calls the "hidden ground" of history.

But media determinism has also been used in a far more extreme and restrictive sense. Consider, for example, the perspective of Jacques Ellul (1964, p. 321), who sees the human/technological relationship as something akin to "a fly on flypaper." For Ellul, technologies (including of course technological communications media, going at least as far back as the printing press) are utterly dominating, irresistible, and destructive forces, in whose grasp we poor humans find ourselves helpless and hopeless. Although few scholars fully accept Ellul's apocalyptic perspective, it is ironically this type of media determinism—perhaps because of its boldness—that has caught and fired the public's attention, and indeed has served as the basis for some serious suggestions concerning social policy. The view of television as an irresistible and dangerous force, for example, has motivated many of the claims that TV is responsible for violence in the real world, and has even been offered as a *legal* defense for an act of murder in Florida, and a bank robbery allegedly committed by a small boy in New York City.[1]

It is this second type of media determinism that I shall address, for there is much evidence and good reason to conclude that, contrary to the premises of this severe, pessimistic perspective, the effects of our communication technologies are neither disruptive of human life and society nor irresistible.

ARE MEDIA ALIEN TO HUMAN SYSTEMS?

Much of the view that media are at odds with human interests comes from the notion that technology is in some way fundamentally alien to natural patterns of life and communication. Ellul (1964, p.321) makes this point quite vividly when he writes that the human being "was created for a living environment, but he dwells in a lunar world of stone, cement, asphalt, glass, cast iron, and steel." Mumford (1970) makes a similar claim when he describes modern technology as encroaching upon "organic" ways of life. Similarly, an "anti-natural" notion of technology animates much of the more recent criticism of media, such as Mander's (1978) all-out attack on TV.

One possible way of countering such views is to contend that there is no simple "organic" or "natural" standard of human life and communication against which to gauge the performance of technologies and media. Meyrowitz (1979/80), for example, criticizes Mander on the grounds that all human communication, whatever its biological or organic components, is inevitably filtered through some sort of cultural overlay—so that when Mander calls for an end to television, he is not really calling for a return to the "natural" (as he claims he is), but to an earlier *media* environment (e.g., print). While such observations may be well-taken as a critique of Mander, they are of little value in assessing the fundamental issue of Ellul's sweeping media determinism, for they leave unanswered the underlying question of how print, TV, or any technological medium may distort or contradict the organic components of human communication, whatever they may be.

---

[1]The Florida case involved Ronald Zamora, who pleaded that he fatally assaulted an elderly woman while under the "intoxication" of the violent programs he watched on television, especially the *Kojak* detective series. The jury rejected this defense and found Zamora guilty; Zamora appealed on the grounds that his lawyer's invocation of TV was an "incompetent" defense; the conviction was upheld ("Conviction," 1979). In the recent New York case, the defense lawyer pleaded that his 9-year-old client had walked into a bank and pointed a gun at a teller because the boy "spent most of his time watching crime shows on television" (Shipp, 1981).

Another way, then, to approach the problem of media determinism is first to identify the natural aspects of life and communication that communications technologies are thought to encroach upon, and then see in exactly what ways various communication technologies work against these natural roots. As I have suggested in some detail (Levinson, 1979), the task of identifying the organic components of communication may be greatly simplified if we dispense with such controversial terms as "organic," "natural," and even "biological," and confine our search for elements of communication that may be termed "pretechnological"—i.e., those elements of communication that everyone would agree are present either before or without the introduction of communication artifacts or humanly-produced technologies. We might identify as "pretechnological" or "deviceless," for example, such elements of human communication as color and depth perception, appearances of stillness and motion, and sights usually synchronized with sounds. All of these aspects of communication are functions of our naked mentalities and unaided sensory systems.

When we plot the performances of various technologies on such pretechnological coordinates of communication, we discover a most interesting pattern. In the case of photography, for example, we find that the earliest photographs were still, silent, colorless, and two-dimensional—i.e., sharply at variance with elements of pretechnological communication—but that with the successive development of motion pictures, "talkies," color, and, most recently, three-dimensional holography, the photographic process has moved to a closer and closer approximation of pretechnological communication. The evolution of the telegraph, and its mechanical clicks, into the vocal capabilities of the telephone, and, more recently, into the facial expressions communicable via video-phone, suggests a similar line of convergence between communication technologies and pretechnological features of communication.

These developments seem to be part of a general pattern of media evolution, in which we as media consumers unconsciously select for survival those technologies that bear an increasing correspondence to our pretechnological modes of communication. Furthermore, since the transmission and reception of information (communication) is essential to the survival of organisms, any naturally-developed mode of communication (e.g., color perception) would necessarily have a high degree of efficiency or otherwise suffer extinction. Therefore, it is not surprising that as we strive to make our technologies more efficient, they inevitably and increasingly resemble elements of communication hammered out in the organic foundry over millions of years.

But whatever the mechanisms responsible for the development of more "human"-like media, the growing presence of these technologies poses a serious challenge to media determinism. While *any* difference between a technology and a human communication system could surely prove to be fatal for the human system, the general reduction of such differences surely diminishes the likelihood of such disruptions. Of course, an insistent media determinist could argue that as media become less distinguishable from living systems they become even more treacherous, leaving us less able to recognize that we are involved with an artificial device. In concrete terms, such an argument would claim that color TV is more distracting than black-and-white, and video-phone a more tempting substitute for in-person conversation than conventional telephone. But given the fact that we wish to converse with someone who is not physically present, aren't we better off doing so with a medium that is as close as possible to the real thing? And in any case, the very development of these more life-like technologies, whatever their ultimate consequences, suggests a profound reversal of the traditional media determinism equation. The evolution of technologies that recapture elements of human communication suggests that, rather than technologies programming us, *we* are determining the course of technological development, and devising media that are coming ever closer to our human specifications.

ARE MEDIA EFFECTS IRRESISTIBLE?

The issue of control is, of course, along with the artificiality of technology, the second great pillar of media determinism. Ellul sums up the supposed human inability to resist technology quite well in his allusion to the "fly on flypaper," but this perspective is actually very widespread and deep-rooted in many 20th century philosophies. We see it in all the theories that view appeals to the senses, emotions, our irrational unconscious, etc., as overwhelming our intellect and rationality. Media determinism is, in other words, predicated upon the notion that our intellect is too weak to rationally control our inventions.

Since communication inventions presumably "get to us" by restructuring our perceptions, it might be useful to consider briefly the role of perception independent of technology. Psychologist Donald Campbell (1974) has provided an ingenious explanation of perception's biological basis. All perceptions, he explains, are in effect substitutes for touching. All that amoebas "know" or "perceive" of the world is what they find from bumping into it—a no doubt "truthful" but highly dangerous process. In more highly evolved organisms, systems such as vision and hearing provide vicarious experiences of the outside world—"stand-ins" for touching—which are likely to result in more error than touching (i.e., our eyes may lie to us), but are a good deal safer. Human beings attain an additional level of vicarious experience in their thinking (e.g., seeing things in the "mind's eye") and their culture, which inject an additional dose of noise or possible error into our perceptions, but provide commensurately greater survival benefits. Although Campbell does not discuss media, it may be argued that technologies such as television and telephone are similarly "third level" perceptors, providing vicarious experiences of seeing and hearing which are themselves vicarious forms of touching the world.

Campbell's evolutionary account of perception and cognition thus explains these functions as successful "trade-off" mechanisms, providing a vast amount of safety, insulation, and flexibility, but also making possible a large degree of error (as in the case of hallucinations, misjudgments, etc.—the amoeba, remember, can neither hallucinate nor commit a logical fallacy). At the apex of this evolution, humans are the most capable both of dodging dangers in the real world, and of creating them with misperception and misunderstanding.

But this raises a very important question. How is it that, beset as we are with the immense possibilities of error given us by our multiple systems of vicarious experience, we have somehow managed to flourish as a species? How does any human individual remain sane at all in the myriad of perceptions and perceptions of perceptions that bounce around the mind? The answer is quite obvious. Humans not only have a multiplicity of perceptions, but the capacity to mediate these perceptions through logic and rationality— to assess, criticize, and even reject any perception that they find wanting or in error. We see this process in operation quite clearly when we drive down a highway on a hot day, spot a patch of shimmering water in front of us, but take no evasive action because we know that what we are seeing is an optical illusion—i.e., that in this case our senses are lying to us. A similar process occurs when we cry during a sad movie even though we know full well that what we are watching is fiction.

This process of rational assessment is so common that it is usually taken for granted; but I would like to propose that rationality is a biological necessity in humans, a corequisite, in evolutionary terms, of the many layers of perception that humans are capable of generating. For without the mediation of reason, we *would* be lost in a thicket of various perceptions, and, indeed, the numerous levels of vicarious experience of which we are capable would be as valueless—and as counterproductive—as a system for ingesting food without an accompanying system of digestion. I am suggesting, in other words, that logic and rationality are far more than niceties of our civilization— that they are fundamental biological properties of the human species, evolved as a necessary complement of our powers of imagination and abstraction, with the ability, but of course not the certainty, of transcending appeals to the senses.

In the days of Descartes, few people doubted the primacy of reason, but this "clear light" of the intellect was thought to be a gift from God. And as religious belief waned in the second part of the 19th century, so too did the confidence in human rationality (see, for example, the writings of Nietzsche). But the development of Darwinian theory during the same time has provided the means of understanding the centrality of logic on grounds that are biological rather than religious or moral—of reintroducing the notion of reason's indispensability as a natural, not a supernatural, necessity.[2]

What does all of this mean for media determinism and its presumption that the effects of our media are irresistible? It means, simply, that the effects of media, like all our perceptual encounters with the world, are subject to the scrutiny of our rational intellect, and therefore not in principle irresistible at all. It means that we can even indulge our media fantasies—engage, as Coleridge put it, in a "*willing* suspension of disbelief" (my emphasis)—see sad movies, violence on television, whatever our bent, and resist whatever tendencies we may have for generalizing these experiences to the real world. The reality of rational choice means that we are automata only in the eyes of technology's critics, not in our relations with technology itself.

The power of reason can also be used to assess and criticize not only the content of media, but the structure as well; and such criticisms of media structure can serve as a spur for development of new "remedial" media that address the structural problems. Consider, for example, the case of television, which has long been criticized for its immediate and irretrievable presentation of information, and the incompatibility of such a mode of presentation with the traditional processes of contemplation and reflection. The introduction of home video recording devices has now rectified this shortcoming, and given the TV viewer the same opportunity for leisurely re-examination of information previously possible only with books and acoustic recordings. (The price of these devices is, of course, still quite high and beyond the average consumer; but such has been the case shortly after the introduction of virtually all new technologies, including the book.)[3] In other words, though introduced to make money, the home video recorder nonetheless addresses a technological problem rationally; or rather, the commercial success of this adjunct to television will depend upon how well it remedies TV's "instantaneous" drawback, and how disadvantageous this drawback really is.

Of course, there is much that is *ir*rational and dangerous in ourselves, our technologies, and our world; and our rationality provides no assurance that it will always transcend these other aspects of life, or even that it is free

---

[2]Campbell (1975, p. 96) calls attempts to give an innate, Darwinian account of various aspects of human mentality a "recurrent heresy" against behavioral psychology, and cites 47 such biological interpretations (mostly off-hand and minor) made between 1897 and 1973 (Campbell, 1974, pp. 460–63). Other than Campbell's (1974), the most important contributions in this growing discipline of "evolutionary epistemology" (Campbell's term) have been made by Konrad Lorenz (1975) and Karl Popper (Popper, 1979; Popper and Eccles, 1977).

[3]Whetmore (1979, p. 19) reminds us, for example, that as recently as 1800 the price of a book ($1.00) amounted to an average wage earner's weekly salary.

of error itself. Indeed, quite to the contrary, human rationality, like all evolutionarily-derived capacities, is groping, inexact, and fallible. But the knowledge that reason is a fundamental part of the human species, coupled with the recognition that our media are growing closer to, not further from, our human systems of communication, means that the severe type of media determinism propounded by Ellul and Mander, and so popular with much of the intellectual community and the general public these days, is not tenable. The flypaper we are stuck upon may be no more fatal or irresistible than the words on this page.

REFERENCES

CAMPBELL, D.T. (1975). Reintroducing Konrad Lorenz to psychology. *In* R.I. Evans (Ed.), "Konrad Lorenz: The Man and His Ideas," pp. 88–118. New York: Harcourt Brace Jovanovich.

CAMPBELL, D.T. (1974). Evolutionary epistemology. *In* P.A. Schilpp (Ed.), "The Philosophy of Karl Popper," pp. 413–463. La Salle, IL: Open Court.

Conviction of youth upheld in "TV intoxication" case. (1979). *New York Times* (Dec. 19), A24.

ELLUL, J. (1964). "The Technological Society." Trans. J. Wilkinson. (Original ed., 1954). New York: Knopf.

EISENSTEIN, E. (1979). "The Printing Press As an Agent of Change." New York: Ca bridge University Press.

INNIS, H. (1951). "The Bias of Communication." Toronto, Ontario: University of Toronto Press.

LEVINSON, P. (1979). "Human Replay: A Theory of the Evolution of Media." Unpublished dissertation, New York University.

LORENZ, K. (1975). Kant's doctrine of the a priori in the light of contemporary biology. (Originally published in 1941. Reprinted and translated by D.T. Campbell.) *In* R.I. Evans (Ed.), "Konrad Lorenz: The Man and His Ideas," pp. 181–217. New York: Harcourt Brace Jovanovich.

MANDER, J. (1978). "Four Arguments for the Elimination of Television." New York: Morrow Quill.

McLUHAN, M. (1962). "The Gutenberg Galaxy." New York: Mentor.

MEYROWITZ, J. (1979/80). Review of "Four Arguments for the Elimination of Television" by J. Mander. *The Structurist 19/20*, 102–107.

MUMFORD, L. (1970). "The Myth of the Machine." Vol. 2: "The Pentagon of Power." New York: Harcourt Brace Jovanovich.

POPPER, K. (1979). "Objective Knowledge." Rev. ed., London: Oxford University Press.

POPPER, K., and ECCLES, J. (1977). "The Self and Its Brain." New York: Springer International.

SHIPP, E.R. (1981). Armed robbery is court charge faced by boy, 9. *New York Times* (Mar. 3), B3.

WHETMORE, E.J. (1979). "Mediamerica." Belmont, CA: Wadsworth.

23

Interactive Video Communication*

BRUCE C. JEFFRIES-FOX
American Telephone and Telegraph Co.
Parsippany, New Jersey 07054

SUZANNE JEFFRIES-FOX
Institute of Communications
Cedar Crest and Muhlenberg Colleges
Allentown, Pennsylvania 18104

BACKGROUND

Electronically-mediated personal communication (EPC) has been a part of American life since the days of the Wild West, yet is as new as the computer age. Technological developments in the electronics industry have brought consumers new personal communication media, and additional forms can be expected to proliferate in the years ahead.

The distinguishing characteristic of EPC is that it involves two-way communication between people who are geographically separated. One person sends a message through some electronic medium and is responded to by one or more persons through the same medium. It is a personal form of communication because it takes place between people. (Interactive behavior in which information is obtained electronically from data bases is not viewed as EPC.) EPC is personal communication because it takes place between private individuals, rather than between business persons or representatives of institutions acting in their professional roles.

Many types of EPC are familiar: telephone conversations, telegrams, citizens' band (CB) and short wave radio conversations, call-in radio and television talk shows. Other forms of EPC are much less familiar: for example

---

*This paper is the sole responsibility of its authors and in no way represents the views of the American Telephone and Telegraph Company.

picturephone and interactive video conversations. Personal communication through interactive video is the focus of this paper.

Interactive video communication (IVC) requires that participants have some form of terminal in their homes, allowing them to encode a message for transmission to another person or persons. Typically, such terminals have alphanumeric keyboards and are electronically linked by telephone or cable television lines. These terminals may be home computers or special terminals designed specifically for this type of communication. Messages typically appear on a video screen, which may be built into the terminal itself or may be a common television set. The routing of messages is controlled by large, central computers operated by so-called "personal computer utilities" (Nilles, 1980).

This form of communication is not widespread at present. "The Source" and "CompuServe," the largest of the personal computer utilities facilitating this type of communication, jointly reported 11,000 subscribers in the United States as of November 1980; and most of these subscribers utilize the personal communication features.[1] Industry estimates indicate that there are approximately two million terminals in American homes capable of interactive video communication. About 250,000 of these presented are equipped with the hardware to allow IVC, while most of the remainder could be so equipped with the addition of peripheral devices (Payment Systems, 1980; CSP International, 1980; Noll, 1980; Link, 1980).

Several factors suggest that this form of EPC will proliferate rapidly in the 1980s. Advances in electronics and new, highly-efficient production methods are making rapid and steady progress toward bringing the necessary equipment into a price category low enough to support mass marketing.

Soaring energy costs also are expected to contribute to growth in interactive video communication. As people increasingly are forced by the high cost of energy to stay at home, IVC will provide a cost-effective means of facilitating contact with others.

Consumers' acceptance will be aided by growing familiarity with similar electronic devices in the form of electronic and video games. The equipment necessary for IVC is becoming increasingly easy to use, which should facilitate expanding the market beyond computer hobbyists to the general population.

The cable television industry is clearly interested in the possibility of providing equipment and service for IVC. Representatives of the industry at a recent National Cable Association seminar indicated the high probability that the cable industry will embrace this service and increasingly make it available to the public. Interest in offering IVC undoubtedly is motivated

---

[1]Features in addition to personal communications are offered by "The Source" and "CompuServe."

by the political reality that communities granting cable franchises are beginning to demand interactive systems (Cable TV, 1980). As more cable companies offer IVC, the price of terminal equipment and service will come down while the number of potential consumers will multiply.

If the home computer market and interactive video communications grow to the mass-market proportions predicted by industry experts, this could have a significant social impact. New forms of communities could develop, the democratic process could be altered, and the present trend toward cultural homogeneity could be reversed. For this potentiality, it is important that we understand the nature of this new form of electronically-mediated personal communication. In addition, the emergence of IVC provides an opportunity to investigate a dramatically new form of communication in the process of its introduction and acceptance into American life.

TYPES OF INTERACTIVE VIDEO COMMUNICATION

Figure 1 presents a typology of personal communication, including examples of video, electronic, and nonelectronic forms of personal communication that are similar in terms of temporal synchrony and conditions of access.

A unique characteristic of IVC is that there is a choice of communicating in real time or in "delayed time". People engaging in personal communication may address their messages to one individual (private conditions) or "to whom it may concern" (public conditions). The following is a brief description of the four major types of IVC identified in Figure 1.

FIGURE 23.1. Forms of Personal Communication (Video, Other Electronic, Non-Electronic), by Temporal Synchrony and Conditions of Access.

	Temporal Synchrony	
	Real Time	Delayed Time
Conditions of Access Private	VIDEO CHATTING Other electronic: telephoning Non-electronic: face-to-face interaction	VIDEO-BASED ELECTRONIC MAIL Other electronic: telegrams Non-electronic: postal service

Public	VIDEO FORUM
	
	Other electronic: short wave,
	  CB, radio and TV call-in shows
	Non-electronic: town meetings,
	  conventions
		VIDEO BULLETIN BOARD
		
		Other electronic: telephone
		  answering devices
		Non-electronic: personal/
		  classified advertising,
		  conventional bulletin board

Real Time/Private Access IVC

Here, a person creates and sends a message to a person known to be at his or her terminal. Upon reception, this message is responded to relatively quickly. When the response is complete it is sent back to the conversation initiator who remains at his or her terminal. No other parties are privy to the conversation. This form of IVC is highly popular and, despite charges levied on the basis of time spent at this activity, users spend a great deal of time chatting.

Delayed Time/Private Access IVC

The most widespread use of this type of IVC is electronic mail. Messages are sent to specific others and stored until retrieved. Only the specified other has access to the message. A second manifestation of this type of IVC is the advice column called "Dear Lore" offered by "The Source." In this instance people send messages to "Lore" who responds confidentially some time later.

Real Time/Public Access IVC

This is a highly popular form of IVC. People "call up" specific topic categories, such as "politics," on their terminals. They are presented with whatever messages are passing between people who are at that time conversing about politics. Messages can be entered and directed toward specific others, but it is known that all people in the "politics" category at that time will have access to the message. The number and range of categories, determined by the system operator, changes frequently.

Delayed Time/Public Access IVC

This form is similar to real time/public access IVC but messages within categories can be entered and remain available for viewing and response until they are erased.

IVC CHARACTERISTICS AND THEIR IMPLICATIONS

Purposive Communication

Interactive video communication clearly requires intentional participation. Since one has the option of scheduling such participation, one has the luxury of participating only when so inclined. Other electronically-mediated communication, such as telephones, offer less choice in this respect. When the phone rings there is both the normative expectation and, from an auditory comfort standpoint, a practical necessity of answering it.

IVC is purposive, in that all messages must be typed into one's terminal. This requires, even for the most skilled typist, that messages be brought to consciousness for encoding. Hence, it is relatively difficult to communicate unintended messages, unlike face-to-face interaction, where the involvement of multiple communication channels may yield unintended information.

Spatial Separation of Participants

Participants in IVC are geographically remote. It is unlikely that people in the same home or in the same room would engage in IVC. IVC between geographically-remote people can aid in the creation of new publics in which mutual interests and views bring people into communication. From a preliminary and unsystematic scanning of "The Source," it appears that membership groups form around a variety of topics. People appear to seek out and then maintain communication with others having similar computer gear; those interested in discussing politics tend to do the same.

IVC can also facilitate lively debate between people holding contrary views on a topic. This has occurred on Knight-Ridder's experiment "Viewtron" system in Coral Gables, Florida. Currently, the numbers of characteristics of IVC participants are too restricted to conduct meaningful investigation on this subject. When a more heterogeneous group comes to engage in IVC, we might expect to find it providing participants access to and interaction with a broader range of ideas and perspectives than is available to them through face-to-face communication.

Semi-anonymity

Participants in IVC typically are semi-anonymous to each other. Messages usually are signed with a first name (or first name and initial), which may or may not be the person's real name. In this way, one can receive direct responses to messages while revealing very little about oneself. Over time, as certain participants develop an IVC "relationship," full names and even telephone numbers may be exchanged. This progression appears to be rare, suggesting that participants find value in anonymity.

If one is semi-anonymous, one can "speak" one's mind without fear of sanctions. A person who, in face-to-face settings, would never reveal communist leanings for fear of losing job or friends, can become a rabid Marxist when engaging in IVC. Such a person may well find others of similar views and even become an opinion leader, enjoying a kind of status within the IVC community, all without fear of retribution. Also, since a participant can back out at any time, and re-emerge under a new name, IVC may be a particularly "low-risk" system of interaction.

Finally, semi-anonymity permits an equality of access to communication with others. For example, in face-to-face settings one's name alone can be the basis of attributions. Some people will decline interaction with others because of the social position, ethnicity, race, or religion implied by the name. IVC offers participants the opportunity to choose and manipulate their identity.

Lack of Portability

Another characteristic of IVC is that participation does not permit mobility. Unlike a letter, which can be written anywhere, or a telephone, which can be found nearly anywhere, a terminal capable of IVC is relatively bulky and too delicate for portability. While it is true that computer companies (including Panasonic and Nixdorff) are marketing terminals that are small enough to fit in a briefcase,[2] the interconnections necessary for IVC between these devices and the telephone lines and video screens are sufficiently complex to discourage carrying a terminal outside the home.

The potential significance of this non-mobility lies in the fact that people are not at home at all times. It is probable that IVC will be an "after-hours" form of communication for most participants, and this likelihood is supported by a favorable rate structure for evening use. The absence of terse messages transmitted "on the run," as is so common in telephone conversations, may mean that this form of communication might be characterized as tranquil, unhurried, and protracted.

Technological Characteistics

In IVC, typed messages are displayed by a CRT (television screen). This is likely to influence the type of people who engage in IVC. Most obviously, the vision-impaired will not use this medium. We also know from consumer research that there are many types of people who simply do not like to sit in front of a TV screen, typing and reading. Many people do not know how to type and have no desire to learn. Many people have back problems that make sitting in one place for an extended period of time an unpleasant experience. Assessment of the significance of technology-based participant

---

[2] The devices are designed for and marketed to businessmen who find it useful to have a terminal with them as they travel, and are not used for IVC.

selection must await larger numbers of IVC users. It seems likely, however, that, more than other forms of personal communication, the technology of IVC will play an important role in determing who participants will be and to what uses they will put the medium.

The technology of IVC also plays a large role in determing the norms of interaction and interpretation. The fact that home computers and home terminals are new and that IVC itself is new clearly lends "play value" to participation. Monitoring of "The Source," "CompuServe," and "Viewtron" indicates that much of what is communicated is frivolous. A recent *New Yorker* cartoon on IVC illustrates the point: the caption reads, "I've heard of small talk . . . but this is microscopic." The computer hobbyists who now make up the majority of participants in IVC clearly enjoy the transmission process in and of itself.

The IVC technology itself frequently is the opening topic of conversation between two IVC participants. People often begin "chatting" by asking about the type of equipment the respondent is using and how long he or she has been on the system (A prophetic chat, 1981). In the future, when IVC is more commonplace, one would expect that this "opening pattern" would be altered.

IVC interaction norms are influenced also by the constraints and limitations of the technology. As with CB radio, only one person can "talk" at a time. There can be no interruptions, although it is possible while interacting with one person or data base to get a signal indicating that another person is trying to get through. Consequently, participants develop means of signaling that the message is completed, and other participants wait until that signal if received before responding.

The attributions participants make when reading others' messages is greatly influenced by the IVC technology. The following story illustrates a case of mistaken attribution that would have been impossible in a face-to-face setting. The author, a "Source" user, responded in the affirmative to an inquiry from a person named Jon about whether he would like to chat electronically:

> Jon, who was obviously facile with the Source, came right back, impatiently, I had obviously delayed too long for his skilled fingers. I couldn't remember how to break out of what I was doing to answer him.
>
> He wanted to know if I were into games, what equipment I used, and how long I had been on the Source. I answered him meekly, knowing he was looking for more than just another novice user.
>
> I asked him why he was on the Source. He quickly, even disdainfully, replied that he was interested in games of all types. His style was authoritative, sharp, and experienced. I felt somewhat intimidated. . .

(After another fifteen minutes of feeling intimidated by this experienced user, the author learned that Jon was an eleven-year-old who was sneaking his time on the computer while his parents were out of the house. The account continues:)

. . . I was stunned. Eleven years old and on the Source. I had no idea until that moment that I was talking to anyone less than an Apple-owning, Source-subscribing adult. And an articulate, competent, impatient one at that, who couldn't know that bumbling me was a fifty-one year old computer amateur. (*Sourceworld*, 1981).

This example makes two points. First, proficiency with the medium itself is recognizable and meaningful to IVC participants. Second, this competence plays a part in one participant's attributions about the identity of the other. The salient dimensions of proficiency as well as the inferences participants make based on perceived proficiency warrant further investigation.

Systems offering IVC typically provide editing functions so that one can correct typographical errors before one's message is sent. It is likely that this feature plays a role in the interpretation of IVC. If, for example, each participant has the editing capability and knows that the other has it as well, spelling and typing errors allowed to remain in the message could imply to a respondent that the message initiater is a sloppy, imprecise person. This attribution could influence how one responds to such a message.

As discussed earlier, IVC may take place in real or delayed time. Temporal synchrony in communication has important implications for expectations of intersubjectivity and for level of control. When speaking with another in real time, we assume a certain degree of shared consciousness. However, when one transmits a message that will not be received until some unspecified time in the future, one cannot assume the same degree of intersubjectivity; events transpiring in the meantime could well influence how the message is interpreted. This situation is familiar to all letter writers. The longer the delay, the less will be the shared experiences of sender and receiver and, *ceteris paribus*, the lower one's expectations of intersubjectivity. The significance of this situation for the content of IVC bears investigation.

Forgetting the name of the person with whom one is talking in face-to-face interaction can be embarrassing, if not debilitating to a relationship. In contrast IVC offers the opportunity to surreptitiously refer back to your addressor's signature and/or to any other previously-transmitted information. Through these means, one can avoid uncomfortable situations and give the illusion of paying close attention.

Finally, IVS's reliance on visual display facilitates its use by the hearing impaired. IVC may provide a new and simple means for these people to communicate with others and foster their greater participation in society.

IVC VIEWED FROM A SOCIOLINGUISTIC PERSPECTIVE

Further understanding of IVC may be achieved through a sociolinguistic analysis, as set forth by Hymes (1972). Analysis of "ways of speaking" focuses on the components of speech in the verbal channel rather than in other communication channels. Given IVC's reliance on the lexical mode, this framework is particularly appropriate and useful in highlighting issues and questions for sociolinguistic research.

It is also interesting to note that IVC's reliance on the lexical mode presents conditions which elicit elaborated coding in Bernstain's sense (Bernstein, 1972). Since participants do not have many cues for inferring the knowledge and experience of others, meanings must be made relatively explicit compared to face-to-face communication. Elaborated coding also implies complex and careful editing at the grammatical and lexical levels. This is clearly the case with IVC. The technology requires that messages be brought to consciousness and encoded into words that will be understood without reference to a specific context. The relative permanence of video displays compared to the spoken word compensates for temporary lapses of attention and facilitates careful formulation of responses. Similarly, the ability to edit one's messages before transmitting them allows participants great control of what is communicated. Day-to-day practice in elaborated coding varies with social factors, and this has resulted in class-related differences in children's performance in situations that reward elaborated coding such as school. If IVC becomes available to people of all socio-economic levels, children may gain competence in elaborated coding through practice in IVC.

Also, with IVC, the key, or tone of a speech act must be communicated using words alone. Hymes (1972, p. 62) points out that in fact-to-face speech key is "often signaled non-verbally, as with a wink, gesture, posture, style of dress." In IVC, the burden of communicating tone falls on verbal forms. One way in which key might be signified is for participants to frame their message by a comment. For example, at the end of a message whose lexical content could be interpreted as mock or serious, one might add, "P.S. Just kidding." As a more heterogenous group engages in IVC, means of signaling key will become increasingly important.

The absence of para-lexical cues may be expected to affect the potential for intimacy in this channel compared to face-to-fact conversation. IVC may have relatively high potential for intimacy because of its semi-anonymous nature. It may be easier to speak of personal topics in IVC than in face-to-face settings. Monitoring of "The Source" indicates that many persons speak of important personal problems through this medium. For example, "The Source's" advice columnist is presented routinely with personal problems such as race relations, job mobility, and management of children's social concerns (On line with "Dear Lore," 1981).

IVC's potential for intimacy may be limited, especially in certain areas. Since para-lexical cues are often used in face-to-face communication to approach a very private area (e.g., to express sympathy for someone who has lost a loved one), IVC's limitation to lexical cues may not permit such personal expressions.

Several research questions are raised by the above two possibilities. Under what conditions can intimate communication take place in IVC? Is this intimacy essentially different than that experienced face-to-face? If IVC fosters intimate communication, what are the implications for those many persons who today feel alienated from others?

DISCUSSION

This paper is an introduction to an area of inquiry which is likely to grow as rapidly as the medium itself. Our observations are organized to emphasize the many fascinating research questions raised by this new form of communication.

Our concern with the technology and characteristics of IVC is necessary because this form of communication is so new. Use of sociolinguistic analysis was equally obvious, due to IVC's reliance on the lexical mode. However, preliminary observations suggest that several other analytical frameworks could yield fruitful insights into the nature of IVC. For example, institutional analysis would highlight policy issues such as censorship. Among the companies currently offering IVC, those which grew out of traditional news media (e.g., "Viewtron") are more concerned with and active in censorship than are those companies whose executives typically have a computer-industry background (e.g., "The Source"). Another topic for institutional research is the agenda-setting role of the systems operators who decide which topics are to be indexed for electronic forums.

A functional analysis of IVC might point out that for the individual IVC can have the manifest function of providing users with a community of others with a common interest in computers, while at the same time having the latent function for society of contributing to the maintenance of cultural diversity.

A technology assessment of IVC could highlight the implications and consequences of this communication form's technological characteristics. Since users must necessarily "log on" to the interactive system to initiate communication, a record of the message's originator is available to the systems operator. Likewise, a record of whoever responds to the message is available to the operator. Such a situation raises the important issues of security and confidentiality, which are likely to influence the rate of IVC's acceptance (as it has with electronic funds transfer systems), and the role of regulation in the development of the industry.

An examination of IVC from the perspective of diffusion of innovation might note that, as with most technological innovations, the early adopters tend to be relatively young, well-educated, and affluent. Moreover, it is likely that the particular market segment first using IVC will shape the nature of this form of communication. Norms for interaction, including protocol and jargon which are appropriate and typical for this first group of users, may come to be characteristic of IVC, as we have seen in the case of CB radio.

We are witnessing the birth of a new form of communication. Since it is through communication of ideas that cultures evolve, it is possible that IVC will come to play a significant role in our own culture's natural history. Investigation of the processes and effects of this new communication form will surely yield valuable insights into the dynamics of cultural change.

REFERENCES

BERNSTEIN, B. (1972). Social class, language and socialization. *In* P.P. Giglioli (Ed.), "Language and Social Context." Harmondsworth, England: Penguin.

Cable TV, the race to plug in. (1980). *Business Week* (Dec. 8). pages?

CSP International. (1980). "In Context." (Research Report.) London: CSP International. (Report 5.)

HYMES, D. (1972). Models of the interaction of language and social life. *In* J.J. Gumperz and D. Hymes (Eds.), "Directions in Sociolinguistics: The Ethnography of Communication." New York: Holt, Rinehart and Winston.

Link, Inc. (1980). "Videotex; A World Wide Evaluation." (Research Report.) New York: Link, Inc.

NILLES, J.M. (1980). "The Confluence of Personal Computers and Telecommunications." (Paper presented at the 8th Annual Conference on Telecommunications Policy Research, Annapolis, MD.)

NOLL, M.A. (1980). Teletext and videotext in North America: Service and systems implications. *Telecommunications Policy* (March). pages?

On line with "Dear Lore. (1981). *Sourceworld* (Feb.) pages?

Payment Systems, Inc. (1980). "Home Terminal Services." (Research Report.) Atlanta, GA: Payment Systems, Inc.

A prophetic chat. (1981). *Sourceworld* (Feb./March). Pages?

Sourceworld. (1981). (Feb.), 127, 41.

24

Some Aspects of Telephone Socialization

GARRY MITCHELL
Nassau Community College
Garden City, New York 11530

When it was a relatively new phenomenon, the telephone was regarded by many as a miracle. Many others, however, adamantly refused to own one, feeling it was a burdensome intrusion. Yet in 1975 the U.S. federal welfare agency ruled that the telephone was no longer to be regarded as a luxury. It had become a necessity.

By Marshall McLuhan's definition (1964), the telephone is a relatively cool medium. The voice must express all that there is to say. It must cover both the content of the message and the necessary nonverbal instructions on how to interpret that content. Thus, talking by telephone demands a good deal more attention to vocal nuance than face to face communication does.

In addition, we try to visualize the person on the other end of the line. Such a need for visual fulfillment can be explained by McLuhan's theory of the interaction of the senses. As our ear "channel" is "hotted up," the other senses are stimulated but remain unsatisfied. So we fill our hands (and sense of touch) with doodling pens. We fill our mouths (and sense of taste) with cigarettes or gum or, failing all else, the ends of our doodling pens; and we "see" the person to whom we are talking. Some of us go so far as to ask, "What are you wearing?" or "What are you doing?" Many just volunteer the information in an apparent effort to help the caller visualize them.

The sense of the visual is so strong that we will sometimes say, "I'll see you later," when we mean that we will call later. But this visual orientation is not powerful enough to supply all of the nonverbal details of important social rituals like parting. As a result, unless we make a special effort to compensate, saying goodbye on the telephone becomes a much more difficult task than in person. Many phone conversations end with repeated closing cues, goodbyes, and reassurances from both parties.

The telephone has created strong social rituals of its own. Even more than radio or television, it has distorted our sense of distance. Its function is to allow us to communicate verbally with anyone, almost anywhere, instantly, without having to leave our present space. For our voices, distance has become almost meaningless.

We take this ease of access to others for granted. Yet it is a learned behavior. Little children, when first allowed to talk to a spatially-distant grandma on the telephone, invariably shout into the mouthpiece. Perhaps even Alexander Graham Bell *shouted*, "Mr. Watson, come here. I want you," into his new toy. Even he would not have realized that the essence of his invention was intimacy.

This is the strange paradox of the telephone. It is at the same moment both public and intimately private. In Edward Hall's terms (1966), it is simultaneously intimate and social. The voice on the other end of the line speaks quietly into our ears from an intimate distance of less than an inch. But at the same time our response is audible to whomever is in our immediate vicinity. So, unless we have been able to sequester ourselves, our response to the intimate stimulous must be a social one. We are forced to play two roles simultaneously.

Erving Goffman (1963) has described this situation for us in his famous theatrical metaphor. On the telephone we are in a position where one aspect of our performance must be "front region" (that is, an intentionally and carefully monitored presentation of ourselves to another) and one aspect is "back region" (in which we can relax from our front region performance). In addition, especially in the case where there is another person present in our back region, we engage in what Goffman calls "teaming." That is, we share an insider's knowing attitude with those we include in our back region. Thus the telephone creates an almost unique dichotomy. Both the social role demanded by the space from which we are calling, and the intimate role associated with the actual telephone contact, are interchangeably front or back region.

Let me give two contrasting examples. Many business calls are made while trainees or customers or even friends of the caller are looking on, sharing the insider's experience, watching the call take place — all without the knowledge or consent of the party being called. The caller is presenting him or herself alone over the telephone — a front region activity — and at the same time sharing his or her end of the call with the others present — a back region activity. During the call, he or she may make faces to companions, cover the mouthpiece to comment on the call, and so forth. By providing them with such a commentary, he or she is able to keep them informed as members of the team.

But we have all experienced the complete opposite of this behavior as well — a call in which the parties on the telephone are teamed in a conspiracy to present a particular front region performance to persons present at only one end of the call. Perhaps the most familiar example of this type of manipulation is teenagers calling while other members of their families are present. In this case we have guarded remarks and cryptic comments and a variety of paralinguistic signals that contribute to the creation of a mediated back region.

This dichotomy is the key to understanding the impact of the telephone on our behavior. It is simultaneously intimate and social in nature, demanding the mastery of two separate roles. At the same time it can be either a front region or a back region for either or both of the parties to the call. With so many possible role variants facing us each time we answer a ringing telephone, we experience a degree of tension, of heightened uncertainty, or unpredictability. The more experience we have with the telephone, the more competent we become at straddling the dual roles and shaping the performances we want to present. But a degree of unpredictability is always present. To the extent that we cannot predict our caller's behavior, we will feel ill at ease — uncomfortable with the call.

I call this the "predictability principle." As outlined by Hannemman and McEwen (1975), the predictability principle holds that we are comfortable only so long as our immediate environment is predictable. To the extent that unpredictable elements are present, we will be wary of them and unable to fully relax. The greater the degree of unpredictability in any interaction, the greater the tension. This implies that we work to eliminate our tension by making our environment predictable again. But the most predictable behavior for each of us is usually our own, and so we seek to control the environment to make it predictable for ourselves. In this sense, all communication is, at best, a negotiation for predictability; at worst, a struggle for control. This is certainly true of the telephone.

When we make a telephone call we can predict at least the beginning of it because we have control over it. But when we receive one, we can expect only that someone will be on the other end of the line. The event of a ringing telephone is an intrusion into personal privacy and individual predictability. Few can ignore this imperious summons. It constantly interrupts both business and pleasure. Those who can afford it, might have housemaids or butlers to screen their incoming calls, thus providing a degree of protection which enhances their sense of predictability. Many businessmen have secretaries to do this, and some people pay a monthly fee to an answering service in order to maintain control of the access to their intimate, personal, psychological space.

The intimate nature of the telephone and our need for predictability combine to make it an instrument of both bonding and attacking behavior. Those who are close to us we allow to call us, even in the middle of the night (though we may grumble a bit). So, exchanging telephone numbers has become a bonding ritual for us — a symbolic gesture of invitation to closeness. On the other hand, we may resent those who call us without "permission" as unpleasant or aggressive. And those whose prurience is excited by the sudden forced intimacy of calling unknown victims to spout lewd remarks at, or heave amorous sighs to, are a problem in all wired societies. To help us counter this sense of unpredictability, we have developed a number of conventional types of behavior — behavior that allows us to predict our caller's actions and so give release to our tensions.

The first convention is that callers must first identify themselves and state the purpose of the call. This is why we answer the telephone with a questioning or a demanding, "Hello!" The second convention is that we expect to reach a correct number. We are always surprised by a wrong one. Conversely, we expect whomever calls us to actually *be* calling *us* and we are annoyed when the party asks for someone we don't even know. The third convention is that we are hesitant to point out a calling error. We couch our corrections in such phrases as, "I'm sorry but . . . ," or, "I think you may have a wrong number," or, "There isn't anyone here by that name," so that the caller must realize his or her own error. We are allowed only to *suggest* that there has been one. Fourth, an error demands an apology, and fifth, such an apology *must* be waived and dismissed as not necessary. Finally, after the apology (or even after the avowed purpose of the call has been achieved), we are obliged to get off the line. And we feel uncomfortable when we are not allowed to do so.

Overall, the real effect of the telephone on our daily lives lies in the blending of three main elements. We are forced by the telephone to respond to dual conflicting behaviors demanded by our cultural use of distance; we are forced to respond to the front or back region others thrust upon us with our own front or back region interactions; and we are forced by our own need for a predictable and secure environment to respond to calls either in certain accepted conventions, or by aggressively pursuing an environment structured by us to our own ends.

We are increasingly dependent on the telephone. It is a prime tool for dissembling, procrastination and romance. It has become a vital means of shopping, conducting business and knitting families together. And, technology is rapidly expanding its role in these areas. This rather insignificant looking technological toy has woven itself into the fabric of civilized life and has done so almost without our notice. The time has come for it to receive more scholarly attention.

REFERENCES

GOFFMAN, E. (1963). "Behavior in Public Places." New York: Free Press.

HALL, E.T. (1966). "The Hidden Dimension." Garden City, NY: Doubleday.

HANNEMAN, G.J., and MCEWEN, W.J. (1975). "Communication and Behavior." New York: Addison Westley.

MCLUHAN, M. (1964). "Understanding Media." New York: Signet.

25

The Chamberpot: A Most Private Medium

Suzanne Claire Schick
New York University
New York, New York 10003

Picture a scene that might have occurred in *Masterpiece Theatre's* "The First Churchills." Young John Churchill is on a diplomatic mission on the Continent. As the scene opens, we see him finishing a letter to his dear wife Sarah. He signs the letter with a flourish of his quill pen, seals it with sealing wax, and presses the hot wax with his signet ring. Turning the wedding ring on his finger pensively, he glances through the windowpane and sees that his horse is saddled. He leaves the building, mounts the horse, slips his feet into the stirrups, and rides away. John Churchill uses many technologies in this brief scene. There is one thing, however, that John does not do, and will not do throughout the 13-week series; he will not use that new and fashionable item, the chamberpot, nor will he relieve himself in any of the older, less convenient places—the midden heap, the privy, or the garderobe. This peculiar state of affairs derives from our notions of privacy rather than his, for, because of the differing state of technology, people in Churchill's own day were much less delicate about mentioning such things, which were, understandably, much more of a problem. For instance, here is what Samuel Pepys has to say about the subject:

> September 28, 1665, and so I to bed, and in the night was mightily troubled with a looseness (I suppose from some fresh damp linen that I put on this night), and feeling for a chamber-pott, there was none . . . so I was forced in this strange house to rise and shit in the chamney twice; and so to bed and was very well again.

The chamberpot is only one of a series of solutions for that basic human problem, what to do with our bodily waste products. This paper traces the history of these solutions from the Ancient World until the 19th century, when modern sewage systems and flush toilets were being developed. This history will be examined with regard to three interrelated factors: existing technology, the attitudes people had toward collective life and community, and notions about privacy.

Technology and techniques are obviously very important in a study of this kind. For instance, before one can have an instrument that qualifies as a "knife," one must have both a material capable of being sharpened and a method for achieving the sharpening. That is not all. One must also have a need which is fulfilled by the knife, and a set of social attitudes and conventions that supports the use of this particular instrument to fill that need. The same holds true for the disposal of human wastes. It turns out that sewer systems and toilets appear very early in man's history, and chamberpots very late, and this paradox occurs because of people's attitudes toward community life. There may be a continuum, at one end of which is an attitude rooted in things of this world. People with this point of view are practical and provide practical and technologically-skillful solutions to problems, including the problem of sewage. At the other end of the continuum is an attitude rooted in things of the next world. People with this attitude we would call impractical and idealistic, and consequently their solutions to practical problems are not very sophisticated. Mankind moves back and forth between these point of view, especially in the matter of cleanliness. As Terence McLaughlin says:

> Cleanliness and urbanity go together. The Romans were clean because they set great value on public and collective life . . . This same urbanity and interest in social life was anathema to the rising cult of the Christians, who were firmly convinced that the things of this world were vanities, and they tended to reject all other Roman values, including cleanliness, along with the theological ones. (McLaughlin, 1971, p. 6).

Thus, solutions to problems of this sort rest not only on the state of the technological art, but also on the values of the particular culture. Notions of privacy, on the other hand, seem to have traveled in one direction only, from unabashed "publicness" to shame-ridden privacy. However, even the notion of privacy is related both to technology and to social attitudes. Norbert Elias (1976, p. 139) says:

> But this isolation of the natural functions from public life . . . was only possible because, together with a growing sensitivity, *a technical apparatus was developed* which solved fairly satisfactorily the problem of eliminating these functions from social life. (Emphasis mine)

Thus, the state of technology, attitudes about community and collective life, and notions about privacy are highly interrelated.

Evidence about ancient plumbing is scanty at best. Early man probably developed the need for an organized method of getting rid of waste when he changed from a nomadic life to agricultural communities. The most basic idea, says Alexander Kira (1976, p. 7) is a container of some sort with which to catch bodily wastes. The wastes were then disposed of either by return to the soil or by washing away with water. Thus, the basic idea for the chamberpot appeared very early. What is interesting about ancient civilizations, however, is that some of them created quite elaborate ways of dealing with waste. The earliest evidence we have of what may have been either a continuously flushing toilet or a built-in chamberpot utilizing stored water for flushing is at the Cretan Palace of Knossos, c. 2000 B.C. J.D.S. Pendlebury (1954, p. 55) writes:

> The Queen's Toilet Room is a room with a stone seat on the West Wall and traces of a W.C. in the south-west corner.

Sir Arthur Evans (1927, p. 228) continues with a description of the plumbing:

> The stone channels themselves, ventilated by air shafts and made accessible by manholes, were so roomy, that, in the course of their excavation, my Cretan workmen spent whole days in them without inconvenience. It thus would have been easy to clean them out when necessary. At the same time, their use in connection with latrines would hardly have been tolerable unless they were pretty constantly flushed.

We also have evidence that the Romans, engineers of both sewer systems and "civitas," had flush toilets or, at least, convenient places where one could dump human waste into the sewers (Kira, 1976, p. 6). Yet, while the ancients had the technology for organized sewage systems, this knowledge was later either lost or ignored. The Minoans and the Romans were empire builders and, at the height of their powers, each controlled most of the then known world. Peace reigned, and man, the center of the universe, was in control. The Minoans and Romans achieved this state of affairs because they tended toward that end of the continuum that was practical and rooted in things of this world, and they maintained their situations for the same reason. Furthermore, community life and the city were cornerstones of their empires, and so their solutions to human waste disposal were civic in nature. Thus, the technologies and the world views of the Minoans and the Romans were interrelated and, in a sense, inseparable from one another. As for the notions of privacy held by these two ancient peoples, we may infer, from the fact that athletes practiced and performed nude and that the Baths were a social congregating place, that they were much less modest (or prudish) than later cultures.

But darkness fell on the noon that was the Roman Empire; the Visigoths invaded, and the "pax romana" was over. Writers and philosophers of the time, such as St. Augustine and Boethius, expressed the despair that people felt, and the conviction that something outside man was in control. Thus Christianity triumphed and Roman values were rejected. In particular, cleanliness was rejected, because the baths, which had become little better than brothels, were symbols of Roman decadence. Holiness and saintliness became equated with dirtiness. The genuine anchoret was disgusting and dirty, and the angelic rule of Tarbenne forbade bathing (Kira, 1976, pp. 11-12). The beginning of the Dark Ages also saw the death of the city as the Romans knew it. People moved to small villages organized in a feudal manner for protection. The Roman systems of roads, aqueducts, and sewers were allowed to decay. The economy and the constant state of siege had much to do with this disintegration; also, the value system (shifting as it was toward the end of the continuum represented by idealism and belief in the next world) made other things more important for the people. The sewers were allowed to collapse because the people were not interested in cleanliness, but in holiness.

At this point the most common solution to waste disposal was the "garderobe" or "longaigne" (far-off place), which we would call a privy. The people of the Middle Ages would not have called it a "privy," because they usually visited the place in groups, and it was arranged to hold several people at once, as it had a succession of holes (Levron, 1968, p. 42). In royal households, such as the castle at Salisbury, there was often a special latrine tower to which users were escorted and assisted by a chamberlain (Holmes, 1952, p. 97). Private homes in London and Paris had garderobe pits near the kitchen fire, in a projection of the foundation wall. The waste fell neatly into the spaces between the houses. Wealthier people probably had lids on these pits, but the odor of excrement was prevalent, despite the fact that a "maistre fifi" came every so often to remove the waste in buckets (Holmes, 1952, pp. 38-39, 92). Andreuccio, in the *Decameron*, is tricked into a garderobe in a courtesan's house and falls through the floor into the filth underneath (McLaughlin, 1971, pp. 27-28). In some castles, the longaigne opened onto the moat, which shows that it took more courage to swim in it than any movie hero could possibly imagine. Swim it they did, however, for the opening of the longaine was often used as an entrance for an attack, as Philip Augustus used Chasteau-Gailliard's while beseiging Richard the Lion Heart. A basket of straw "torche-culs" or a curved stick, called a "gomphus," was always provided for the user (Holmes, 1952, pp. 188-189).

What do these examples tell us about technology, social attitudes, and, especially, privacy? Medieval solutions were technically simple, and reflected the piecemeal character of society. People did not care whether fifth fouled their neighbor's drinking water. Indeed, in 1355 London's Fleet River was choked by filth, and in 1347 two men were prosecuted for pumping ordure into a neighbor's cellar. Evidently, the plaintiff failed to notice that anything was amiss until the cellar began to overflow, which gives one some idea of how London smelled in 1347 (McLaughlin, 1971, pp. 27-28). The Roman sense of "civitas" was gone.

Medieval society, although in some senses more technologically advanced than the Romans, put energy into other things, most notably *warfare* and the *Church*. Although the society was very systematized (as reflected by Church and State hierarchies) it did not organize sewer systems. In Medieval times, eyes were firmly fixed on the hereafter. The public character of the privies, where people might have gossiped agreeably, shows that privacy was rare and not considered very important. Elias (1978, p. 134) points out that Medieval social commands and prohibitions surrounding this issue were few:

> Neither the functions themselves, nor speaking about them or associations with them, are intimate and private, so invested with feelings of shame and embarrassment, as they would later become.

Thus, its sewage technology and design reflected the social attitudes and notions of the privacy of the Middle Ages.

The Renaissance and the 16th and 17th centuries might be considered the golden age of chamberpots. Buildings, at least public ones, had become bigger and more elaborate, and government had become mush more centralized around the monarch, whose person was supposed to reflect the glory of the nation. Therefore, while Philip Augustus may have attacked Richard the Lion Heart by way of the privy, it became inconceivable that the Virgin Queen or the Sun King, whose very lives were an elaborate presentation of self and nation, should take a day's march through their ornate palaces to get to the kitchen pit. Thus, chamberpots came to be the fashion for the monarchy. Such devices had to be luxurious. For example:

> Padding was added to the most unexpected pieces of furniture. A close stool make in 1547 for the "use of the Kynges mageste" was covered in black velvet and garnished with ribbons, fringes, and quilting . . . thus allowing Edward VI to relieve himself in comfort. This commode was like a box with a lid and had two leather cases to carry the actual pot and a "sesstorne" or cistern for washing it out . . . A similar piece of furniture, used by Elizabeth I and later by James I . . . has a lock for the lid, so that no one of lower order than the sovereign . . . could tamper with it. James in particular was terrified of poisoning, and might have thought that poison in his close stool would have been a particularly nasty kind of death in the pot. No one seems to have used this piece of furniture since James I, which is not entirely surprising. (McLaughlin, 1971, pp. 39-40).

In terms of technology, social attitudes, and the notion of privacy, this period was one of transition. The Renaissance and Reformation had brought about a new sense that man was the center of the universe, and the rediscovery of the classical world confirmed this point of view. Thus, it was no longer a sin to make life as pleasant as possible, and social attitudes began to shift to that end of the continuum concerned with practicality, urbanity, and systemization. This shift is reflected in the chamberpot, an immense improvement over the longaigne, although, at first, only royalty benefited from it. Sometimes, incidentally, they did not. In 1530, Erasmus wrote *De Civilitate Morum Puerilium,* a book on etiquette for boys. Although *De Civilitate* was the precursor of a new standard of shame, it still speaks as a matter of course about things which, by present standards, we do not mention in company, much less in books on etiquette. Obviously, it was common in Erasmus' time to meet someone "qui urinam reddit aut aluvum exonerat" (urinating and defecating) (Elias, 1978, p. 135).

It is clear from Erasmus' writing that notions of privacy, as well as social attitudes, were in transition. The chamberpot afforded, for the first time, the possibility of privacy, but not everyone used it in such a way. At the court of Louis XIV, people would bring their chamberpots with them, gather in groups, and, like their medieval counterparts, gossip in comfort (Leuron, 1968, p. 42). The first chamberpots were bigger, more luxurious privies. Even the Sun King himself overlooked the possibility of privacy, for he received visitors while sitting on his "chaise percée," which was padded with fringed velvet, provided with an earthenware basin, and had a folding table enabling Louis to read or write while upon it (Leuron, 1968, p. 42). Of course, the organizational benefits of the chamberpot had not yet reached the lower classes. The absence of privies was a constant problem. Pepys' wife had a colic when they visited the Duke of York's playhouse, and she "did her business" in a corner of Lincoln's Inn Walks. Not surprisingly, the 1660s were plague years, for public sanitation was as bad as ever, or even deteriorating, as a result of overpopulation (McLaughlin, 1971, pp. 88-89). Thus, although attitudes and ideas about privacy were changing, the technology had not yet quite caught up or become widespread enough to do any good. Thus, peculiar paradoxes were produced, as Jonathan Swift satirized in *Directions to Servants*:

> Do not carry down the necessary Vessels for the fellows to see, but empty them out of the Window, for your Lady's credit. It is highly improper for Men Servants to know that Fine Ladies have occasion for such Utensils, and do not scour the Chamberpot, because the smell is wholesome. (McLaughlin, 1971, p. 100).

In the 18th century the transition that had started in the previous two centuries ran its course and headed towards a well-organized sewage system. During the Age of Reason, man was again, triumphantly, the center of the universe. It is not surprising, therefore, that the benefits of the chamberpot reached the middle and, sometimes, the lower classes. However, such benefits were not without drawbacks. G.M. Trevelyan, in his *English Social History,* writes of early morning hazards in the 1750s:

> Far overhead the windows opened and the close stools of Edinburgh discharged the collected filth of the last twenty four hours into the street. It was good manners to shout "Gardy loo!" (Gardez l'eau) before throwing. (McLaughlin, 1971, p. 101).

Naturally, 18th century scientists tried to invent more practical ways of dealing with human waste, and the nobility wanted a status symbol to distinguish it from the lower classes. So, attempts at built-in flush toilets occurred throughout the period. An important precursor of this movement was Sir John Harington, who proposed, in *The Metamorphosis of Ajax: A Cloacinian Satire*, a valve water closet, which he subsequently built at his home. The only other "Harington" was built for the Palace at Richmond, and fell out of use after 1612, when Sir John died, because no one could fix it (McLaughlin, 1971, p. 52). In the 18th century, the Duke of Bedford had four water closets installed at Woburn Abbey, one of which, it was proudly noted, was inside the house (McLaughlin, 1971, p. 109). These new inventions, however, presented problems. A Mr. Melmoth of Bath, who was enterprising enough to build a water closet in his house in 1770, was ordered to remove it because it was wasting valuable water (McLaughlin, 1971, p. 105). Although the new water closets got the waste out of the house, that was about all. It eventually choked up the rivers instead of being carted away for use on the land, as had been done formerly. Thus, the rivers became more polluted than ever, and the incidence of typhoid increased.

As we have seen, technology became much more sophisticated in the 18th century, but it was incomplete and in the beginning, made more of a mess than it had cleaned up. However, the social attitude tended toward the practical, civic-minded end of the continuum, and this attitude, combined with the fact that things became more nauseous than they had ever been before, caused collective action to be taken for the first time since the Romans. Water closets, which had been looked upon as wasteful and expensive, began to appear in the better-class homes, and sewer systems were proposed. Again, however, the attitude appeared before the thing itself:

> For the mass of people, the eighteenth century closed little better than it started . . . Many of the improvements of life did not reach the poor at all: the rich had the water closets the poor merely had more sewage in their drinking water. (McLaughlin, 1971, pp. 110-111).

In the 18th century the sense of privacy and modesty was firmly established. In the 1729 edition of La Salle's *Les Règles de la Bienséance et de la Civilité Chrétienne*, the author demands that all natural functions be done in private, but he still goes into great detail, and one gets the feeling that people did not do what the fashionable arbiters of etiquette were demanding. In the 1774 edition of the same book, however, the recommendation about natural functions was made without the details (Elias, 1978, p. 137). By this time, it was considered indelicate to mention such things.

Thus, privacy had arrived, but why? It was noted earlier that an apparatus had to evolve before natural functions could be taken out of the public arena. The chamberpot and the WC fit the bill. Elias states:

> After a reshaping of human needs has once been set in motion with the general transformation of human relations, the development of a technical apparatus corresponding to a changed standard consolidates the changed habits to an extraordinary degree. (Elias, 1978, p. 140).

Thus, privacy occurred because technology made it possible. The changed attitudes of society gave impetus for the new technology.

By the turn of the 19th century, then, some few aristocrats possessed early models of the water closet, some more efficient, some less so. The vast majority of the upper- and middle-class people had chamberpots, and the poor had either privies or nothing. However, the industrial revolution was encroaching. The great demand for goods during the Napoleonic Wars created idle money for the middle class to spend. Some of this money went into the demand for luxuries and some was invested in the great new factories using labor-intensifying machinery to turn out these luxuries. Jobs in these factories attracted agricultural workers to the towns, and this tremendous influx of people created unbelieveable overpopulation and crowding. The demand for cheap housing led to crowded double rows of houses, jerry-built, with a pump at one end and a privy at the other. In St. Giles, London, a whole large square was gradually filled up with these row houses, until it resembled a maze. Here, there were no sewers or drainage whatsoever (McLaughlin, 1971, pp. 120-121, 132). Predictably, this unprecedented acceleration in growth led to things that made the 17th century chamberpot dumping look like model sanitation. The untreated sewage was still pouring into the main rivers, which were also used for washing and cooking. Cholera epidemics in 1848-49 and 1853-54 resulted (McLaughlin, 1971, p. 139).

The cholera, which affected the rich as well as the poor, was the final impetus for what had been coming for a long time. Reformers demanded action. The push came just at the time that factories came into being which could produce the necessary materials cheaply. As before, the attitude came first; but technology, social attitudes, and notions of privacy all interacted, and the movement toward unified and sanitary sewage systems began.

Chamberpots were still used in some large houses at the turn of the 20th century. Typically, such a house would have one modern bathroom, but bedrooms were supplied with chamberpots. However, the twentieth century might be called the "twilight of the chamberpot." Modern sanitation and sewer sytems had made the chamberpot almost extinct.

REFERENES

ELIAS, N. (1978). "The Civilizing Process." New York: Urizen Books.

EVANS, A.J. (1927). "The Palace of Minos at Knossos." London: Macmillan.

HOLMES, U.T., JR. (1952). "Daily Living in the Twelfth Century." Madison, WI: University of Wisconsin Press.

KIRA, A. (1976). "The Bathroom." New York: Viking.

LEVRON, J. (1968). "Daily Living at Versailles in the Seventeenth and Eighteenth Centuries." New York: Macmillan.

MCLAUGHLIN, T. (1971). "Dirt: A Social History as Seen Through the Uses and Abuses of Dirt." New York: Stein and Day.

PENDLEBURY, J.D.S. (1954). "A Handbook to the Palace of Minos at Knossos." London: Max Parrish.

Author Index

Subject Index